PENGUIN BOOKS

Just in Time to be Too Late

Just in Time to be Too Late

WHY MEN ARE LIKE BUSES

PETA MATHIAS

PENGUIN BOOKS

PENGUIN BOOKS
Published by the Penguin Group
Penguin Group (NZ), 67 Apollo Drive, Rosedale,
North Shore 0632, New Zealand (a division of Pearson New Zealand Ltd)
Penguin Group (USA) Inc., 375 Hudson Street,
New York, New York 10014, USA
Penguin Group (Canada), 90 Eglinton Avenue East, Suite 700, Toronto,
Ontario, M4P 2Y3, Canada (a division of Pearson Penguin Canada Inc.)
Penguin Books Ltd, 80 Strand, London, WC2R 0RL, England
Penguin Ireland, 25 St Stephen's Green,
Dublin 2, Ireland (a division of Penguin Books Ltd)
Penguin Group (Australia), 250 Camberwell Road, Camberwell,
Victoria 3124, Australia (a division of Pearson Australia Group Pty Ltd)
Penguin Books India Pvt Ltd, 11, Community Centre,
Panchsheel Park, New Delhi – 110 017, India
Penguin Books (South Africa) (Pty) Ltd, 24 Sturdee Avenue,
Rosebank, Johannesburg 2196, South Africa

Penguin Books Ltd, Registered Offices: 80 Strand, London, WC2R 0RL, England

First published by Penguin Group (NZ), 2009
1 3 5 7 9 10 8 6 4 2

Text copyright © Peta Mathias, 2009
Illustrations copyright © Penguin Books, 2009

The right of Peta Mathias to be identified as the author of this work in terms of
section 96 of the Copyright Act 1994 is hereby asserted.

Extracts have previously appeared in different guises in the *Australian Women's Weekly*
and the *Herald on Sunday* and are reproduced here with permission.

Illustrations by Donna Cross, threeeyes.co.nz

Designed by Anna Egan-Reid
Typeset by Pindar NZ
Printed in Australia by McPherson's Printing Group

All rights reserved. Without limiting the rights under copyright reserved above,
no part of this publication may be reproduced, stored in or introduced into a retrieval
system, or transmitted, in any form or by any means (electronic, mechanical, photo-
copying, recording or otherwise), without the prior written permission of both the
copyright owner and the above publisher of this book.

ISBN 978 014 320246 2

A catalogue record for this book is available
from the National Library of New Zealand.

www.penguin.co.nz

Contents

	ACKNOWLEDGEMENTS	6
	INTRODUCTION	7
1	RELATIONSHIPS: SUPERFICIAL MANIPULATIVE BITCH SEEKS NICE GUY TO EXPLOIT	15
2	FATHERHOOD: STARK RAVING DAD	45
3	SEX & LOVE: IF YOU WALK AWAY FROM ME, I'LL LOVE YOU FROM BEHIND	71
4	SPORTS: CONTROLLED AND CHANNELLED BARBARISM	107
5	FASHION: THE GAME FOR THE YOUNG AND THE DEAD	135
6	GAY MEN: BOYS ON THE PINK EDGE	169
7	HEALTH & EATING: THE ROAD TO SELF-RIGHTEOUSNESS	199
8	WORK: AGE ONLY MATTERS IF YOU ARE A CHEESE	223
9	HAPPINESS: DON'T OVERDO IT	249
10	WHY MEN LIE: FEEL FREE TO KISS MY ASS ON THE WAY OUT, HONEY	277
	SELECTED BIBLIOGRAPHY	300

Dedicated to my father, Harvey
My brothers, David, Jonathan and Paul
My brother-in-law, Ian
My nephews, Hugo, Tom, Harrison, Conor, Denis and KJ
My deceased husband, Alexy Zabiego

ACKNOWLEDGEMENTS

Thanks to my publisher, Dorothy Vinicombe, for her brains, support, lunches, help and unbelievably sweet temperament. Every time I got tired of writing she sent me intellectual stimulation in the form of research findings, news and meaningful proverbs like, 'If you think the way to a man's heart is through his stomach you're aiming too high.'

Thanks to all the gorgeous men who allowed me to interview them – without you I would never have known what I missed by not marrying you.

Introduction

In *Can We Help It If We're Fabulous?*, my book on women, I said men were not the enemy and that I now have only a low level of animosity for them. This was not strictly true – I said that so I would look better-adjusted and more socially evolved than I actually am. The truth is that I didn't and don't hate men, but I have almost always disrespected them. Not men *friends*, of course, but all other men – lovers, work colleagues, other women's husbands, the rubbish collector (I don't leave my rubbish bin open and lying on the street for him so why does he do that for me?), any man who uses the toilet before me and leaves the seat up (do you think I *want* to touch it?).

It's easy to write a book celebrating women if you're a woman because you have intimate, readily accessible knowledge of your subject. My friends and I were the subject. When my publisher suggested I write a book on men, I laughed. It would be *work*. Moreover, how hazardous would it be to look into the heart of the male species? Although I have an adorable father, a deceased husband, a brother-in-law, three brothers and five nephews, I don't pretend to really know men. I just treat them as I would a charming foreigner who speaks an obscure Mongolian dialect – I nod my head in faux comprehension and, in some situations, hope they don't notice that I only speak high Kazakh. A virgin would know more about men than I do because she's probably listened more. Not only did I not listen, I never asked. I had no idea what men wanted, how they really felt (difficult to hear someone when they're not talking), or how they saw me as I stalked off into the sunset, voluntarily or not.

Compared with the number of books on women there are not many books on men, for men, by men, and very few uplifting or witty ones. In *The Myth of Male Power* it turns out that it's all our fault and that men are the powerless ones. In *What Men Don't Talk About* it turns out they lack the ability to show affection and we have to help them get their acts together. Please. As I started to read earnest books on men I began to build a picture I had never seen before. I suspected that a book on men was going to be rather sad and depressing and that I was going to wish I had never looked into the topic. As time went on, though, I found a different story from interviewing men themselves. Men told me they didn't feel useless or rudderless at all. They said they welcomed women's social advancement; felt that women needed and wanted them just as much as they ever have; and that while their male roles were changing they still feel 'relevant'.

I wanted to call this book *Often Licked but Never Beaten*. This suggestion made my publisher smile that kind of smile you give people who have forgotten to take their medication. When I said I was interviewing men for this book, people said, 'Men won't tell the truth, they will exaggerate and make their lives more interesting than they are. Either that or they will be intimidated by you and do the still-waters-run-deep thing.' The opposite has been true. With a few exceptions, men are dying to talk, have a great sense of humour about their lives, and admit to vulnerability and doubt. When I tell them my joke, 'If they can put a man on the moon, why can't they put them all up there?' they have the courtesy to offer me another cocktail.

What can I say about relationships that hasn't already been said? In the first chapter I discuss the concept of the veneer of monogamy, the demise of the Alpha Male, the meaning of a mate, how to know if a man is talking and what happens when they have negligent mothers. I have devoted a bit of space to the incorrigible habit men have of lying and the inexplicable habit women have of choosing bad boys. You will hear the sad story of what happened to the biggest liar of all. I have also looked into the mysterious cult of male enthusiasm for sport. According to my research, sport is how men bond, teach each other life skills, develop their fabulous personalities and grow up. Hello? Don't make me weep. In the sex chapter you'll learn that a hard-on does not count as personal growth. The famous book *The Joy of Sex* has been updated, which is most heartening because apparently we are still desperately in need of a bit of basic instruction. When I delved into fashion I found the most wonderful book by Hardy Amies, who rightly noted 'black is a colour much loved by Italians and Americans, best suited to swarthy Latin types and totally inappropriate to the russet-toned Anglo-Saxon gentleman.' Did you know that in popular culture 'Men in Black' describes men dressed in black suits who claim to be government agents and whose job is to harass into silence

UFO witnesses? Either that or they are Johnny Cash.

Just the mention of the word 'childbirth' while I was researching the fatherhood chapter reduced one of my interviewees to tears. A lot of men said having children changed their lives – it was the single most creative and rewarding thing they had ever done. In fact men like having children so much that quite a few of them start over again with a younger wife and have some more. Happily for the new wife they are unlikely to do a runner as they can no longer run. In the health and food chapter we find out why my sister-in-law Sharyn gave up teaching my brother to cook. It turns out men hate going to the doctor just as much as you thought but not for the reasons you thought – they hate having to wait at the doctors so always turn up just in time to be too late.

You may be interested to know that most men do not decide to be gay just to get on their father's nerves, to possess a bigger and better wardrobe, or because they want to go into interior design. It is simply the way a portion of the population expresses human love and sexuality. In this chapter you will find out how to marry a gay man and how to tell whether the one you already have is gay. I also make some comments on happiness – it's catching, just like beauty, but if you're too happy there's probably something wrong with you. Happiness cannot exist in a vacuum – it needs the contrast of sadness. Both states should be embraced. Our preoccupation with happiness has come at the cost of sadness, an important feeling that we've tried to rub out of our emotional repertoire. And, at the risk of giving a little too much away, I discovered that men have three brains and don't seem to know how to use any of them, especially when it comes to Christmas and women.

INTRODUCTION

I interviewed men for this book because, well, I can't make EVERYTHING up. I wanted to ask some real men why most of their species haven't yet worked out that the way to get a woman to do anything they want is by submitting to us. These guys also helped me get away from writing about sport before I lost consciousness and interviewing them was a great excuse to have meals with interesting, intelligent men.

Anthony Grayson

Ant is a 49-year-old corporate banker whose partner's name is Gorgeous Sue. He's a good-looking man with piercing blue eyes, an engaging manner and is possibly the only man I know who has an armchair positioned right beside the kitchen bench so he can watch Sue cook. After the interview he insisted I view his downstairs man cave. I expected a utilitarian room with tools, computers and pictures of naked ladies. What I got was a very slick boy parlour complete with gigantic screen, state-of-the-art sound system and a luxuriously long golden couch for the boys to line up on while they watch rugby. He treated me to his DVD of The Eagles reunion concert – a banker who rocks! I chose to interview him after I met him at a party. We had a wine-fuelled conversation about how much he admired his father and the people he works with.

Jimmy Keogh

My friend Jimmy Keogh lived with his family at Manly on the north coast of Sydney and started surfing in 1948 at the age of twelve. A wonderful old salty dog, he lives with his partner Sue and paints and writes, and also fishes in the harbour bordering the bottom of his garden. Jimmy is a great storyteller and

I knew he would offer me a good surfing yarn. His brother, Danny Keogh, invented the famous Keyo shortboard.

Greg Blake

Greg is fifty years old. He is a handsome old devil, very funny, warm, affectionate and self-disclosing. He has a lot of friends who are very attached to him; a daughter; and has recently married his gorgeous Italian sweetheart, Fausta. Greg and I have had lots of talks about the meaning of life, sexuality and relationships over the years. It's rare to find a man who is so open. He turned up for the official interview bang on time with the opening sentence, 'God, I was terrified of being late because you're so controlling and I might have got a slap.' In his dreams.

Richard Pringle

Richard Pringle is a senior lecturer in the Department of Sport and Leisure Studies at Waikato University. I have never met him but his nephew at Penguin Books said he was very knowledgeable and had interesting views on sports. I interviewed him on the phone and the recorder picked up only my voice – he had to repeat everything he had said to me by email later. Richard is married with two children.

Jeff Avery

Jeff is a cameraman and editor with his own television production company. He is thirty-eight, Canadian, attractive and easy-going. He has been happily partnered with his wife Jane, a television producer, for ten years. They have one son 'who slipped past the goalposts'. Jeff normally uses one-word sentences in emails, but when I interviewed him he became a silver-tongued orator.

INTRODUCTION

We yelled at each other throughout the interview at an outdoor café specialising in heavy truck traffic.

David Horsman

David Horsman is a sculptor, artist and designer. He lives with his French girlfriend, Florence, in India and France. David is tall and handsome, makes great cocktails, cooks well, tells exciting stories and is always the last person to go to bed. He dresses beautifully in pale, loose, Indian-style clothing. He is my business partner in the gastronomic tour company I run. I interviewed him in Marrakesh on the roof of a riad, over many glasses of red wine. No topic is taboo for this erudite man.

Steve Yeoman

Steve Yeoman is sixty and thrilled to announce he is almost at the stage where he doesn't have to work any more, but does. He is currently an IT teacher and website designer. In the past he has been in publishing and sales, was once a potter and the owner of a café called Jolt. He is a SNAG (Sensitive New Age Guy), but only because he was born that way. Steve was a stay-at-home dad and almost bursts into tears every time he talks about being present at the birth of his daughter, or if you ask him about his grandchildren. He has been happily partnered with his girlfriend Jill for twelve years. He is funny and warm and has a lot of friends.

Linz Ariell

Linz Ariell is a clothes designer who also owns several menswear stores in partnership with Sam Gray. He is tall, slim and softly spoken, with floppy grey hair like Hugh Grant.

1
Relationships
SUPERFICIAL MANIPULATIVE BITCH SEEKS NICE GUY TO EXPLOIT

HOW NOT TO IMPRESS A WOMAN

Some years ago I lived in an apartment in Cannes, the most glamorous town in France. I knew no one there and believed I would write, because unless you're a film star there's nothing else to do in Cannes. It wasn't film festival time and Hollywood hadn't called me. I rented an apartment in Le Souquet, which is in the old Cannes. Cannes is commercial, touristy and festival-oriented now, but it is in a beautiful setting on La Napoule bay and has a stunning climate through both winter and summer. Before it was discovered by the English aristocracy in the mid-1800s it was just an old fishing village on a hill with a particularly beautiful port. It took its name from the reeds (cannes) that grew everywhere. In those days, the ice-cream-cake lookalike 'Hotel Splendid' hadn't been invented; the famous Croisette promenade lined with palm trees and gardens didn't exist; and there was no casino, conference centre or rue d'Antibes, which is now full of designer shops. All that came later, but even now, in old Cannes, people still hang their washing from lines outside their windows like flags in the wind – a habit forbidden in Paris.

So, there I was on the Riviera with, as it turned out, writer's block. Day after day the heat never let up; even when it was cloudy it was there, like an unresolved argument. Two days of not being able to write, talk or email and I was weeping into my fish soup. Why was I there? Why had I done this? Why wasn't life a party any more? And why was I depressed in one of the world's most beautiful seaside towns? You mention Cannes or Monte Carlo or Menton, which is up the road, to anyone outside France and they faint with envy, imagining casinos on the beach and half-naked starlets more beautiful than the mind can bear without going into synapse meltdown. On the third day, after reading late into the night – a desperate 'best seller' full of predictable American tear-jerking/God-loving/perfect-love-lost crap (I wept uncontrollably) – I rose from my cool, darkened sarcophagus-like apartment and took myself in hand. The thing that annoyed me most about the book was the sex scenes: no truly erotic stuff but nevertheless they both came at the same time on their first lovemaking session and she even had multiple orgasms. Please. I thought male authors gave up the multiple-orgasm-as-a-synonym-for-true-love shtick in the seventies.

I needed to clear my head, so I went down to the beach for a swim. Going to the beach in Cannes was quite a treat. There was a young woman with long purple fingernails in a silver bikini with her mother – she of lengthy red nails in a white bikini edged in gold. There were African women with hair extensions, who sat their high, shiny shoes in the sand beside them. Old people, having long ago given in to their addiction to the sun god, stretched out like goat skins which had gone black from having been outside in the wind too long – hideous, grilled skin-clad skeletons.

The Croisette had chic beaches with sun chairs, comfortable mattresses, restaurants, attentive service and flapping umbrellas of lollipop pink, ochre and tangerine, black and tan. Every morning all the beaches, whether expensive or free, were combed by staff with big rakes to pick up the syringes, condoms, rubbish and other unthinkables that had been left as souvenirs of the night.

Suffering from writer's block is boring and you can hear your mother saying, 'There's no such thing. Writing is *work* – you just sit down and *work*.' I went upstairs to pay rent to my landlady, Veronique, and mentioned in passing that I was about to defenestrate myself from the third floor. In the nicest possible way and with the most beautiful smile, she advised me to get over myself. She softened the blow by saying she would have cocktails and invite me.

Her friends were most interesting. I met Roman, a suave, middle-aged Russian businessman. His money ensured he was well-kept – designer teeth, surgically perfected face, expensive clothes, even tan and a chillingly smooth, soft voice. I distrusted him instantly, partly because of his voice and partly because he wore gold chains around his neck. Men in the South of France have a tendency to wear gold chains but for him there was no excuse. Roman made his money in a telecommunications business – and a number of other less 'obvious' businesses I reckoned. He spoke good English and had recently moved to Cannes to live.

We fell into a long discussion about Russian women. He told me they were the most beautiful women in the world, but stupid and empty. He lamented that young women these days were incapable of real love, commitment and devotion to a man. He was looking for someone intelligent, deep and interesting – beauty was no longer enough for him. The next day I received a message from Veronique. Roman wished me to join him and friends for dinner; I was to be ready at 8.50 precisely. At 8.55 he knocked on the door – I didn't bother to reproach him for his tardiness. A big, shiny car was idling in the narrow street outside. What did I see sitting in the front seat, but a creature who fitted the exact description of the beautiful-young-stupid variety he told me he had sworn off. This one was so stupid that speech beyond the predictable one-word signals of aerated agreement seemed beyond her. But, dear reader, the height of her and that breath-taking figure! Her black designer clothes looked painted-on; she had long honey-blonde hair, a high, baby-like voice. Perestroika Barbie.

Over drinks at the Carlton Hotel, where this Euro Barbie arched back on her chair like a praying mantis, Roman informed me she had just got divorced from her second husband, had an 11-year-old son and had also recently moved to Cannes to live. I asked her through him what she did for a living (my first and only stupid question). Of course she had never worked in her life, she never would, and only a blind-deaf mute living in a catacomb wouldn't have realised that immediately. When I told my friend Michele this story she blew smoke in my face and reminded me how ridiculous I was and what a danger it was to let me out of the South Pacific. Barbie was obviously a high-class call girl and he and his associate were obviously gangsters. All rich Russians are gangsters, she pointed out to the blind-deaf mute. Everybody knows this.

The 'business associate' was an older, overweight man with a New York accent and lots of stories to tell. He was mildly entertaining, but they both had that certain way of behaving with women that I found very distasteful. With the vulgarity that new money brings, they ordered 'the best wine in the house' without looking at the list. The American knew nothing about anything – he couldn't talk about art, literature, cuisine or culture. They could only tell stories about junkie associates, the models they had 'known' and make murky allusions to 'business deals'. It was like going backwards on a Concord to the days when men were men and women were pieces of cotton wool. At the end of the night, the old guy drove me home pointing out all the expensive hookers on the Croisette on the way. In a final, delusory touch he thought he was going to spend the night with me. I love saying 'no' to men – I get so little practice.

MATE

Mate: a deck officer on a merchant ship subordinate to the master.
Informal: a person's husband, wife, or other sexual partner.
Origin: late Middle English: from Middle Low German māt(e) 'comrade'; of West Germanic origin; related to meat (the underlying notion being that of eating together).

One theory is that the word 'mate' started being used by dock workers in the Victorian era. It is a cultural idiom with connotations of equality, loyalty and friendship. The meaning of mate has evolved to embody notions of sticking together in adversity; actually helping a friend to survive; a them-against-us camaraderie; and sharing experiences. It has an egalitarian ethos, especially among working-class white males, but about ten years ago, the flat white class took it over. They turned it into an ironic, jokey term and changed its pronunciation into the drawn-out 'ma-a-t-e'.

HOW TO RECOGNISE MATES

1. No one's talking. They're all staring into space or the fire and revelling in the fact that they don't have to use their daily quota of 3000 words. Like warriors they are listening to each other's non-verbal communications and not showing any emotion, as that would jeopardise the safety of the tribe. To show that they are listening they grunt.
2. If they are in a life or death situation, like at the bottom of a mine shaft, a conversation might go like this: 'How are ya, mate?' 'Okay, mate.' 'Are ya hurt?' 'Yep.' 'Bad?' 'Yep – the coal trolley has cut me in half at the waist.' 'Oh, mate.'
3. When they do talk it is about sports, work, the car, politics, how to poach foie gras in a tea towel (they love aspirational recipes) and wine (lots of technical details).
4. There is no sex talk – if a mate did that his mates would get nose bleeds and vacate the premises.
5. In a mate relationship everyone is always right, there is no criticism, no one asks for advice and no joke is too stupid.
6. They will be hunting in packs using a sophisticated system of body language signals known only to themselves; otherwise, they're in the shed together doing stuff in silence.
7. To keep real intimacy at bay mates call each other affectionate names like loser, dickhead, wanker and poofter.

RELATIONSHIPS

Steve Yeoman

PM 'Okay, friendship. Do you have mates?'

SY 'Not really – I'm too much of a loner. Most of my friends are women because women use their brains a lot more when they are talking.'

PM 'Why don't you have male friends?'

SY 'Because I don't like sport or politics.'

PM 'Does that mean you would have nothing to talk about?'

SY 'Yeah.'

PM 'But you could talk about clothes, Steve.'

SY 'I think I might be an awkward person to talk to. I only really like men who are very interesting and with whom I can talk about lots of different things.'

PM 'I would like to have more male friends but the sex thing always gets in the way.'

SY 'It is hard to start up a friendship with a woman because you have to go through that stage of figuring out what the relationship is.'

ALPHA MALES – YOUR COFFINS ARE READY

The definition of an alpha human (which can be male or female) is the dominant, most powerful and most admired person in the tribe. The word 'alpha' comes from the first letter of the Greek alphabet. It is a term used in astronomy to denote the chief or brightest star of a constellation. Alpha people are also described as Type-A personalities. I, for example, although a woman, would describe myself as a borderline Alpha Male with a slack attitude.

I'm impatient, time-conscious, a bit aggressive, have trouble relaxing but can goof off at the drop of a hat. I appear to be relaxed during the day but my inability to let go manifests in sleeping problems. Sometimes I am literally speeding while relaxed in bed and my heart is thumping, but I think a lot of hard-working people are like this. That's why I am not attracted to Alpha Males – too much bossiness and strutting going on. It's not that Type-A women are desperately controlling (although we are), it's that we respond badly to people trying to control *us*. The perfect match for a Type-A woman is a Type-B man – an easy going, patient, unambitious guy who says 'whatever' a lot and smiles when we are being insane.

The Type-A personality used to be considered an at-risk one because of coronary heart disease. Alphas are high-achieving workaholics who multitask, drive themselves to meet deadlines and get driven nutty by delays. They get the work done on time/ are never late/are reliable no matter what – so why isn't everyone? They don't permit themselves to get sick but if they do get sick they work through the illness and they disrespect people who 'give in' to sickness or emotional stress. How any of them live past fifty is a complete mystery to me. Strangely enough, a lot of alpha people are insecure and have tragic self-esteem, but this is usually very well hidden in their bluster and scene-stealing behaviour. When I see high-achieving, hard-working women with what appear to be useless, passive husbands I now look twice. I now consider that they have made a good choice because no other kind of guy could live with them. People have always said that the upside to an Alpha Male is that he is the person who gets things done – the leader, the inventor, the creative.

RELATIONSHIPS

Medical research has now shown that Type-A, high-achieving men are actually not at greater risk of having a heart attack than their relaxed brothers. What is now thought to be an influencing factor in heart attacks is anger and hostility constantly being expressed. First psychologists told us we were repressed and had to get our anger out; now they are saying expressing it makes us sick. No wonder we get irritated – I'm going to keep screaming till the debate's resolved.

The reason women tend to seek Alpha Males as partners is that we have a biological drive that compels us to choose the strongest male – the one who will provide for our needs and with whom we can make the strongest babies. We don't tend to seek 'nice guys' because in nature nice equals weak and weak means being left unprotected and in danger. The tricky part is, the Alpha Male is genetically programmed to spread his seed; in other words, staying on the veranda with one woman doesn't come naturally. However, we women have now been socialised to the point where we no longer admire men who spread their seed. Never fear. That women have been socialised into monogamy means men can be too. They may even end up being happy about it. My friend Harry is a borderline bad boy who has been married for thirty years – he is successful, sophisticated, funny, drinks, smokes and flirts with women. His wife, my friend, is beautiful, gentle and smart. She has managed to work it so that he is a faithful bad boy, thus proving it can be done. He always says, 'Men who like women are already living with one.'

Alpha Males constantly remind us they are irresistible; they get away with murder, are sexy, charismatic and big earners. However, this ape's days may be numbered – characteristics such as being insufferable and vainglorious when he's on the up, but pathetic and whingey when things go wrong (not to mention his pathological philandering) are starting to annoy women and beginning to look less sexy. They will start hearing us say, 'If I gave a shit, you'd be the first person to know, honey.' We don't really feel like tolerating their arrogant behaviour any more and it's only going to get worse in an economic downturn. When the shit hits the fan, Alpha Males start to look like throwbacks from a backward era – just in time to be too late. Poor societies don't have Alpha Males because they can't afford them – they're too much trouble. Women now want Mr Type-B, who doesn't behave like an arsehole, gets in and helps with the housework and can at least think about something other than his fabulous self and his big dick. You'd be surprised at how good Type-B men are in bed.

Greg Blake

PM 'If you are faithful, why are you?'

GB 'Because I know how easy it is not to be. It feels easy for me to be faithful now with my wife, but if in the past I have been unfaithful in previous relationships it was because I just wasn't ready for that kind of commitment. Meeting the right woman is not so much about the woman – no matter how fantastic she is – it is more about being ready yourself. Being ready can come at different ages for different people. I think when people get married young it can be because they think that's what they're supposed to do. They feel a biological urge almost. You might be interested

RELATIONSHIPS

> to know that Aristotle Onassis said "Monogamy is for the poor". But once you have decided to go down the track of monogamy, you stick to it.'
>
> **PM** 'Do men find women difficult to understand?'
>
> **GB** 'Oooh – that is a dark road you don't want to go down! But there *are* certain qualities you look for in a woman, such as trust. One of the things that most attracted me to my wife was her loyalty – along with her beauty. You have to choose a woman whom you can just hang out with at ease; who you enjoy doing both everything and nothing with. You also have to respect women and let them be who they are – if you lose respect, you're done for.'

A VENEER OF MONOGAMY

A lot of men think monogamy is like mahogany: you don't need the real thing. No one will know – a veneer will do. Mahogany is a very large canopy tree. It can reach over fifty metres in height and its trunk may be greater than two metres in diameter. Mahogany generally has a straight grain and is usually free of voids and pockets. The wood matures with age, has integrity and is warm. It has excellent workability, and is very durable. It polishes to a high lustre, and has excellent working and finishing characteristics. It responds well to hand and machine tools, has good nailing and screwing properties, and turns and carves superbly. Mahogany is perhaps the most valuable timber tree in the whole world and has been heavily exploited for most of the last century. It is becoming increasingly rare, is already extinct in parts, and is listed as threatened.

See how easy it is to confuse mahogany with monogamy? A monogamous man shares many of the same qualities: tall, good-looking, strong, free of voids, matures with age, has integrity, warmth and great screwing abilities. He is the most valuable man in the world and is listed as threatened.

In the heterosexual world, monogamy is when one man is permanently mated with one woman. Other monogamous creatures are geese, eagles, some monkeys and foxes. Cavemen were genetically compelled to have sex as often as possible with as many cavegirls as possible to ensure the survival of the species. Unsurprisingly, 80 per cent of all human communities have been polygamous through time. That was then – this is now. Modern man has outrageous quantities of testosterone, which exceed today's biological requirements and create havoc.

The principal reason relationships end is because of unfaithfulness. There's no longer a biological reason for men to endlessly chase women – it is an anachronism. I can sympathise with them, though, and not all men are like that. A lot of men want to be monogamous, and not just in a veneer-like fashion, and a lot of men have no trouble achieving that. Just because you are programmed genetically to do something, doesn't mean you have to do it, especially if the result has been proven again and again to be destructive.

When I asked Jeff Avery, who's been happily partnered for ten years, about monogamy, he said fidelity is important in a relationship because everything is based on trust and security, and infidelity is the first thing that would undermine security. You can't get away with it by thinking you will keep it a secret, because even one person knowing – the one straying – changes the relationship. You'll never actually get away with it because then you have to live with guilt. 'Not all men would feel guilty,' I suggested to Jeff.

'True,' he answered, 'if you're devoid of sentiment and conscience – sure. Men are very good at justifying things – they'll think up any excuse for infidelity and for not owning up. They use the children, the money, the whatever. But, if it was a sanctioned event – "Honey, you go and have a fling while you're away in Japan, I wish you all the best" – they would regard their spouse as a saint, fuck with reckless abandon and be guilt-free! However, a man knows that this situation is unlikely and would generate a quagmire of complexities that would surely come back to haunt him in some way. So, we continue to live in our fantasy worlds.'

I asked Ant Grayson if fidelity was important. He answered, 'Absolutely, yes, but it depends on the couple. In some couples, in order to keep the relationship together, they have to be a bit flexible and understanding on that. People do have indiscretions and forgiveness is important. How it works in those situations is because there is a meeting of the minds. It's not something that works for me. I'm quite traditional – reputation and integrity are important to me. I love Sue and I wouldn't want to ruin a good thing.'

HOW TO TALK TO A MAN

1. Men are not mind readers. They can't even read body language so you have to actually ask for what you want using clear simple words and, sometimes, combine this with sign language. Although it doesn't appear so, if you are in England they usually speak English, in France they speak French

JUST IN TIME TO BE TOO LATE

and in Outer Mongolia they speak Mongolian or Russian, et cetera. Hints, subtle or strong, don't work – too open to different interpretations for people with tunnel vision.

2. If you have a problem, only confide in a man if you really want a solution. Every woman knows there is nothing more irritating and insulting than someone giving you solutions to your problems if that's not what you are seeking. Sometimes, both men and women just want someone to listen to them and sympathise. Men only want you to bother them if they can do something concrete about your situation. They have evolved to problem-solve and not show fear or uncertainty. If you say to a man, 'The cat ate the baby', he might say, 'And your point is?' because he knows it's too late to do anything.

3. Don't ask men unanswerable questions like, 'Are my ankles thick in these shoes?' This is passive-aggressive behaviour because you know perfectly well there is no correct answer to this particular question. You're just looking for a scrap.

4. Try not to make statements which can be interpreted in two ways. By the time his corpus callosum has caught up, he will have interpreted it the wrong way anyway. This is your fault for being obtuse. Men can't follow multi-track conversations and they get bored easily.

5. Talking to a man while he's watching television is just you looking for trouble again.

6. A man only has a quota of about 3000 words a day and once they're said, that's it. A woman has up to 8000 she must get rid of. Women could try talking less, using fewer words to say what they have to say, or using any surplus words that they can't direct at men on other women.

HOW TO KNOW IF A MAN IS TALKING

1. Generally, his lips will be moving, but not necessarily.
2. A man talks *in* his head. He needs lots of time to think silently while showing no expression on his face – but it's all happening in there. When I asked a hotel clerk in Vietnam why the women worked so hard and the men did practically nothing, he earnestly explained to me that men need a lot of time to think and solve problems. Brain scans have shown that a man staring into space is having an animated conversation with himself. If the man is disturbed by the woman he will bite.
3. For women 'yes' and 'no' are words; for men they are sentences. Men don't think in grey areas. Many of them think the words 'yes' and 'no' are *entire* dialogues and that you should be satisfied with them.
4. Anything a man said six months ago is inadmissible in an argument; in fact, all views expressed are null and void after seven days.
5. If you ask a man what he is thinking and he says nothing, he is telling the truth.
6. If he compliments your red dress and it's green, he can't help it, it's genetic – it's a Y chromosome thing. For a man peach is a fruit not a colour; cappuccino is a drink not a colour; dove is a bird not a colour, et cetera.
7. If you ask a question you don't want the answer to, expect an answer you don't want to hear.

USELESS WAYS TO PUNISH A MAN

1. Banishing him to the couch – he loves it on the couch. He can watch television, enjoy a bit of peace and quiet, and pretend he's camping.
2. Refusing to do any housework or dishes until he does his share. Fine with him. The house looks okay as downtown Basra – you're the obsessive-compulsive one anyway.
3. Withholding sex – this is very dangerous and it'll usually be you who breaks down first.
4. Asking him to stick his head up his bum – this is misplaced optimism. Scientific studies have shown this is not possible.
5. Sulking. This is his number one dream – silence and peace.

OEDIPUS AND JOCASTA

In Greek mythology, Oedipus was left to die on a mountain by his father, Laius, who had been told by an oracle that he would be killed by his own son. The infant Oedipus was saved by a shepherd. Returning eventually to Thebes, Oedipus solved the riddle of the sphinx, but unwittingly killed his father and married his mother Jocasta. On discovering what he had done, he put out his own eyes in a fit of madness, and Jocasta hanged herself. In Freudian theory, the Oedipus complex is a group of ideas and emotions aroused in a young male child, typically around the age of four, by an unconscious sexual desire for the parent of the opposite sex and a wish to exclude the parent of the same sex. In other words the boy wishes to sleep with his mother and kill his father. This also happens with girls and their fathers and is called the Electra complex. In real life a normal child is not consciously aware of this and quickly represses it. Most psychologists today say this is rubbish.

BAD MUMMY

A boy's relationship with his mother affects his entire life because she is the first woman he loves. He grows inside her and when born, is nourished by her body. As any woman knows, most men have never got over the fact that their mothers stopped breast-feeding them. It is really only now that we are beginning to understand the impact mothers have on their sons in early development. Men who do not progress properly through phases of their development can still be playing out its psychodrama in various displaced, abnormal, and/or exaggerated ways. According to Freud, the very act of entering into civilised society entails the repression of various archaic, primitive desires. If a boy is ripped away from his first love – his mother – at a formative stage, he may get stuck or fixated and, for example, often be attracted to older women and have to punish them for his mother's desertion. If the man does not adjust and move past his initial experiences to go on to lead a normal life, as he gets older sexual behaviour may become more and more extreme, leading to perversion.

You can always tell a man who loves his mother – he loves women and treats them well and guess where he learned it? Some people find mother love unattractive in men; it's considered uncool, as if he hasn't quite grown up. They're wrong – it is very healthy. The mother–son relationship is a deep and intense one during childhood. The man in the chapter on why men lie hated his mother when he was a young man and had a terrible relationship with her. This has since been repaired, but like all repair jobs with mothers, it's too late – the damage has been done. You can both grow up and understand each other's positions, forgive and forget, let go the rope around their neck and even learn to appreciate their qualities – something you were previously blind to – but the damage is done in childhood and adolescence and that stays put in terms of men's attitudes to just about everything, especially women and relationships. This man's mother 'deserted' him in childhood for a few years then came back, but the trauma had sunk in.

Another man I was involved with on and off for twelve years was very charming but couldn't express any emotion with women and was pathologically unreliable. His fear of abandonment drove him to get in first. Well on into the affair, he finally told me about his mother. His parents separated when he was a little boy and went to live in different countries. He was sent off with his father and his sister went with the mother. He didn't see his mother again for years. He never recovered from the feeling of having been abandoned by her and the shock and psychological damage of the little boy losing that important love made great scars grow over his heart. To this day he doesn't like either his mother or his sister. This was compounded by the fact that there was abuse from the father and step-mother. How could this person grow up to have normal relationships with women? Of course he doesn't trust us – why should he? Of course he can't forge intimate connections – what training did he have? This left him with only one skill with which to attract and keep women for any length of time – his sexuality. What he doesn't know yet is that even his good looks and sexual prowess will abandon him – then what will he be left with?

A man who was abandoned by his mother or who had a cold, emotionally closed one, aches all his life for her missed warmth and maternal energy. The sadness and bitterness poisons all his dealings with women, whom he fears. Boys need lots of kissing and cuddling when they're little so they learn to appreciate close physical contact, emotional safety and the connection between physical pleasure and love. If a boy doesn't develop a range of emotions with the guidance of his mother, basically the only one he will be left with is anger. This is not terribly drastic if he has a warm loving father, but if he has neither, he is in big trouble because a man without emotional intelligence can't deal with change and can't empathise with other people. They may do well in life professionally, but they probably won't succeed in intimate relationships and probably don't even have a lot of close male friends.

GOOD MUMMY

My friend Diana always used to say, if you want a good man, look around your happily married friends and steal one. Men who love women are married or in a committed relationship. I'm not talking about men who like fucking women – I mean men who *love* women. Men who like women have lots of women friends, adore their daughters and are nice to their mothers. In Mexico they call mother 'she who loves us before she meets us'. The first word a baby boy says sounds like ma or mama. Both physically and spiritually his system is tuned into 'woman' right from the start. My mother was in love with her sons, one in particular who still calls himself 'Number One Son', and my sisters and sisters-in-law all have special bonds with their boys. Most of the men I interviewed spoke positively of their mothers as being very nurturing – even nurturing to the point of claustrophobia sometimes.

In a sense boys are harder to bring up than girls because often a mother has no experience of boys before she has one and boys are all over the place, noisy, silly, game-playing, making faces, bouncing off the walls, making messes and igniting farts with matches. Good Mummy in her wisdom absolutely creates the well-adjusted man of the future if she gets it right.

One little complication can be when the mother is single or has a useless partner. She might then go overboard and subconsciously treat the boy as the man in her life which feels suffocating to the child and creates an untenable pressure. I'm sure all that stuff irons itself out – how can you have too much love? We still tend to be tougher and less emotional with boys but in fact they are just as sensitive as girls, so always appreciate tenderness, understanding, respect and tips on essential life skills like how to never stop being goofy, how to save the world and how to be a man. Boys and teenage males are absolutely brilliant, gorgeous and funny. In her book *He'll Be OK*, researcher and social commentator Celia Lashlie gives a lot of great, no-nonsense advice on raising boys – ensuring they survive fast cars, alcohol and drugs to become good, articulate men. She admires men for their skill, intuition, pragmatism, humour and ability to become children again at a moment's notice; and considers an adolescent boy's mind to be a sacred, magical place.

When I was a child you didn't have to worry about children's feelings because 'feelings' didn't exist. We, the baby boomers, invented feelings at the same time that we invented sex, brown rice and non-prescription drugs. Now we're stuck with all these people – even babies – who have feelings. Good Mummy treats her boy like the prince he is and lets him go (I know it's difficult) when the time comes. Celia Lashlie's advice to mothers (especially white middle-class ones) is to not get over-involved in the lives of their adolescent sons. She describes adolescence as a bridge that boys have to cross over and suggests that mothers get right off the bridge, in fact don't get on the bridge at all – this is man's work, not women's work. Boys should be on the bridge only with other males. If there is no father in the picture, there are usually other friendly males who can stand encouragingly at the other end of the bridge. The message from boys to their mothers is 'chill out'. There's no point in telling a teenage boy to fold his clothes if he leaves them on the floor for a month – he knows he'll wear them regardless. Boys find these kind of orders incomprehensible. In my childhood I had my clothes folded and colour coded in my drawers – my brothers used to look at this with pity.

Ant Grayson

PM 'What do you think women want?'

AG 'Commitment. Guys have a slightly different agenda around that compared with women. It depends on what your connection is. If it's a marriage, commitment means love, support, flexibility. You have to find someone who has the same values as you but who is her own person. That way you are aligned. Marriage is probably the biggest single decision you make in your life.'

PM 'Do you need a woman in your life?'

AG 'Yes and not just one. I need a whole bunch of women – friends, sisters and colleagues. The best advice I get comes from women – they're not afraid to tell it like it is. There are some feisty women at work, who I adore, and they have made me a better person.'

PM 'Do you think men make good companions?'

AG 'We're not bad but women are better at companionship. Sue and her daughter are soul mates; they do everything together, talk all day.'

PM 'How do you resolve disagreements?'

AG 'Sometimes we agree to disagree, but we don't have huge arguments. I like to win, but I also like to think I take all views into account. Someone has to make the decision and it's usually me. If I've not been nice and I've pushed too hard I always apologise.'

PM 'Women have big expectations of men and relationships – do you think men do?'

AG 'No. Men are less "desperate", if you like, and it also depends on who is the breadwinner. If the male is the breadwinner then the female has big expectations. If, as in our case, we are both breadwinners, then automatically expectations level out.'

PM 'How do you think men are doing these days?'

AG 'Look, if men are not comfortable with themselves then they will have major problems. If you know who you are, you can ride with changes. Women are far more comfortable in themselves, I think. It's really interesting for me watching my sons with their female friends – they're very relaxed and close with each other in their friendships – more so than I was at that age. They confide in girls, they're smart and they have fun.'

PM 'Is it important for boys to have a good relationship with their mother?'

AG 'Hugely important. My ex-wife is very knowledgeable about anything to do with our boys – their sports, et cetera – she's involved with them on every level.'

PM 'Is it good to be a man? Would you rather be a woman?'

AG 'Ha ha – no, I'm suited to being a man.'

AG's partner, Sue, shouting from the kitchen:
'He would make an appalling woman.'

CAN YOU JUDGE A BOOK BY ITS COVER?

You can tell a lot about a man just by looking at him. The ancient Greeks believed a person's character could be glimpsed in their face. This idea became popular again in the eighteenth century, when Swiss poet Johann Lavater called it 'physiognomy', and by the time Charles Darwin came along it was an accepted 'science'. Then in the nineteenth century it became associated with phrenology, the detailed study of the shape and size of the cranium, a supposed indication of character and mental abilities, and lost favour. But now there is a resurgence with 'new physiognomy' – researchers are wondering if we really can judge a book by its cover, or even predict its destiny. We all know that first impressions count – within a tenth of a second of seeing a stranger's face we have judged it as caring, trustworthy, aggressive, extrovert, competent, et cetera. Once that snap judgement has been made, it is very hard to yield to another impression. The interesting thing is that if your first impression of someone is that they are slimy, most often others will get the same impression – it is unusual for several people to get completely different impressions. We act on these snap judgements: politicians with competent-looking faces get elected; CEOs who look dominant are more successful; compassionate-looking faces become doctors and social workers. If a baby-faced man appears in court he is more likely to get off a criminal charge than a mature-faced man. Also, if a man is handsome, life is handed to him on a silver platter – he gets more Valentines, more attention from women and is judged, solely on the basis of his good-looking face, to be more outgoing, socially sophisticated, powerful, sexy, brainy and healthy. People are automatically nicer to handsome men.

But are baby-faced men really naive and submissive? Are strong-faced men really dominant, or are we just jumping to superficial conclusions? Why do we so strongly judge a person's character by their face? How many 'honest' faces have you met who turn out to really be honest? Personally, I always trust gut reactions, but my friend Gwendoline assures me that that is just gastroenteritis.

Some scientists think there must be an evolutionary advantage to judging a book by its cover. In a study in Canada last year it was found that men with wide faces (cheekbone to cheekbone distance) were not only judged to be aggressive and dominant, but were actually more given to violence and had a higher level of testosterone. In evolutionary terms we judge these men as more likely to attack us. This could also be rubbish. My friend Mike is tall, big, has a deep voice and has a wide face. He is a lamb.

What about self-fulfilling prophesies? If you judge a person's face as untrustworthy and treat them that way they end up behaving that way. If you give a baby girl a name like Peta, she will become that name – she will become tough because of the constant teasing and attention attracted to an unusual name. I'm sure if I had been called Mary, I would be a different person. The French say you end up with the face you deserve, so maybe you can judge character better on an older face.

HOW TO IMPRESS A WOMAN

In the days when I often visited Greece it still cost practically nothing to holiday there and the only requirements were a swimsuit, toothbrush, birth control and a copy of Lawrence Durrell's *Reflections on a Marine Venus*. Getting off the plane in Rhodes, one is immediately hit by the roasted incandescence of the climate. I settled into a pension where my breakfast of eggs fried in green olive oil was prepared for me every morning by the lady of the house. On a melting Olympian morning I was sipping my sweet, grainy coffee at my usual little café when Theo sat down at my table. Theo was a Greek God who lived on Rhodes, sent by Aphrodite for me to lavish my tenderness on. I was recovering from an incident involving an old man flirting with me, a spilt glass of Ouzo (at ten in the morning) and a backhander. I'll leave you to figure out who got what but here's a hint – there was also an old lady involved. But back to Theo. He smoothed over the fracas and gently smiled his way into my veins.

For two glorious weeks I read and wrote by day and trysted by night. Theo smoked tarry, short, Greek cigarettes and my hair became more tangled and snake-like by the day. There's something about Rhodes with its dry, dusty streets and relaxed pace of life that is very healing if you've been living in mad Paris. What's not relaxing is that they speak a language that seems to be made up entirely of 'x's, 'th's and thirty-seven-letter words. I don't speak one word of this ancient language and Theo didn't speak English or French, but we communicated effortlessly. Of course lust is by its nature impermanent and passion cannot be confused with real life, but one forgets all those things when faced with an Adonis. Theo slept by day and sang by night. Greek men tell you how they feel all the time; their emotions are obvious and flirtation is always in the air. He was brown of skin, eyes and hair, had a truly Greek body and as is completely normal after knowing someone for only three days, he declared his undying love for me. He was inventive and romantic. He sourced all sorts of idyllic settings for our trysts. The fact that we could have got a ten-year prison sentence should we have been caught only made it more exciting. One of the most memorable locations was the garden of a private mansion under a voluptuous bower of lilacs and honeysuckle.

He sang traditional Greek songs in a nightclub, to which I was invited every night, and sent the most expensive wine the house could produce to my table. Then he sent me little delicacies, little tokens of his affection from the kitchen. These were laid out before me like his feelings in all their simplicity and complexity. I tasted succulent baby octopus marinated in olive oil, lemon juice, garlic and parsley; tiny deep-fried sardines with their tails pressed together to form a fan shape and fresh grapevine leaves stuffed most delicately with shallots, rice, tiny black Corinthian currants, pine nuts and dill. I managed to soar to great heights of culinary ecstasy while still technically attached to my chair.

This was truly the food of the gods and my senses were infiltrated with the mélange of Theo's perfume, the spices and herbs and the aroma of Greek wine. He explained to me in great detail how these dishes were made. When you tell someone a recipe you tell them a love story – it's sublime alchemy.

Lust is an ideal fantasy that I think modern people seek like the courtly love of the fourteenth century. It remains artificial, a literary convention, a fantasy – like pornography – more for the purposes of discussion than for everyday reality. It is like the concept of paying for sex. The minute you involve money, the minute the fantasy is lived out, the party's over. The opposite is true of psychoanalysis, for example. The minute you involve money the party really starts – it only works if it costs you your first-born son. Craving an object of desire who can never be domesticated and the gluttony of lust makes the impossibility of it all the sweeter.

In the legend of the Châtelain de Coucy, the hero fell for the lady of the castle, an event she bitterly regretted and which ruined her taste buds forever. The fruits of love would never taste so foul. Her husband, the lord of the castle, got wind of the wooing, moaning and general subterfuge and, as anyone would do in such circumstances, sent the hero off to the front line where he belonged. Before he died from a poisoned arrow wound the hero wrote one last passionate love letter, instructing the dispatch person to deliver it to his lady love along with his heart and a lock of her hair she had given him. The lord of the castle got hold of the barbaric little present, cooked the heart up and served it to his wife for dinner. Upon finding out what she had eaten she swore it was the most noble, tasty meal of her life, declared that she need never eat again, and didn't. Call me old-fashioned, but I miss those days. This legend is much more erotic than pornography because it has melancholy, tension, depth and an unusual recipe.

At the end of my holiday I returned to Paris, and Theo and I wrote love letters to each other with the help of the bewildered owners of the Greek restaurant down the road, who wished they'd never spoken a word of Greek in their lives. Unfortunately, Greek Gods are for myths. We both wanted nothing more than to play house forever because we fitted each other like satin slippers, but I started to say au revoir to Theo from almost the minute I met him. The heat and purple dusks of Rhodes were soon undone as the reality of a grey, dreary Parisian autumn drowned out mythology. The rain made the words in his letters run; I recommenced eating croissants instead of dripping baklava and knew in my heart that Theo could not survive the trip into my quotidian life. Eventually, we gave up writing to each other as lust is by its nature transient. Most normal people and house plants know this, but I am a slow learner. I decided to keep his letters for emotionally rainy days.

LESSONS LEARNED

- None.
- Mahogany seems to be the way to go, but few of us can see the forest for the trees.
- Teenage boys are fabulous and we should listen to them.
- I love saying 'no' to men – I get so little practice.

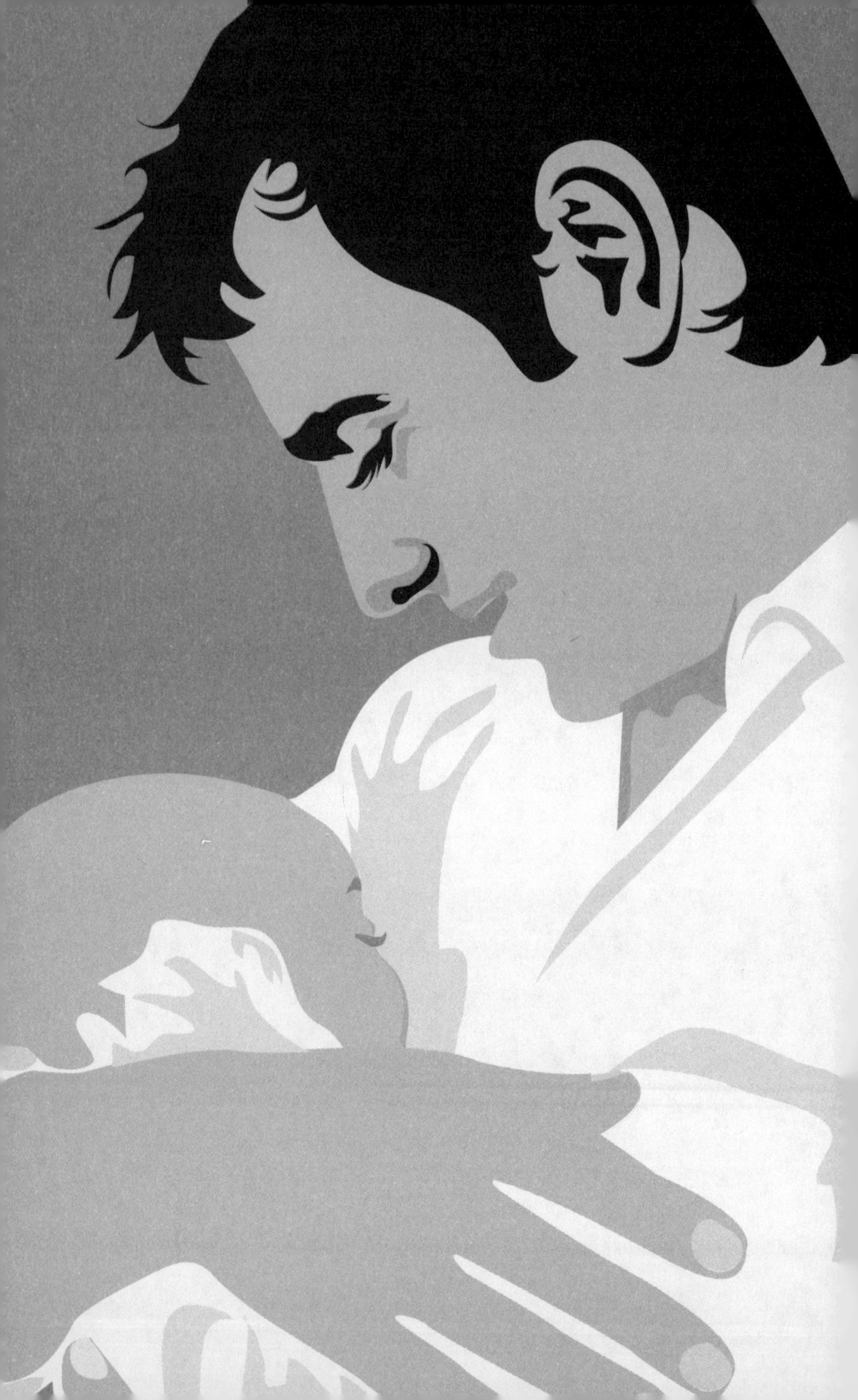

2
Fatherhood
STARK RAVING DAD

NEW MILLENNIUM FATHER

The baby boomer generation was brought up by rather cold, controlling and intrusive parents who, along with school teachers, used physical discipline. This was thought to strengthen the backbone and prevent children from running the world or thinking they had rights. Those baby boomers grew up and exploded into a life that was the sexual revolution, prosperity, television, flower power and mung beans. They said, 'No, no, no. We are free of the strictures, we will do what we like, we are at one with the little flowers in the fields and we will never treat our children the way we were treated. They will be free, loved, indulged and happy. We will be their friends, not their jailers.' Those children now have no idea how to be parents and their little darlings well and truly rule the roost. So now we have the terrifying backlash where tough love and hard care is back in vogue – witness the popularity of nanny television shows using rigid behaviourist principles to rein in naughty children and strict regimes for regulating a baby's eating and sleeping. Even government agencies now crack down on parents who do not control their children.

What makes a man a man is not the ability to have a child, but the courage to raise one. It used to be that fathers knew what their job was – it was to earn money and support the family, otherwise they would be destitute. Nobody asked fathers to sweep the floor, do the washing or stand up straight on Saturday night (except in my house). My father was a complete anachronism in our neighbourhood because he not only earned money, but he also changed nappies and hung a machine load of washing out before he went to work. He also baked cakes, strangled chooks and every so often did completely insane things like buy a house without telling my mother.

Fathers' narrow roles changed when women started working outside the home and earning money – the power balance changed. Then, because they had money, the women had choices and one of them was not to stay in bad relationships. So, now there are fewer fathers around but the ones who *are* stable fixtures in their children's lives are very embedded. They want to be like Brad Pitt – babies strapped to every arm and leg. It's considered sexy now to be a good father. Divorced men find that it's a great way to pull women – 'Oooh, look he must be nice if he's involved with his children' (by and large this is probably true). A baby buggy is a now a woman magnet; even a man with a dog seems nice.

There is a school of thought that says boys don't miss out on one single thing by not having fathers – there's nothing magical about them and it's very simplistic to think that fathers are important, simply because they're male. What if Dad's a pimp,

FATHERHOOD

what if Dad's violent, what if Dad thinks McDonald's is food? I tend to think men do things differently just because of testosterone and that's enjoyable for a male child to witness. Research shows that when men are separated from their children they suffer and so do the children. Unless the father is really bad, even a hopeless father is better than nothing. I suppose one has to remember that the mother and child have different relationships with a man: for the woman, he was someone she slept with; for the boy, he is his father.

Greg Blake

GB 'When you have a child, this inexplicable thing happens. Everyone tells you it will happen but when it does, it's very strong and you feel biologically connected to this person who you want to look after, no matter what. I had separated from my daughter's mother before her birth but I absolutely wanted to father her. That's the worst thing a father can do to their child – to desert them.'

PM 'What's your relationship with your daughter like?'

GB 'I enjoy her and we're very close. One of the most amazing things you can hear is the laughter of your own child.'

PM 'Children must teach you things – they must make you grow up, although that doesn't seem to have happened in your case, Greg.'

GB (Laughs) 'Thank you, Peta. Actually, not having your child all the time, as is the case with me, does make me stop everything for her when she is with me. I don't socialise much, don't drink, don't work – I just concentrate on her.'

PM 'Do you think she's like you?'

GB 'Yeah, in some ways. She has this thing where her eyes go out of focus. She's there and she is hearing and can respond but is somewhere else at the same time. I do that. She was pleased when I told her I do it too.'

PM 'What about older fatherhood? You're fifty and your wife is quite a bit younger. They say older men make better fathers.'

GB 'Yeah, they probably do, not only because they don't have the work pressure but also because they don't have the biological sexual pressure they had when they were young. You're not as obsessed with chasing women as you get older, especially if you are happily married. Anyway, you're only as old as you allow yourself to be. It's your responsibility to keep young and interested in your life.'

David Horsman

PM 'Tell me about your relationship with your father.'

DH 'Not easy. I've done a lot of work on myself over the years – therapy, Hoffman process, et cetera – learning to understand patterns of behaviour. The main thing I learned from all of that is that you are your own person. You can't blame your parents for anything and you must have the courage and strength to accept

> that. When you get to that stage, the ties that bind just fall away. It's only in recent years I've been able to confront all my father stuff.'
>
> **PM** 'Did you feel loved by your father?'
>
> **DH** 'Love is a really, really tricky one, especially father–son love. A parent can't help but naturally love their child (with a few exceptions), even if they can't show it. During my childhood you could maybe talk about it but didn't show it. Humans are a species who recognise very quickly the difference between what is being said and what is actually happening. You can't trick children – they know perfectly well if they are being lied to. This leads to a lot of confusion and takes a long time to work through later, in adulthood.'
>
> **PM** 'They say that in order to really become yourself you have to kill the mother or father metaphorically.'
>
> **DH** 'That's exactly what happens in the Hoffman process. You even get to dig a hole and bury them.'
>
> **PM** 'I did a similar thing and it transformed me. It got so bad with me I was having violent, murderous nightmares. It's amazing how much these primary relationships affect you. And then once it's gone, it's gone and you actually get to have an adult relationship with them and appreciate them as interesting, complex people.'

TEACHING BOYS

I know of a preschool that's run by a bloke. This is like saying I know of a butcher shop run by a vegetarian. The little boys there play with swords and toy guns while dressed up in superhero outfits. There is a wrestling mat for play-fighting, because boys have to be 'boysterous'. The theory is that because there are fewer and fewer male teachers and classrooms are becoming increasingly feminised, boys' natural behaviour is being inhibited. Some primary schools have no male teachers whatsoever. Boys seem to be struggling academically, although that does iron itself out. But 80 per cent of naughty kids at schools are boys; 75 per cent of teenagers who end up before the courts are boys; and the majority of those who develop serious psychological illnesses are male, as are those who commit suicide. Some people feel that it's not that men are better teachers than women; it's that they have emotional and social roles to perform which can't be done by women. Because there are so many single-mother families, sometimes a boy won't come across a man in any real, dynamic sense until high school. The only role models they know are sports players and we all know how admirable they are. A mature man knows how boys are because they were the same once – they know they play fight quite aggressively, get morose, and can't sit still. They get the physicality of it. A man will stand back and let them get on with it when boys are in conflict; a woman will intervene to stop the aggression.

Men encourage risk and go beyond what women will consider safe. If you want a child – male or female – to grow up creative and innovative, you have to let them take risks and restrain yourself from being over-protective. I can spit this out easily, because I don't have children. If I did, I would lock them in the toilet until they were twenty-one – I would be so fearful that they would trip on the front step.

What boys have to figure out is what it means to be male and

FATHERHOOD

how you turn out to be a good man. A lot of male teachers don't think women teachers really know enough about male behaviour. Of course there are many people who say that's rubbish – it doesn't matter who teaches boys so long as they're competent. One of the main reasons men don't want to go into teaching any more is the stain of sexual abuse accusations in the school system – they are afraid of being stained themselves. Another reason is the all-female work situation and yet another the pathetic pay. Some feel we need to attract more good men into teaching because it's not just a question of doing well academically, it's about turning boys into proud men who do men's stuff and feel happy with who they are.

Steve Yeoman

PM 'Were you present at the birth of your daughters?'

SY 'When my first daughter was born, we had to apply to the medical commissioner of health for permission for me to be in the room for the delivery. By the time the second one came, they were asking for fathers to be present. I think it's a really good thing for fathers to be there for their children's births because they are part of it – why wouldn't you be there? I didn't find it terrifying – don't make me blub – I found it incredibly important and deep. It's life and death you know. I saw my mum off at the end, too, when she died and it was the same feeling. I get this every time I have anything to do with birth – it's a profound, gutsy experience – it is one of the sublime moments of life and it gets me every time. Birth helps you to understand yourself in a way that nothing else can. In terms of birth and death, I think the person who is doing it, should make the decisions as to how it will be – this includes caesareans, assisted death et cetera – it's their business and right, not anyone else's. With my second daughter's birth, we adopted her, but the parents were friends of ours. I arrived at the hospital about an hour after she was born. I walked into the room and said, "I'm the father." The other bloke said, "I'm the husband."'

PM 'Did you have a good relationship with your own father?'

SY 'Yes. He was a lovely, gentle old man – he was forty-nine when I was born. He was a war hero and we were surrounded by his soldier cronies. He had lots of family who all liked each other. My father taught me how to be a man, was a good role model, and shaped an awful lot of what I do and think – little things like be nice to others, leave a place tidier than when you found it, and don't shout when you can use gentle words. When I find myself shouting I always remember him and think, "Oh I'm not explaining myself clearly." He was a gentleman with good values who doted on his children. He never expected to have children because he was injured in the war and my mother had had polio.'

PM 'Was he emotional – did you have an emotional connection?'

FATHERHOOD

SY 'No. Men didn't do emotion in those days, but we knew he loved us. He was a stiff-upper-lip Englishman. When one of my daughters turned out to have serious health problems I just accepted it and got on with things as my father would have done. Now I'm going to blub again.'

PM 'Do you think that the ways you cope with life's bad spots are coloured by the way you were brought up?'

SY 'Yes, absolutely – my father taught me that there is a right way of doing things and you just do it. He had no time for people who he thought were wrong and would tell them so, but not in a demeaning way. I am not half as good as him but I have tried to teach my children to be like that. I love being a father and a grandfather.'

FATHER'S DAY

Father's Day was invented in America in 1908 so that men wouldn't get jealous of Mother's Day. As if they didn't already get enough attention. I happen to have the father most people wish they had – kind, gentle, loving, witty and taken to bit of a flutter on the horses. As a child, I went up the road to the trots and to the TAB with him, enjoying the indescribably wonderful smell of horses and the camaraderie of the betting shop. My mother was considerably less enchanted with his betting. My father, as luck would have it, was also a good cook, especially of sweets, for which his teeth were specially made. He never got tired of them and still isn't – dessert every night and always lots of cakes and biscuits in the tins. He still makes the best scones this side of the black stump. I interviewed the fathers in my family for this story and they all said Father's Day for them meant being with the family, especially their sons, and eating. Nobody mentioned presents but they would accept cards with outrageous messages like 'You are the best father in the whole world'.

This is also a day where you are free to adore and worship other men who have helped father you, like step-fathers, uncles, friends and grandfathers. If you do want to give gifts, please stand back from ties, socks and books with titles like *How to Access Your Inner Tantric Sex God* – most men already have these things. Better to veer towards gourmet food packages like organic pork, a case of pinot noir, or remortgage the house and have some black truffles sent up from a faraway place. Better still, shout your father a holiday to a faraway place where men are men and if it's not brown with froth on top, then it can't be good wine. None of the men in my family specified *exactly* what they wanted to eat, but I know deep within me they will be unable to refuse my home-made baked beans. Home-made baked beans are great on burnt toast with sausages for breakfast; on bruschetta as an antipasto; and are fabulous for brunch, a light lunch or an easy supper. In fact, they are always sublime. They will keep in the fridge for up to a week and also freeze well – all of which is very handy for men, who are fond of saying, 'There is *absolutely nothing* in this bloody fridge.'

HOME-MADE BAKED BEANS

Serves 6 fathers

500 g haricot beans, soaked overnight
2 tbsp extra virgin olive oil
300 g bacon in one piece
2 small onions, chopped
4 cloves garlic, chopped
¼ cup white wine
3 x 400 g cans diced tomatoes
2 tbsp brown sugar
2 tbsp molasses
1 tbsp Dijon mustard
2 bay leaves
1 tsp sea salt
1 tsp black pepper, freshly ground
½ cup fresh basil, chopped
½ cup fresh flat-leaf parsley, chopped

1. Rinse beans and boil until almost tender (approximately 30 minutes).
2. Heat oil in large, heavy-based pot, add bacon piece, onion and garlic, and sauté until golden.
3. Add wine, tomatoes, brown sugar, molasses, mustard, bay leaves, salt and pepper. Cook for 30 minutes on medium-low heat, stirring from time to time.
4. Add beans to sauce. Cook a further 30 minutes, stirring occasionally. Remove from heat, add chopped basil and parsley. Salt if necessary.
5. To serve: Slice up the bacon and serve warm with beans.

Jeff Avery

PM 'I think the nuclear family, which is still being doggedly held up as the ideal to strive for, is actually too big an ask for most people. Mum, Dad and the kids seems to create too much pressure. Do you agree?'

JA 'Yeah. In a way we need to completely restructure the system where you need ten people to bring up a child, work the farm, survive, work together.

PM 'Also we had a lot more physical freedom when we were children. We were out in the bush all day building tree huts and stuff on our own. Your mother just said, "Be home in time for dinner." No parent would do that now – we are very over-protective. We are stifling their adventurousness.'

JA 'If you don't let kids make mistakes, they will be unable to learn about calculated risk, about good decision-making'.

PM 'How do you get boys to do things?'

JA 'My method is opposite to my wife's. Women are very ordered and responsible, but boys (and men) just like playing, so you have to turn chores into games that appeal to their brain. Boys hate being told what to do; you have to be creative about it. My son responds better to this method because boys are not about time frames. They are like goldfish – all over the place. If he comes home in a bad mood, as soon as things turn into fun, he's over it in a second. I mean, you go to a party of gay men – they're having a ball.'

FATHERHOOD

PM 'Because they're not being controlled by women. What was your relationship with your father like?'

JA 'Very different from how I am with my son. I play and hang out with my son a lot. My father was down in the wood shed, but he was always supportive and "there". He went to all my sports games. Our relationship was based on sports and that was mostly what we talked about – that's still what we talk about.'

PM 'Did you feel loved by him?'

JA 'Totally. I can remember coming home every day and jumping into his arms. He led by example – there were no heart-to-heart conversations. His morals are mine: if he says he will do something, he does it; if he makes a mistake, he puts his hand up; he treats people the way you wish to be treated. My mother was devoted to me.'

PM 'Which is why you are good to women and like them. Were you present at your son's birth?'

JA 'Yeah. I think it's very important to do because during the pregnancy you're the back-rub guy, but you're not really connected with it and there's still only the two of you. You're a bit worried, especially if it's a surprise pregnancy, and you're thinking "Oh my God, my life is going to be over, I won't play music any more, et cetera, et cetera." So if you are present at the birth it snaps you into reality. The moment you take your baby from the hospital to the car, you change. You become a protective father and start screaming at all the bad drivers on the road who are endangering

> your child and wife. You don't really connect with the baby until it distinguishes you from a chair and smiles. You change from being free of responsibility to realising you must now provide for this child, feeling it is now your purpose. In fact, nothing changes really and your life isn't ruined – I still do everything I did before. We chose for Jane to stay home and me to work while Angus was young. We thought it was really important for one of us to be at home because it gives the child security.'
>
> **PM** 'Did you have any ideas about fathering before Angus came along?'
>
> **JA** 'No, but it's just common sense and I had a good example with my own parents. I would never force a child to eat, for example, because it doesn't make sense to me.'
>
> **PM** 'What is that thing where children won't eat and parents have to force them?'
>
> **JA** 'Children are grazers – they don't want three meals a day. They like small amounts of food often.'

GOOD OLD DAD: YOUNG AT HEART

Stand back. Older fathers, or SODs (Start Over Dads), are on the increase. In 1971 the average age of a new baby's father was twenty-seven years; by 2004 it was thirty-two. In the United States there has been an 18 per cent rise in fathers aged forty and above over the last ten years. In Great Britain one in ten babies is now born to a father over forty and one in a hundred is born to a father aged over fifty, which is probably a conservative estimate.

FATHERHOOD

In 2004 in Australia the percentage of married men having children at forty or older had tripled from thirty years ago. In New Zealand the average age of a new father is now thirty-three. Paul McCartney was sixty-one when he had Beatrice, Rod Stewart was sixty when he had his most recent child, Eric Clapton was fifty-six, Rupert Murdoch seventy-two, and Luciano Pavarotti sixty-seven – to name but a few.

Young fathers pay more attention when they have children in the car, but old fathers are hysterical about it – they suffer from baby-in-car rage and have huge flashing lights and signs on their Range Rovers. Late fathers make very good fathers the way most men make good grandfathers – they are just wiser, more relaxed and much more involved with their kids. The list goes on: more mature, tolerant and affectionate; help more with housekeeping and washing; are probably more obedient. They are less likely to do a runner on the young wife because they can no longer run.

Older fathers are also not in the 'making it professionally' demented phase of their lives, which psychologists call 'provider fever'. When men are young they are very bound up with anxiety about their careers and succeeding. There is the concern that the age difference between an older father and his children is so great he can't relate to them but I think that is just a matter of attitude – plenty of younger fathers can't relate either and older ones are so patient and sweet with their kids. Even if they don't really wish to start a new family with the younger wife, most older men say they don't regret it and enjoy their second family much more than their first.

Why do they do it? Why would you go through all that with your first family – earn a bit of independence and peace – only to start from square one again? The answer is much higher divorce rates – some of these jokers are on the third wife (they catch them in bars or at their grandchildren's play centre). They believe that life is too important to be taken seriously and what the hell, they're not old in their outlook anyway. It's a way of keeping young and keeping on learning – late babies remind you of the forgotten, imaginary world children indulge in and how charming it is.

THE HAZARDS OF LATE FATHERHOOD

1. If he misplaces the Viagra, he's done for. Also, elderly sperm has trouble swimming in a straight line – I'm serious – which makes it hard to get to target.
2. His sperm is no longer tip-top quality, and the risk of Down syndrome, autism and schizophrenia in children increases.
3. He can't move fast when the projectile vomiting starts.
4. If he's left his glasses upstairs it's almost impossible to measure the milk formula properly in the middle of the night.
5. His children are embarrassed to have a craggy father.
6. His children and grandchildren are the same age and they all think he's Daddy.
7. Late fatherhood can be dangerous for a man's health. The father of crooner Julio Iglesias had a heart attack at the age of ninety, days after hearing he was expecting his fourth child. Just in time to be too late.

Richard Pringle

PM 'You're a university professor, Richard. Tell me about how men are seen in terms of research.'

RP 'The subject of men wasn't really examined until the late 1980s. Research wise, the topic was invisible. There have been a lot of women's studies, but very few men's. The initial research was quite negative in that men were seen as the problem, they dominate prison populations, they die seven years earlier, cause the majority of the car accidents (which is interesting because men think they can drive better). Within literature, masculinity was looked upon as a problem. This was the result of a Marxist view that men held all the power. Only a few men actually had this power but the rest were complicit in the idea of powerful manhood, and yet many men were suffering with this concept of the dominant male, not showing pain, not admitting weakness, et cetera. Then there started to be a backlash – men didn't want to be portrayed as violent losers.'

PM 'Yes. There are the ads on TV where men are portrayed as hopeless and figures of fun.'

RP 'Most men don't care about those ads but there are a minority who do and they are provoking a small backlash.'

PM 'The courts are much fairer now regarding custody arrangements. Nevertheless, aren't there some fatherhood groups who are quite strongly anti-feminist?'

RP 'I am not sure about whether the fatherhood groups are anti-women or more concerned that the laws don't recognise the value of fatherhood equally. But there have been "backlash" groups against feminism, such as the Promise Keepers movement – an American conservative religious group making inroads into other countries. They argue that men need to recognise that they are leaders in the family and men need to promise to recognise that they are the ones (given God's word) who should make decisions, because women's leadership in the family is leading to problems. In a similar manner, there are groups concerned about education and some blame feminism for supposedly "failing boys". Evidence suggests that boys and girls prefer teachers – irrespective of gender – who are good teachers.'

PM 'What do boys *want* to excel in?'

RP 'Sport, to a large extent. Boys would rather fail in the classroom than on the sports field – as failing in sport is failing to be manly – so I think in some respects boys' ideas about "masculinity" may play a major part in shaping how they value school and how they do in school. In this sense, it is social conditioning rather than inherent genetic biological differences that appear to have most input into shaping success in schools. But the bottom line – irrespective of qualifications – is that males still tend to earn more than females in the workforce.'

PM 'Can you expand on the Marxist approach to

masculinity as opposed to the poststructuralist one?'

RP 'With respect to Marxism and masculinities, the theory is linked strongly to Robert Connell's work – who is now known as Raewyn Connell. (S)he promoted the idea of hegemonic (dominant) masculinity, which draws from feminism and neo-Marxism, and argues (in a more complex manner than I will describe) that the leaders in society, for example businessmen, priests, principals, politicians and army leaders, are overwhelmingly male and therefore these leaders are in a strong position to shape policy and ideology. With respect to gender, they promote a form of masculinity (via ideological means) known as "hegemonic masculinity" (for example, movies like *Rambo* and the James Bonds, and sports like rugby) which informs people that the dominant and most respected way of being manly is to be tough, aggressive, heterosexual, pain tolerant, competitive, et cetera. This dominant form of masculinity (apparently) works in insidious ways so that people in general think it is normal or natural for males to dominate females, and for "strong" males to dominate weak or effeminate males. So this ideology supposedly works to legitimate male power in institutions, shapes gender relations in favour of men and discriminates against gay men. This theoretical perspective was popular with academics in the 1980s and 1990s, but many have also criticised it. Like all theories, it has strengths and weaknesses – I like the idea that this theory helps explain why females (who are known to be safer drivers) often let males drive. Yet I think the flaws of the theory outweigh its strengths.'

PM 'So what's poststructuralism?'

RP 'Poststructuralism is a social theory linked to the rejection of the idea that individuals can know the correct structure of the social world. For example, in the 1960s some people started to question whether Marx's view of the world was correct. A prominent poststructuralist is Michel Foucault, who died of an AIDS-related illness in 1984. His basic idea was that the "meanings" we create about our social world influence how we operate within, so he was interested in trying to understand how people create meanings (which he termed discourses) about social life and themselves. These meanings then influence how people know themselves and each other and how we interact and treat each other; they are therefore connected to the workings of power.

'For example, men in the 1950s were known as intelligent, strong and adventurous and this helped legitimate their position as social leaders in social institutions and in the family. Women on the other hand were perhaps known as nurturers, kind, loving, but also weak and not as intelligent as men. Such knowledge, or discourse position, supported the idea that women should not have strong leadership responsibilities. Our knowledge about men and women has changed greatly since the 1950s. And a

Foucauldian approach is interested in understanding what has helped change these knowledges – how these changes have influenced the lives of men and women and changed power relations. A poststructuralist approach does not position men as holders of power but accepts that we are all able to exercise some degree of power and shape other people's views (for example your books, Peta, will have an impact on how people "know" men and women).

'More generally, this theoretical view does not overtly worry about whether men are driven by hormones or the so-called nature–nurture debate but is concerned with how we "know" males; that is, there is the common knowledge "boys will be boys", so how does this knowledge influence teachers and parents? Do they treat boys differently? Are they forgiving if they have been in a fight? Thus, a poststructuralist view accepts that men and women all help shape knowledge about boys and men and therefore we need to be careful with how we parent and school our boys (and girls). A poststructuralist view allows us to consider research questions, such as: "How does rugby influence men's understandings about masculinities?" More generally, such an approach would reject the idea that boys need "male" role models in education (that is, male teachers) but would be interested to understand how boys construct meanings about female and male teachers and how those meanings influence their views and values of education. The subsequent research results suggest that boys prefer teachers that help them learn irrespective of whether they are male or female.

'There is a recognition that the clear majority of males are doing many wonderful things – they are taking an increased interest in their children, changing nappies, are critical of violence and alcohol abuse, are also critical of the ideas that men should not cry or show emotions. Many men are also critical of sexism and a smaller number of homophobia (yet the clear majority would advocate that it is wrong to "beat up" gay men). Although I would not say that there has been a radical revolution in masculinities, the boys of today are being raised in a very different context from the 1950s and for the large part, these changes are positive. Many men, and of course women, are concerned about domestic violence – how would the story of a sportsman's violence against his partner have been treated in the 1950s? Would it have even got into the media?'

CUCKOLD DADDY

A research study conducted in the 1950s concluded that about 10 per cent of all babies born in America were fathered by someone other than the man who raised the child. The study was considered to be too scandalous to be made public and the findings were hushed up. In about 1990, a new paternity research study was conducted. This study confirmed the accuracy of earlier statistics. This time the study's findings were made public along with the results of the 1950s study. It is actually believed that the percentage is much higher – probably 30 per cent. Women have been having babies with men other than their significant others since the beginning of human time. In addition, adoption and the raising of other people's children has also taken place since early civilization, and children will thrive in a loving home with committed parents – no matter who their biological fathers are.

Anthony Grayson

PM 'Tell me about your father.'

AG 'My father was an orthopaedic surgeon. He was the only orthopaedic surgeon in the area so worked very long hours – eight to eight basically. He is famous for doing the first hip replacement in the mid-sixties, in fact his registrar phoned in sick one day and he asked me into the theatre to assist. And I wasn't just standing around – I was in the thick of it. It was an amazing experience mostly because he had complete trust in me. If I wasn't a banker I would be a surgeon, in fact, I idolise my youngest brother for being a surgeon.'

PM 'I come from a large family too. Do you think that the position you held and the role you played in your family is the role you play throughout life?'

AG 'Yes I do. I would probably be the glue in the family with three older siblings and three younger, and as a banker I am essentially a middleman. Bankers only exist because the people who have got the money don't necessarily trust the people who want the money.'

PM 'Did you feel loved by your father?'

AG 'Not necessarily loved in those words but supported. He was the sort of father who led by example. Dad did his absolute best for all of us. What I loved about my upbringing was we enjoyed a lot of autonomy and trust. When I really, really needed to call on Dad was when my marriage broke up. I was bawling my eyes out and said, "Dad I feel like I've dug a hole, jumped into it and now I'm pouring earth on myself." He said to me, "From this day forward, it will only be improvement. You've been dealing with all this and now you'll be fine." I just felt totally comfortable with him. I have been fortunate and done well in my life and to lose my marriage was a great failure. You know the way I feel about my father is that I would hate to damage his reputation. He is a listener and I think I am getting better at that; he is caring, fair, calm and has good judgement – all qualities that I hope have influenced me.'

PM 'Obviously your relationship with your father is wonderful. What's it like with your sons?'

AG 'I had four sons. Two of them died in the womb, which was incredibly traumatic for me and my wife. The other two are great.'

PM 'Were you present at the deliveries?'

AG 'Yes, I was present at all of them. It was fantastic. I was quite comfortable with the whole thing, probably because my father was a doctor. You need to be there to support your partner and to see what you

FATHERHOOD

have created together being born. I think my greatest achievement is to have been happily married and had two children. That's what we're put on earth to do. When my wife threw me out, the most important thing for me was to stay in touch with the boys. I now have a lovely relationship with my ex-wife and am actually able to stay in her house with the boys when I visit them. I think it's good for the boys to see that we can get along even though we're not together. Now the focus is totally on them. I am emotionally connected with my kids and they have done well, so it's good, but you know, these days it's not only parents who are more emotionally open, the kids are very forward and expect it. The aim is to have a relationship with your kids where they can approach you about anything without fear.'

LESSONS LEARNED

- To be a father is a beautiful privilege. A father can help boys become proud men who do men's stuff and feel happy with who they are.
- It's considered sexy now to be a good father – if you're divorced it's a great way to pull women. A baby buggy is a woman magnet.
- It's never too early in the day to have a whiskey if your kid is screaming, 'What fucking planet are you on?'

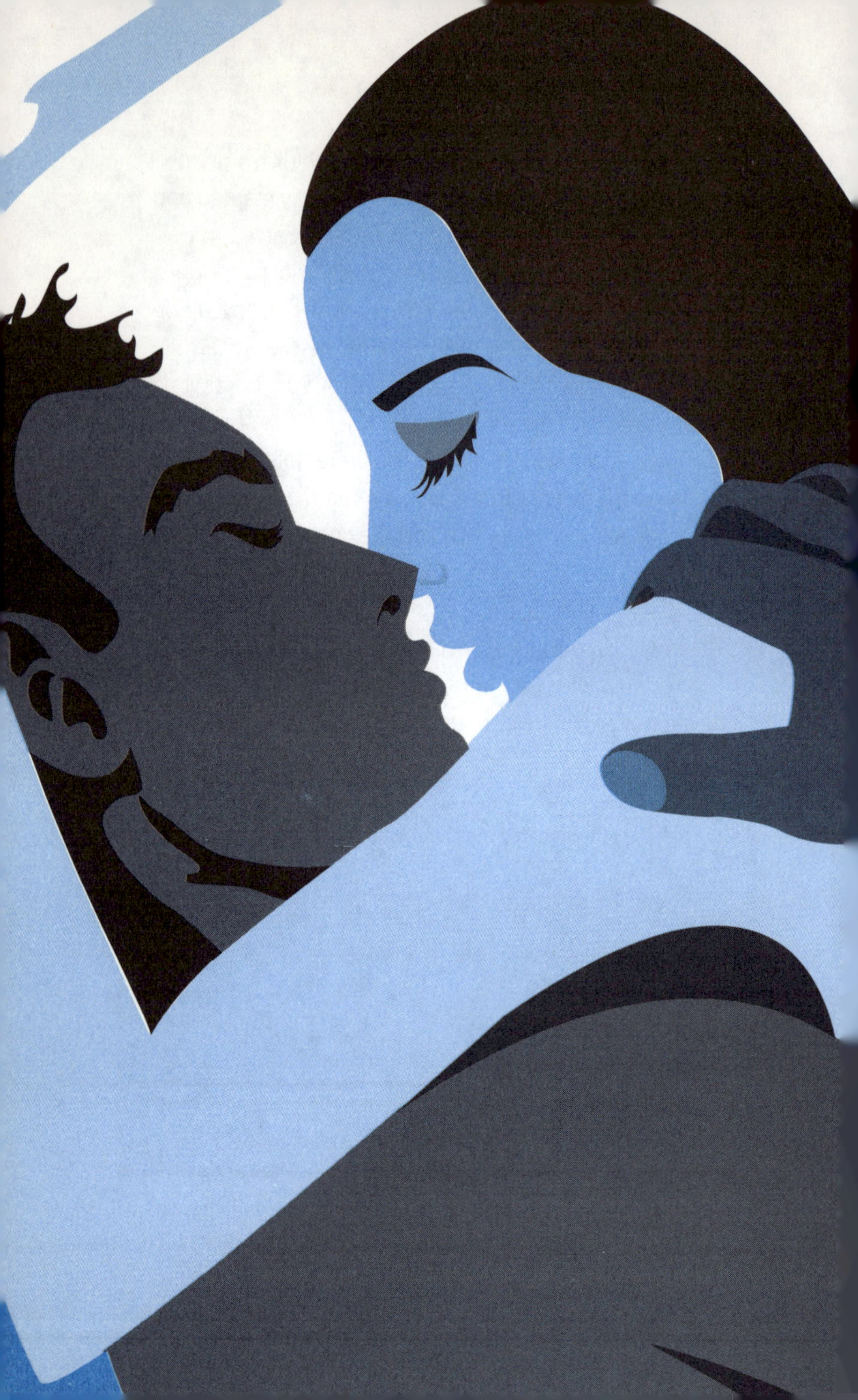

3

Sex & love
IF YOU WALK AWAY FROM ME, I'LL LOVE YOU FROM BEHIND

WHY MEN ARE LIKE BUSES

Men are like buses because you wait and wait and wait then several come at once. The annoying thing about buses all turning up at the same time is they get in your way, are never there in the middle of the night when you need them, cause traffic jams and the bendy ones either run you over or burst into flames. If you end up with a choice of buses/men you could always ride two or three of them, then if you get tired of the ride (as you will because this course of action will be expensive), you can refrain for a while. However, there is a school of thought that says, if you didn't learn anything when the first bus passed by, how can you be sure you'll catch the next one? The key isn't in flagging down the right bus; it's in being the right kind of passenger. Cripes – talk about blaming the victim.

The great thing about a bus, though, is that it is labelled so you know what your destination is and it does what it says it's going to do. If the bus says 'Paddington', it goes to Paddington, not Golders Green. Men are sometimes hard to read, so it would be helpful for service if they had signs on their foreheads saying things like:

'My wife is married but I'm not.' (Run.)

'If one of us dies, darling, I'm moving to the South of France.' (Serial killer.)

'My boyfriend loves marmalade.' (Get him to redecorate your apartment.)

'I'm emotionally available.' (Move in with him.)

'I love my mother.' (Marry him.)

'I am a bus and you have a free ticket waiting for you at the counter.' (Available and funny.)

Interestingly, a fail-safe way to get the man you really want is to go off with someone else. A man will always come running if he sees that other men are attracted to you and you will often find yourself with two or three men competing for your attention, not because you are so fabulous, but because they are competitive and want to be top ape. Take the case of one night in my Paris restaurant in the 1980s. It's always a good idea to have at least one round table in a restaurant, preferably close to the kitchen. This table is for friends and people who wander in on their own and don't particularly wish to eat alone. It is also for you, the chef, to sit down at from time to time with your friends during breaks in the service. On this night an ex, my husband and a current boyfriend walked in over the period of an hour and sat at this table together, not knowing who the others were. It was only when I walked in and they saw the look on my face that they understood. They shouted each other drinks and thought it very amusing to say, 'Is there anyone in the room you *haven't* slept with

Peta, ha ha?' The next day, another man who had been eating in the restaurant called to say he was so impressed with the scene at the round table that he would like to ask me out. This was, of course, in contrast to all the other nights when I sat alone at the table waiting for a bus to come along.

THE JOY OF SEX

In 1975 I was living in Vancouver in a communal house with three wild, feminist women. We were devouring tomes like *The Joy of Cooking* by Irma S. Rombauer and Marion Rombauer Becker; Erica Jong's *Fear of Flying*; *I'm O.K., You're O.K.*, by Thomas Harris; *The Hite Report: A Nationwide Study of Female Sexuality* by Shere Hite; *Our Bodies Ourselves* by the Boston Women's Health Collective and *Delta of Venus: Erotica* by Anaïs Nin – in fact anything by Anaïs Nin. We enjoyed each other's company so much that men almost felt they were intruding when they came visiting. We lay in the sun in the back yard under the grapevine reading passages from Simone de Beauvoir's *The Second Sex* to each other and discussing our relationships in graphic detail. We had the best parties in the neighbourhood, cooked the best food and were intoxicated with the power of being young, free and loving our lives. We were twenty-five years old, warm and charming in an openly fervent way that to a girl like me, born and raised in an emotional vice grip, was almost perverted. In the 1970s everyone was touchy-feely and into 'getting in touch with their feelings'. All new stuff to me but I thought, What the hell, go with the flow, man, and got in touch with a few feelings of my own. It was a repulsive experience and almost turned me off sharing for life.

Another book we devoured, first published in 1972, was *The Joy of Sex* by Alex Comfort. It sold 12 million copies worldwide, which shows you how dangerous a little knowledge is. Every household had a copy. We all devoured it page by page during the day and practised it by night with our boyfriends. It was aspirational and matter of fact, but also sexy and gave the impression that sex was good, natural and healthy, which by that time, we were beginning to suspect anyway. There was a sense of innocence and treasure about it all. The drawings of a hippy-looking man and woman were very explicit without being pornographic. The man had long hair and a beard, which became famous for its ugliness. He looked okay to me. We had been brought up in a world with no sex so we really needed this book.

And, would you believe it, the book that changed what went on in most of the world's bedrooms has now been updated by Susan Quilliam and reincarnated as *The New Joy of Sex*. But why do an update now when the world is so sexualised that even seven-year-olds know everything? According to Quilliam, we need this book more than ever because even though sex is in our faces, a lot of people still need proper sex education and don't know basic things – such as what a clitoris does, why sex is so powerful, what safe sex is, et cetera. *The New Joy* has new sections including phone sex, the internet, sex shops and sex during pregnancy and there is more emphasis on relationships.

Some bad news is that the Kinsey Institute says contemporary lovers have less sex than people did in the 1950s, because they have so little uncommitted time. Cripes. Quilliam says there are an awful lot of pressures on young people – to look fabulous, to have a fabulous sex life, to do well. We're living in a world where it's important to achieve and whether we have a good sex life has become one of our measures of personal validity. Alex Comfort, the original author, took the emphasis off achievement – that is one of the many things he got right in the original book.

WHAT MEN WANT FROM SEX

1. Vocalisation. You know the old joke – what are the words you least want to hear while making love? 'Hi, honey. I'm home.' What men *do* want to hear is *something*, anything – even an enthusiastic sigh is helpful.
2. Oral sex. Another old joke – why do JAPs (Jewish American Princesses) have crow's feet around their eyes? From squinting and saying, 'Suck what?' Men love oral sex, especially when you manage it with no teeth.
3. Enthusiasm. Nobody wants to feel you are just on autopilot – it's deeply unsexy and makes men feel unattractive and unloved. The same goes if you are asleep – wake up.
4. Taking the initiative occasionally. Without that men just feel like they're pestering.
5. Knowing what you want and like. As you know, men can't read body language – this includes gagging, screaming and convulsing while turning red – so you have to spell out whether or not you're enjoying your lovemaking. Personally, I find this extremely annoying – too much like playing charades.

David Horsman

PM 'Why do you have sex and how does it make you feel?'

DH 'We have sex because we are programmed by hormones to reproduce. If you don't get horny you're not going to reproduce. Sex has been made pleasurable to make sure we do it. It is so pleasurable that 90 per cent of internet spam is pornographic. That is the great irony and hypocrisy of our world – that we don't *do* sex. In ancient Indian culture, sex, society and spirituality all went hand in hand.'

PM 'Don't you think that our sex drive is disproportionately stronger than any other drive? It's almost stronger than the drive to eat and stay alive.'

DH 'But of course. It has to be. We have three impulses: to seek shelter, to eat and to procreate. Therefore eating, fucking and sleeping in a comfortable bed are the point of life.'

PM 'So why are we so hypocritical about it? Why do we suppress it so much?'

DH 'Because it *is* so powerful.'

PM 'I like the way the French are unfucked-up about sex; how they are healthily flirtatious. They seem to understand why men and women are on this earth. I think it is my social responsibility to flirt with as many men as possible. Next question. What makes a woman a good lover?'

DH 'That's very easy to answer. Enthusiasm, curiosity and openness, which covers warmth, love, security. The most important thing for both men and women is to feel secure in something as intimate as sex and nothing is more sexy than enthusiasm. You need a combination of selfishness and selflessness, because sex is an exchange. It's still the bloke who has to take the lead to a large extent.'

PM 'Are orgasms important?'

DH 'Of course they are – they give enormous pleasure. It's quite unusual to have a simultaneous orgasm, though.'

PM 'How do you know the woman has had an orgasm? She could be faking. Women are famous fakers.'

DH 'Really? How many women fake?'

PM 'Probably quite a few, but I can't imagine why you would continue doing that with someone you know well – why not just teach him? I read somewhere that some men can ejaculate without having an orgasm.'

DH 'Not that I know of. Maybe they have a leakage problem?'

PM 'Do you have to be in love with a woman to have good sex?'

DH 'Well I'm not exactly an expert in this field. Fucking everything that moves has never been my game. I like to get into the brain before I go anywhere else. You do have to have some other connection aside from sex, be it a shared sense of humour, intellectual, social – whatever. Most men need this mix – that's what sex appeal is about.'

PM 'Yes. In my experience there *are* some men who

are predators, but they are not the majority. A well-adjusted man will not have sex just because it's offered to him if the situation is not right. For example, if he is married, if he is not particularly attracted, if he doesn't know the woman well enough...'

DH 'Having sex with someone you don't care about is always dumb, mostly because it can lead to misunderstandings and hurting people. Women use men just as much as men use women, probably in a more calculating and vile way. Women can go through whole relationships based on mercenary principles.'

PM 'Of course that can go both ways. You know the expression: women fake orgasms, but men fake whole relationships. Do men hate our capriciousness?'

DH 'No. I think women's capriciousness is wonderful. A lack of understanding is annoying – women think we should understand them but they don't think they should make an effort to understand us. In communication, for example, women talk *to* think while men think *then* talk. Women believe men don't talk enough, but sometimes we just need to sit and watch the footy. Men think women use far too many words to say what they have to say.'

PM 'Do men feel used by women?'

DH 'You yourself say in your book on women that the one thing you want is that we should be able to get it up! Men are extraordinarily sensitive and the sexual thing works both ways – men need, require and want foreplay just like women do. Women seem to think that

SEX & LOVE

men are perpetually horny and want to jump their bones at the drop of a hat. To be put upon because sometimes you have an erectile dysfunction...'

PM 'Impotence *sometimes* is fine, but as a routine it is not fine. It drives us crazy.'

DH 'Well if it's all the time, change the bloke! Sexual dysfunction is probably one of the ways men display the stress in their lives, and you can't do much about it, short of sexual therapy. Women can hide it and not suffer loss of face. These days the world is geared more and more towards women – we even tried to be metrosexuals to please you.'

PM 'Well *that* didn't work – no one wanted the metrosexual. What we want is a sensitive Tarzan.'

DH 'That may take about 40,000 years of evolutionary development. You see, this is a conundrum for men...'

PM 'For women too. We are aware of the fact that we want everything and that we are contrary and give mixed messages and we can't wait for thousands of years of evolution. Human sophistication is just a veneer – it's amazing we do as well as we do.'

DH 'I'm interested in anthropology and finding out what human motivations are and how we are programmed, as elaborated in Desmond Morris's book, *The Naked Ape*, which looks at humans as a species and compares us to other animals. It depicts human behaviour as largely having evolved to meet the challenges of prehistoric life as a hunter-gatherer.'

SEX-INDUCED DEPRESSION?

Research has shown that semen makes you happy but orgasms can make you sad. I know what you're thinking – I asked the same thing. Allegedly, mood-altering hormones in semen are absorbed through the vagina. The study showed that women who had intercourse without condoms were less depressed than the others. Please. A thing that could make you really depressed would be an unwanted pregnancy or an STD, ruining all the happy effects of unfiltered semen. Do you ever feel depressed after sex? It might be the fault of your orgasm. Dr Richard Friedman has found that several of his patients don't just feel a little sad after orgasm but experience hours or even a day of intense depression afterwards. He suspects the problem is neurobiological. Not very much is known about what happens in the brain during sex. I don't agree – because the male brain is lodged in the sex organ, nothing happens. Nevertheless, brain scans taken during orgasm have shown a strong increase in activity in the amygdala – the part of the brain that processes fear-inducing stimuli – so maybe people who feel down after sex are experiencing strong rebound activity. Because the most important sex organ is the brain, this doctor remembered that one of the side effects of anti-depression drugs like Prozac was sexual dysfunction. He tried giving his patients an anti-depressive to control the post-coital blues and it worked. They had slightly less intense and pleasurable sex, but no emotional crash afterwards. When they stopped taking the drug, the depression returned, so both sex and depression can be physical when the neurobiological stuff gets mixed up. Who knew?

COURTSHIP

Lust is like a desire to transcend the limitations of self; like a desire for annihilation. Praying mantises have understood this – they copulate and then the female bites her lover's head off. He goes willingly to his ecstatic death. Some men have perceived the significance of this. If only men could understand that the way to get a woman to do anything they want is simply to submit to her. I read in a newspaper that natural selection explains why women's hair grows longer than men's. Its length is due to men's preference for women with long silky hair. Human nakedness resulted from sexual selection by male apes who fancied females with 'naked' or less hairy bodies. We lost the hair that once covered our bodies and were then better able to signal anger, fear and embarrassment. Primitive man was an emotional creature who wished to be rid of the fur suit so he could see facial skin flushed with rage, pleasure, whatever.

Courting someone you like is, along with eating the fat on your meat and singing in the shower, one of the great pleasures of life. Courting, which has unfortunately fallen out of fashion, is a beautiful, delicious dance and should be taken seriously because it gives you time to get to know the person. I know what you're thinking and I'm the same – you are so blinded by sexual desire that you can't see straight until you get that out of the way. That's fine, have sex within five minutes if you want to, but don't bypass the courtship stage. Skipping that stage is like cooking a cake too fast at too high a temperature: it looks good on the outside but implodes as soon as you take it out of the oven.

A British study published in the *Journal of Theoretical Biology* uses applied mathematics to show that, just like your betters said, there are benefits in not rushing into sex. It uses a branch of maths and economics called 'game theory' to explain why men want sex sooner rather than later and women prefer to wait until they are ready. In the 'game' the man wins if he beds the woman quickly, gets her pregnant and shoots through or, as the ghastly expression puts it, 'screw it, kill it'. The woman wins if she holds off, then gets pregnant to a good mate who will stick around to nurture his child. This study opines that a long courtship and delayed mating helps the female gather essential intelligence on the male. A good male is more likely to 'pay the price' of waiting for sex in order to get the prize – he is more persistent. A cad will bugger off if he doesn't 'win' the game fairly quickly.

Of course, the flaw in this study is that it really only works in biological, evolutionary terms, not necessarily in 2009, where these primitive urges are irrelevant and getting together is about more than reproducing. Most people these days see sex as a pleasurable form of communication and only use it for reproduction occasionally, if ever. There are still some primitive societies which have not yet made the connection between sex and babies. Not all women are looking for a mate or to reproduce and what about older women who are past reproducing age? Where does the 'game' go then? In fact, Anne Hollands, the vice-president of Relationships Australia, a relationship advice and counselling service, says there is no hard evidence that waiting to have sex leads to more happiness or success in love (I could have told you that).

COURTING TIPS

1. Let men know: a hard-on does not count as personal growth.

SEX & LOVE

2. Every man is looking for his mother and even if he isn't, he is. Take a good look at his mother and you will know what's expected of you – or what he's going to turn you into.
3. If you think the way to a man's heart is through his stomach, you're aiming too high.
4. Absence makes the heart grow fonder – don't always be available at the drop of a hat and avoid patterns. The boys like a challenge – they don't need security and regularity like you do. They like spontaneity and surprises. Don't forget – they are children all their lives.
5. If proper dates seem too scary (and this goes for any age group), do 'not-dates'. For example, make the outing short and casual; go Dutch; wear nice but not flash clothes; go somewhere public. You will pick up on each other's personalities very quickly and know how, or whether, to proceed from there.
6. Have a marriage arranged for you and go on the dates with your mother (it works for Indian women). The downside to this is that your mother will never think anyone is good enough for you (they're not), but you can't be a virgin all your life. Remember what Lady Nancy Astor said, 'I married beneath me – all women do.'
7. Sweethearts are like birds – you have to build a nice nest for them to come to. If you invite someone home, make sure your house is clean, tidy and welcoming.

THE STAGES OF LOVE

There are several stages in a relationship, as outlined by Dr Gail Ratcliffe in her book *Being Single and Happy*. Stage one is the

HONEYMOON stage, which can last from two months to two years on average. This is the stage where everything the adored one does is wonderful and perfect, you don't see faults, passion is flowing, you can't stop making love and perception could best be described as distorted. You are blind, deaf and dumb; faults are completely ignored. Just being in the same room as this person makes you ecstatic and you talk for hours and hours getting to know each other. This is the stage no one ever gets past in the movies because the other stages are never portrayed, which creates the illusion that this stage will last forever. You are still two individuals but thinking of yourselves more and more as one unit.

Stage two is the **CONSOLIDATION** stage. At this point you are still madly in love but start to notice your partner is human and did not descend from Nirvana. You will fight and make up, learn how to compromise and see each other as one unit – you are a couple. You are on each other's side and you want to stay together long term. You make plans and create dreams together, take holidays together, buy a house and behave in a unified way to the outside world. Your friendships change and you make friends with more couples. This stage is very strong, can go on for a lifetime, even if threatened by an affair, financial problems or illness. If you both feel consolidated and your love is deep, the relationship will probably be successful and will last. What will break it will be if the other person moves on to stage three. This will be devastating for the person left behind.

Stage three is the **WORM-IN-THE-APPLE** stage. You start falling out of love and become disillusioned. Where in stage one, you couldn't see any faults, in stage three, that's all you can see – the person drives you nuts. The problems you were able to rise above in stage two are the things that now define the relationship. The common view you shared of the world no longer has a rosy glow. Things decay and you grow apart – you have developed in different ways and no longer have much in common. Successful relationships thrive on variety and growth and the partners welcome and adjust to changes. A rigid relationship will be threatened by change. I think communication is the secret to just about everything and this is what can save a relationship, but if you've got to stage three, you may be just in time to be too late – but not necessarily. As with stage two, one of the partners will probably have no idea how bad things are and say things like 'I didn't see it coming at all' (lack of communication).

Steve Yeoman

PM 'Do men talk with each other about sex?'

SY 'I have never ever heard men talking about sex. I have spent whole weekends away fishing and we never mentioned sex. We might have mumbled something about relationships, maybe. At this point in my life I am in a happy, stable relationship so there is nothing to talk about. I have heard women talking in great sexual detail about a man from across the bar. To men this is horrifying! Way too much information.'

PM 'Shit, Steve – don't read my book on women.'

SY (Crossing legs tightly) 'I'm not going to.'

PM 'It's true – women talk about sex and relationships a lot. We think men think about sex 100 per cent of the time.'

SY 'No – it's you who think about it all the time, not us. It is women who are after just one thing, not men. You are looking for this sexual reaction in men all the time – it is your first thought and focus. We would be happy to have sexual relationships with you, but it is not the first thing on our minds when we meet you.'

PM 'You know what? Other men I interviewed have told me the same thing.'

SY 'You're going to have to believe it if we all say it.'

PM 'Oh no – men might turn out not to be the arseholes I think they are. I'd have to change my whole thesis.'

SY 'Well don't go overboard. We *are* as bad as you think we are but we're not as *obsessed* as you think we are. We do like breasts because they are lovely and round and right in front of us, so why wouldn't we look?'

PM 'Yeah, but we get really sick of men staring at our bodies.'

SY 'I learned a long time ago how to do it without looking like I was doing it – the rule is not to get caught. It's not hard.'

PM 'Do you think women put more pressure on men for sex than the other way round?'

SY 'I wish.'

PM 'I am looking forward to the day when I no longer think about sex.'

SY 'You know why they call it men-o-pause . . .'

PM 'Ha ha, very good. Do you think men are a lot more sensitive than we think they are?'

SY 'I wouldn't go that far – you have to be conscious to

> be sensitive. Sensitive didn't work at all – when I was a SNAG, all the bad boys got the women. If I had my life again, I'd be a bad boy all the way – that's what women want.'

WOLF WHISTLE

The wolf whistle is a tool of courtship whose use has sadly declined with the advance of civilisation. When I was young, I more or less hated wolf whistles – mostly because they were issued relentlessly. A few would have been fun. When feminism entered our lives we started answering back when boys shrieked from a building site (why was it only building sites?). They'd shout, 'Hey love, pull ya skirt up for us!', and we'd reply, 'Ya buncha losers – we'll raise our skirts when you raise your consciousness.' This was always met with screams of enchantment and appreciation from our oppressors. Recently, wolf-whistling has actually been banned on some work sites on the premise it is out of date in the twenty-first century. A Bristol firm sent around an email explaining that savvy and sophisticated women won't stand for being whistled at by builders. And apparently men find it insulting when their loved ones are whistled at and believe it causes unnecessary tension. Really.

With the sperm count as crap as it is, I'm surprised men still have the balls to wolf whistle – we should clap and thank God that they still think of such things. When this tool of courtship was banned, women rose up from their desks and complained: 'We like it,' they said. 'We like it when the taxi driver calls us "love"; we appreciate men complimenting our dresses; a bit of harmless attention brightens up our day.' What wolf-whistling doesn't do is send us running, tearfully, to the head of human resources, or prompt us to lock ourselves in the bathroom, feeling bruised and degraded. Builders say they just do it for fun and women usually smile at them. One builder interviewed said he even whistled at ugly women to brighten them up. Gee, thanks. A mercy whistle – poor cousin of the mercy lay.

In New Zealand recently, an Israeli tourist got so sick of being whistled at that she took all her clothes off in protest, withdrew money from the ATM she was standing at when said whistles occurred, then put her clothes back on. The police arrested her for indecent exposure and explained that that sort of thing is inappropriate in New Zealand, but the boys are still talking about it. In Mexico they tried to prohibit wolf whistles even though it is 'the most passionate, stimulating and beautiful sound a woman can hear', according to Mexican women. They wax lyrical about the angelic sound of a bricklayer's whistle. They commend construction workers for expressing their feelings. The authorities also tried to ban flattering comments that the women saw as a cordial form of gallantry and praise, such as, 'What would this little bird do without this little nest?', 'Oh look, the sun has come out at night' and 'The flowers should hide in shame when you pass by'. Obviously the blokes are a lot more lyrical in Spanish-speaking cultures. I don't recall comments like that from the construction sites of my youth. In Mexico they say that, if you are feeling depressed, don't waste your money on a psychologist – just walk past a construction site.

Note: The latest intelligence on this subject is that construction workers now use the secret phrase, 'watch the level', to signal that a pretty woman is coming.

KISSING

A kiss is an activity where you press your lips to another person's, swapping mucus, bacteria and God knows what else. Wine is a nice thing to swap. Why did we evolve to start this behaviour of putting our mouths together when we like each other, how and why is it so arousing? Some cultures, like the Inuits, don't do it at all and some, like the French, do it even in public.

Neuroscientists say a passionate kiss immediately and dramatically releases neurotransmitters and hormones, which signal sex and bonding. Anthropologists say the kiss is a relic of mouth-to-mouth feeding, which is how mothers used to feed their young, just as birds do. I think it gives you data on the other person and is a good gauge as to their suitability.

Some people think we like kissing because it reminds us of eating ripe fruit – lips are pink and ripe fruit is often red so the colour means the reward of food. Could this be the explanation for the connection between food and sex? Red has become the code colour for attraction – sexual organs become red when aroused (some female monkeys' posteriors become red when they are fertile), and women wear red lipstick to be more attractive and look younger. Women with full lips are supposed to have more oestrogen, which signals fertility.

A FIRST KISS

A first kiss from someone you really like is extremely important. If it is no good or distasteful or sloppy, it is a complete turn-off. All men reading should take note: get this right and you are in. Women base many judgements on the way a man kisses, just as they do on the way a man dances. A kiss tells them how you make love, how generous you are, how in tune with your body you are, and whether you actually love women or not.

The first kiss is almost spiritual in its magical connection and there's no particular reason why it can't continue that way. Men who like women taught me how to kiss and make love and enjoy it. In truth, some men are hopeless but respond well to instruction. After all, most men want to please you; if they're not doing it right, show them how to. It helps if you've got your own kissing act together. Did you know that two-thirds of us instinctively tilt to the right when we kiss, reflecting our tendency to turn our heads to the right in the womb and for six months after birth?

HOW TO KISS

1. Make sure your breath is sweet – keep your teeth brushed and eat parsley and lemons.
2. Don't rush anything; in fact, the longer you leave it, the better it will be. Do it slowly, but not to the point where the other person starts snoring.
3. Don't have wet lips (slightly moist will do) and don't pour saliva into the other person's mouth – it's disgusting and they feel like they're drowning in snail trail.
4. Some men don't like lipstick but my attitude to that is, 'So kiss it off, honey.'
5. Take note of what he responds to when you kiss. Some people like tongue, some don't. Most men like being kissed on other areas as well as the lips, like the cheek, neck, eyes and around their lips.
6. Most people close their eyes when kissing and enjoy the sensuality of it all.

HOW TO KEEP UP GOOD KISSING

Most women adore kissing and it is very important to them as they have sensitive lips, which seem to have a direct link to the pelvis. Men appear to be less kiss-orientated for the sake of kissing and see it more as the first stop on the journey to the big kahuna. They had better smarten up on this important part of lovemaking, because it's a sure way to keep a woman happy. Men not kissing enough is a real problem, especially as the relationship progresses into a years-long one. Remember those teenage dates when you pashed in the car for hours? That really only happened because you were holding out and there was no question of the big kahuna – he took what he could get. Mysteriously, kissing is the one activity that men can multitask at – they can kiss while watching rugby on TV, kiss while trying to get your bra off, kiss while you are talking to them and kiss while walking down the street.

The true story is men kiss mostly only in courtship. Once they are in a regular lovemaking relationship, they don't really see the point and the guided missile just wants to get to the jewel – pathetic, I know. BUT, you can train them and if you're planning on having them in your bed for years, better start how you intend to continue. Men have to be trained in all areas very early on and this applies to kissing. The upside is they love that you want to civilise them and see it as a game. Men also like unpredictability in women. It's not true they hate our capriciousness – they love it. They initially just go along with your kooky kissing ideas but then, to their astonishment, they find they prefer it that way.

Here's how you get long-term good kissing in the honeypot of your love nest. Right from the moment you meet, gently and lovingly make it clear how much you like kissing and tell your man what a good kisser he is. Explain about your sensitive lips, which have a direct link to your you-know-where, blah blah blah. Remember that men's skin is a lot less sensitive than women's. Explain to the fearless hunter with the guided missile that there is such as thing as just kissing for the sake of kissing and that's it. You have a pash, talk a bit, pash, crack a few jokes, pash, then you stop – it doesn't go anywhere. This is a bit off the topic, but that's how sex therapists cure impotence in men – they teach couples to just make out and do foreplay without thinking about the big kahuna. It's a good and pleasurable way to teach men self-control and if there's one thing that defines a good lover, it is someone who is in control of himself. In this game of just kissing, don't get too passionate because that's just being a tease and teasing pisses people off big time.

Some advice for men: if you don't feel like the kissing game, just do it anyway – you'll be surprised how you get into it. Kissing tells you how your partner feels about you because it's a very intimate thing to do. The absence of kissing is a warning sign – if it gets to the stage of friendly pecking, guys should do something about it, or it'll be as the song title says, 'Get your tongue out of my mouth, I'm kissing you goodbye.'

Sometimes it's just best to not kiss at all. Once upon a time there was a beautiful princess. She often sat by a pool admiring herself and the beauty around her. One day an ugly old pig-dog of a frog jumped up beside her and said, 'Look, I'm not an ugly frog – I'm actually a handsome prince. A witch put a spell on me and if you kiss me I will turn back into a handsome prince again and marry you. You will have my babies, clean my castle, wait on me hand and foot for the rest of your life and be forever happy.' Sometime later, as the beautiful princess sat at her golden dining table eating frog's legs sautéed in Champagne sauce, she smiled and said to herself, 'I don't bloody think so.'

SKIN FLICK

If you flick a woman with a tea towel or your fingers, it hurts her. If you do it to a man it hurts a lot less. The reason for this is that men are thick-skinned in more ways than you thought, which is why their skin ages more slowly than a woman's. The skin on a man's back is four times thicker than the skin on his front – an anatomical hangover from the days when he was still getting around on all fours. He needed this protection from rear attacks while out on the pampas. The male skin is also desensitised so he can brawl with dastardly enemies and rush fearlessly through thorny bushes without the inconvenience of pain slowing him down. By the time he hits puberty a boy has lost most of his sensitivity to touch to get ready for the hunt. When a man is very focused playing sports or in a dramatic situation such as those James Bond is perpetually in, he feels little pain and doesn't notice when someone bites his ear off or cars blow up. He has a mission and forges forward. What I find interesting is that all men's skin sensitivity seems to be in the same area as their brain – the penis. If the man is *not* focused on a dare-devil activity and is at ease, his pain threshold descends by 99 per cent, which accounts for his extreme wimpiness when ill. He can't move from the bed, groans in agony for endless attention from the female, calls his lawyer and stops eating. This is for the common cold. For cancer he makes jokes – see the prostate section in the health chapter.

Jeff Avery

PM 'What do you think women want?'

JA 'Security. It begins and ends there. They want to feel secure and loved. Even if there was no love, I think a lot of women would be happy with just security. They can survive without men but not without security, which is why some women marry for money; and even if the woman is very successful financially, she still needs emotional security.'

PM 'Do you think men make good companions in relationships?'

JA 'By and large, no. I would say maybe 5 per cent of males would be good companions, but keep in mind that 85 per cent of the whole population are not switched on to what's happening in their relationships. A very small percentage have a relationship which is working on all fronts. I personally don't see why women even bother with us.'

PM 'Why do you bother with *us*? Why do men bother with relationships – because it's not hard to get sex. If the worst comes to the worst, you can pay for it. Why do men tie themselves into contracts with women?'

JA 'I don't know – for the most part they shouldn't. One in three marriages split up and of those that are still together, half of them wouldn't be working very well.'

PM 'Okay, so what does a man have to offer a woman apart from security?'

JA 'Love, one would hope, but is that really happening?

Most men don't know what that is. You have to love yourself first. Men are not brought up to love themselves; Western society doesn't expect it of them. Take a guy like our friend Mohammed in Morocco. He's in love with his family; he's in love with life. Put one of us in his life and say, 'Okay now you're going to make your own honey, look after your family, cook your food on the floor, et cetera.'

PM 'But he's a very happy, loving man in spite of the hard life he's had.'

JA 'That's because he's tied to the land, he's connected to everything, he knows who he is.'

PM 'His wife was arranged for him – she was only fourteen, and somehow they're happy.'

JA 'It's because they are connected to everything else – they are part of a whole picture. We are disconnected in our lives. What kind of fathers are most men? They get up at seven, are gone all day, come home in the evening, see their kids for twenty minutes, then sit down and watch TV, play on the computer – anything to distract from the now. I mean look at all those nanny-type shows telling people obvious things that are common sense. There are a lot of dysfunctional parents out there.'

PM 'Do men need women in their lives and if so what for?'

JA 'Yes they do and for the same reason as women – security. They probably feel that if they don't have a woman, they're not part of the herd. Men find a new woman quite quickly after they separate because

they feel insecure and lonely on their own. You see them all down at the pub – single guys in their fifties, alone.'
PM 'But if you see a woman in her fifties drinking in a pub somehow that is not pathetic. First of all she won't be alone, she'll have arranged to meet friends or know she'll bump into people she knows at the pub. Why does it seem sad for a man?'
JA 'Because men think in a tunnel way. They wouldn't think about social networking.'
PM 'And then they go home from the pub to be alone and heat up a TV dinner or eat with their hands or something. I'm going to cry. It doesn't have to be like that.'
JA 'And their house will be a tip. That would never happen to a woman because you are so much better at looking after yourselves. They can't tell anyone they're lonely because it shows vulnerability.'
PM 'I know. That's why men need women – they need us to stop them from becoming savages.'
JA 'Yeah. When you're married your wife keeps the social and home life going, but when you divorce you go back to being in your student flat.'
PM 'How do you and your wife resolve issues on which you disagree?'
JA 'I have to say we're very good at communicating. There's never any screaming and yelling – we usually discuss and compromise. We say what we have to say and it tends to go my way (grins), especially on big

issues. Like I don't say "THIS IS HOW IT'S GOING TO BE." I'll say, "Well you can do it that way if you want and I'll do it my way."'

PM 'What do men expect from relationships? I think women have outrageous expectations on what they think a relationship will be like.'

JA 'Men only expect or dream of one thing and that is to be adored. When you come home you want your wife to open her arms and say, "You're *so* wonderful – I just can't keep my hands off you." What you actually get is, "Hi, can you take the garbage out?" I think men are far too realistic to expect a woman to fulfil all their needs.'

PM 'What do you find attractive in a woman?'

JA 'Obviously aesthetics kick in first, but brains and personality follow rapidly. A woman can be very attractive, but if she's a bitch she loses her sex appeal immediately. Also, insecurity in a woman is a killer.'

PM 'Did your father talk to you about sex and love?'

JA 'No. Not one word. Well he did say one thing when I was a teenager, after a weekend shag session with my then girlfriend while they were away. I disposed of the condoms in the trash can. The raccoons then proceeded to strew the evidence over the front lawn. His words of wisdom were "Don't dump the rubbers in the trash, the raccoons love the sweet stuff". Wonderful.'

PM 'What are you going to tell your son?'

JA 'Mmmm – good question. I think I'm going to wing it. I will certainly tell him about the seriousness of getting a girl pregnant. If you don't understand about sex and pregnancy you can really throw a curve ball into your life. Hopefully we'll have good enough communication so I can explain to him how to pull chicks (kidding), that sex is pleasurable, that you have to be respectful. I don't think I'll have much trouble with him because he's already a passionate person and will maybe be the guy who has one girlfriend.'

PM 'What makes a good lover?'

JA 'Knowing themselves and what they consider to be erotic, being open and not held back, being themselves. Sex is the *only* time when we are out of our bodies, when we don't know what's going on at that moment. If you think too much you're putting yourself out of that realm. When it's at its best, the two of you are one. You have to have rhythm and really love women. Once again, it all comes back to communicating.'

I asked Jeff and Jane about sexual fidelity. This was Jane's answer: 'Jeff instigated the "fat backside clause", that is, if I end up with an arse that looks like a sack of hammers he says he'd be quite within his rights to find sexual solace elsewhere. Just a joke of course! Also we have a top-five celebrity list. Like if Angelina Jolie walked in the door and said, "Do me, Jeffrey", it would be a totally guilt-free fuck. Currently Daniel Craig's up there for me . . . and David Bowie has a permanent place on my top-five list.'

SEX & LOVE

Jeff sips his coffee. 'I belong to a sports group which has a good cross-section of the community – plumbers, lawyers, computer programmers, et cetera, and the conversations in the locker room are a real eye-opener. Most of them are youngish married men with families and no one's getting it or on the rare occasions they do it's with the lights off and the door locked. Their wives' bodies have changed with childbirth and they don't feel comfortable about sex and letting go any more.'

PM 'Well that's more than understandable. After all, a man has children, still looks exactly the same *and* hasn't suffered.'

JA 'The men tell me how frustrated they are but they're not communicating with their wives about their feelings. I have a great sex life with my wife and I think it's all about communication – *all* of it. You have to keep the channels open. I think people don't communicate because it exposes them too much, exposes their insecurities.'

PM 'How do you think men are doing?'

JA 'Generally speaking, I think they are still adjusting to the new role of participation, the fact that women have many more choices now, that they are now contributing financially. Men still feel that they should be the principal supporter of the family and they feel very bad if that isn't happening.'

PM 'Do they feel valued and loved by women?'

JA 'Yes, I think so, but the more important question is,

> "Do they value themselves now that the roles are not so obvious as in previous generations?" At the end of the day, I think the real value is from your family and relationships. When my dad had heart surgery he was most interested to know who had called, who cared. The measure of a life is who you've touched, who has touched you and who cared. It goes back to basics – who loves ya? It's not going to be someone from work, it's not going to be someone from the sports field, it's going to be someone you connect with deeply, and that is your family.'

THE ACCIDENTAL SHAG

The shag is a swing dance from the 1920s, popular among American college students at the time. A derivation called the Carolina shag began in South Carolina in the 1940s and is often associated with beach music. The shag, or cormorant, can also be a coastal seabird, the shag referring to the bird's crest – there are about forty different species of shag. A shag is also finely cut tobacco or a term for rolling tobacco. Shag can also be a luxuriant carpet, very popular in the 1970s in homes and was also a common feature of a Chevrolet van, which had shag carpet on all sides of the interior. I thought this last one was possibly where the word 'shag' came to mean having sex, but further research showed that shag is in fact a very old word. The origins can be traced back to interpretations from the Bible. It began life as a variant of 'shake'. When Jesus walks on water, he does so to reach the disciples' boat 'tossed on the waves'; however, in Wycliffe's version (c.1395), the boat is 'shoggid with waves'. This shaking probably led to the naming of the American swing dance, but was used to describe the act of making love way earlier. The word 'shag' appears in Old English as 'sceacga', meaning hair and eventually all those rough materials. It appears in Grose's *Dictionary of the Vulgar Tongue* in 1788, defined as 'to copulate'. It has always been used in British low comedy and most recently became popular again in Austin Powers films, as in 'shagadelic baby – yeeeeeaaaahh!'

The accidental shag shares some characteristics with the other shags: it's a bit ragged around the edges, has several sub-species and is a very old activity. The accidental shag, technically, is when you 'make love' with someone by mistake, or as my friend Irene puts it, 'It's when a man just accidentally falls over and lands right inside you.' Situations you may find yourself in which could be described as an accidental shag include:

1. You slept with an individual who you don't know. You don't know his name and haven't a clue why he is in your bed in the morning or why your room smells like 37,000 socks. Alcohol and drugs are usually part of this accident. Once consciousness has risen in the temple, you remember this person seemed really hot the night before, but now you would gnaw your way out from under him if you could. However, that would be too obvious, so you behave like an adult. The rudest thing you could possibly do is ask him to get up, get dressed and leave. The most polite thing you could do is treat said individual the way you would like to be treated: make a simple breakfast of toast and coffee (he only get eggs, bacon and Champagne if you are going to ask him to be the father of your babies). Be friendly but firm. Explain briefly that he is not the one for you. Usually

JUST IN TIME TO BE TOO LATE

by this stage both of you are on the same page anyway, and he goes to the door quietly.

2. You slept with a platonic friend who you've known for years and there's never been any question of sex. Alcohol and drugs may also be part of this accident, but not necessarily. It could just be that you were both needing a shag and needs must. But, keep in mind that there is no such thing as a platonic male friend – he always has sex in the back of his lizard mind. The accepted wisdom is that this accident always ruins a perfectly good friendship, but I think that's a bit dramatic. I think you just smile sheepishly, accept that you had fun, don't make a big deal about it and make an effort to get the friendship back on track again. Also there is the distinct possibility that this could lead to a more intimate relationship – it might be an accident with a silver lining.

3. You slept with your ex-partner. This is very common and could be for comfort's sake; could be that the only good thing about him was his shagability; or you may be suffering from misplaced romanticism. When you wake up you remember what your sister said when you mentioned that you still fancied him. At the same time you remember he ripped your still-beating heart out of your chest and that it quite hurt. Be in control of the situation by thanking him for his services and leave the house with a smile. Make sure you don't leave your heart behind by mistake.

4. You slept with your best friend's ex-partner. This is an extremely dumb accident and I would question *his* motives for the shag – he's probably getting back at her. There are a lot of men in the world so for a woman to choose her friend's

ex smacks a little of the sort of competitiveness, which is evident in the worst accidental shag of all, below. There is probably alcohol or drugs in here somewhere to make you think such a stupid thing is okay, but it doesn't make you a criminal. You don't need to worry about how to deal with the man – you need to worry about your friend. Fess up, show remorse, listen to her screaming and agree with her that your friendship will survive this.

5. You slept with your friend or sister's partner. This is 100 per cent competitiveness and a grotesque sort of compliment. You are probably in a position inferior to your friend or sister (that is, she is more beautiful, richer, more successful, younger, whatever) and want what she has because by having that you will be as good as her. Hence Bonnie Raitt's song, 'Women Be Wise', in which she advises women not to advertise their man. As a feminist I would normally say fess up, but this accident does so much damage it's better to keep your mouth and legs shut and never do it again, ever. You don't need to worry about the sort of man who would sleep with his partner's sister or friend as he is from the shallow end of the gene pool anyway.

SAINT VALENTINE'S DAY

Saint Valentine was a priest who lived near Rome in about the year AD 270 and he is the patron saint of lovers. We all need him badly and it only gets worse with age. We were told by the nuns that if we got romantic with boys and then got run over by a car still in a state of mortal sin, we would go straight to hell, where the air is pungent with the aroma of roasting sluts. Call me old-fashioned, but I miss those colourful days when sex was dirty and the air was clean.

According to research, six women out of ten prefer chocolate to sex. This *can't* be true – they must be making love to gerbils. On Valentine's Day, it is not so much what you eat but who you eat it with. Nevertheless, few foods inspire passion and loyalty on the scale that chocolate does and chocolate has come to symbolise this celebration. I think the trick is to combine the two – if your Valentine says, 'Stop eating so much chocolate, you're getting fat', just go straight to the chocolate box and bring it to bed, eat some more, give him some and continue your life as normal. Chocolate releases endorphins, which make you happy, and also anandamide (the brain's own marijuana) which releases serotonin and keeps you happy. Okay, so you would have to eat at least 100 kilograms of chocolate to get as stoned as from one joint, but you *would* be ruining your health and love life by *not* eating chocolate. Eating chocolate is a form of hooliganism – we don't need it, we *want* it and we don't care if it's not sensible, especially on The Day.

The truth is, all food is suitable for romance, all food cooked for a lover is sensual. Food has the power to transport you with happiness and love and we all know that eating and dancing lead to romance. The answer to the question, 'What time of the day on Valentine's Day is too early to start drinking pink Champagne?' is 'It is never too early.' There are only two occasions on which to drink Champagne – one is when you are in love and the other is when you are not. Here's how your Valentine's Day dinner goes: scatter rose petals up the driveway, along the hall, into the dining room and all over the table. The entire house is candle lit. The sound system is playing unbearably romantic music like 'I Can't

SEX & LOVE

Help It If I'm Still in Love with You' (Elvis) and 'If I Fell in Love with You' (Beatles). Dinner is seafood because it's light and you will need to be alert so you don't say something mad like, 'I'm tired – I think I'll have a lie-down'. Dessert is chocolate cake.

> **LESSONS LEARNED**
> - None.
> - A hard-on does not count as personal growth.
> - Frogs are good to eat, but they don't generally turn into princes.
> - The main difference between a man and a bus is that men don't have signs on them indicating direction.

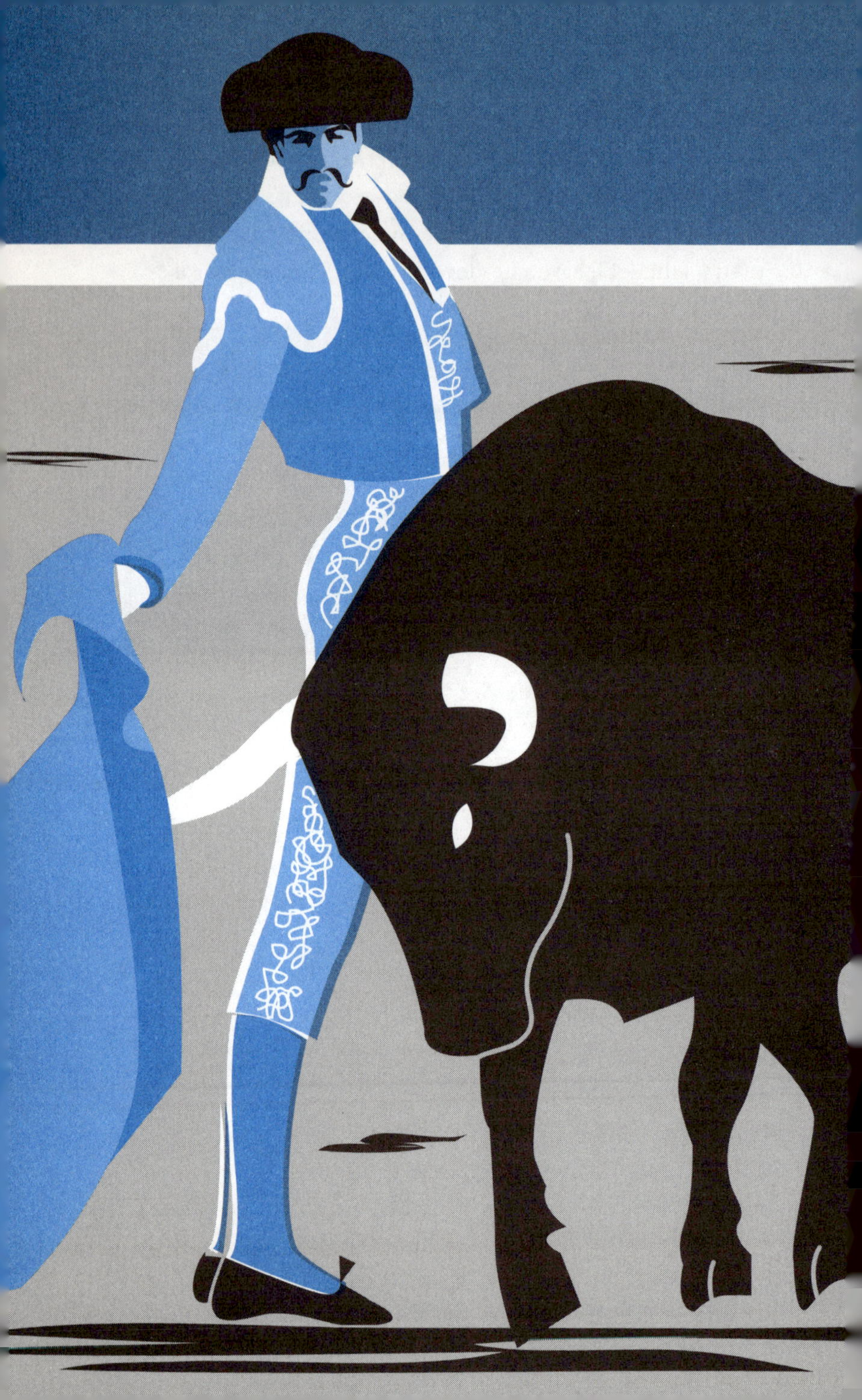

4
Sports
CONTROLLED AND CHANNELLED BARBARISM

A WOMAN'S ISSUE

I am not interested in any way, shape or form in male or female sports, but I should be because sport is a women's issue. It affects us in every way – socially, sexually and culturally – and turns men into boring dingbat warriors. I know a lot of men are interested in sport, so I decided to look into this mysterious cult. Listen closely: all the sporting and leisure activities of men serve a more important purpose than the mere physical activity. Even I know that fishing has nothing to do with fish. Most professional fishermen I have interviewed in my foodie life don't even eat fish – they eat sausages.

My father and two of my brothers were rugby-mad and still are. The third brother refused to have anything to do with it – he called it a dick-head, violent pastime for elitist thugs. As a schoolgirl I noticed that rugby was associated with boys, so pretended to be madly interested in the fact that spotty adolescents the size of articulated trucks were chasing a small, innocent ball around a sea of mud masquerading as a field.

I had learned the correct sideline behaviour expected at rugby games from my enthusiastic mother, who was only one little woman but had the mouth of ten. She planted herself firmly on the sideline, wrapped in woolly hat and scarf, screaming, exhorting, frothing at her sons. 'For God's sake, Mum,' they would say, snuffling into their filthy football shirts, imploding with embarrassment. Opposing teams would tremble if they knew they were scheduled to play Saint Peter's College. Dad and the rest of us kids stood on the other side of the field pretending we didn't know Mum.

My girlfriends and I didn't make fools of ourselves at rugby games because we were far too cool, but we did follow the teams around in a frenzy of barely suppressed oestrogen overdrive. Our testosterone-poisoned objects of desire were far too busy being jocks to acknowledge our presence, salivating over the ball as if it held the meaning of the universe. Which of course it did. Nothing else was more important than rugby, because if you played well enough you might get to be – please stand back – an *All Black*. These rugby jocks weren't particularly charming but at sixteen charm was not a quality we looked for in boys. We were looking for status and good looks. I stood in the rain wearing kit like powder blue bellbottoms, pink mohair jumpers, pale pink lipstick and two ponytails on either side of my head – a look guaranteed to drive the rugby boys mad with desire.

According to my research, sports are really means for men to bond, teach each other life skills, develop their fabulous personalities and grow up. Hello? Don't make me weep. Theodore Roosevelt described sports as 'controlled and channelled barbarism'. It is supposedly about the tribe and essential to a healthy society. It used to be about burning up testosterone and learning values like fairness, team playing and achieving goals. Boys learned respect and consideration of the team and the players were paramount – not the game. Money was never the goal so the player was not forced to take incredible risks. But then in the 1980s, the God of Gold came visiting and everything changed.

My mother's behaviour at her boys' rugby games was the prototype for today's parents who, unfortunately, are not merely enthusiastic but have become sociopaths who cause a lot of damage with their own violence and unfulfilled passion. In many instances, some parents are banned from their children's football games and even banned from transporting said boys to and from games. Boys playing sports should not be carrying the honour of their schools or their parents on their shoulders – they should just be having a good time and learning co-ordination. When boys are put in positions of threat and danger (like being in the presence of their mad parents), their testosterone levels go way up, which leads to aggressive and violent behaviour. Boys have knocked out and even killed others boys in so-called friendly school games. To play to hurt is shameful and dishonourable and shows bad leadership from the coaches. Academics believe that sport is one of the primary ways the defective masculine image is shaped – the arrogant, elitist, violent, unfeeling, individualistic, competitive, sort of sub-human behaviour, and the inability to string two sentences together in an interview. Not to mention the bad dress sense. A game is meant to be empowering and challenging, not humiliating and painful.

The problem with people who inflict pain in a 'playful' setting is that they are likely to inflict or accept pain in other settings as well. This is called sadomasochism. The things rugby players learn are not the skills they need in order to be good human beings. In a normal society, restraint, compromise and co-operation are more typical ways of moving forward. But in rugby you must win and if you have to hurt another player in an underhand way to put him at a disadvantage, then you do it or be 'a big girl's blouse'. Boys need the tribal thing, an initiation into manhood, which if correctly handled, could be through the vehicle of sport. Boys need to hang out with men and men have to deliberately transmit the culture and beauty of being a man to them (if they happen to know what that is).

THE SIGNS OF SOCIOPATHIC DEVOTION TO RUGBY

1. Confusing brain activity or thought with moronic obsession.
2. Displaying an abnormal indifference to wet, cold, testicle-rotting weather.
3. His relationship with his team is the longest, most rewarding relationship he has ever had.
4. Believing that talking about sports is a genuine form of conversation.
5. Thinking the All Blacks losing in France is a cause for national mourning. Responding to this event by questioning the meaning of life and the round earth theory, et cetera.

A HISTORY OF RUGBY

'Folk football' or 'mob football' is the ancestor of this game and in medieval times it was imbued with spiritual and sexual significance. It was played as part of a religious springtime celebration of renewal and fertility. On the day of mardi gras people played with a beribboned, leather football (the shape probably symbolising an egg), which hung off the end of a staff. It was a wild free-for-all and took place between up to five hundred members of opposing villages with almost no rules restricting violence. You could get up to almost anything in the interests of kicking the ball, but not deliberately hurt another player. Needless to say, the game degenerated into a wild scuffle quite quickly with players fighting for the ball. Interestingly, the peasant women also participated: pushing, shoving and kicking with as much reckless abandon as their husbands, sons, fathers and brothers; and they suffered just as much damage with broken bones and cracked heads. Sometimes only women played, with married and single women taking opposing sides. Rugby is still pretty primitive today.

The game of rugby, as we know it, originated at the super-toff Rugby School in England and was played for two hundred years before anyone thought to write a book of rules. I have always been confused about the difference between rugby union and rugby league. Originally, a club with agreed rules was set up in 1845 called rugby union, but in 1895 they had a big fight and split into two sets of rules – the break-off club calling themselves rugby league. Rugby union used to be an amateur sport but since 1995 it has been professional. What does this actually mean to you and me salivating on the sideline? Not that much. Originally, there were big differences in the number of players in a team, the rules, the way the game was played and cultural differences – league was for the working class and union was for the toffs. Differences have reduced over the years as both games are now professional and it's all about money and skill.

My brother Paul says this: 'Before rugby union became professional it was mainly for the private school boys. They went to university part-time and the "old boys club" would then look after them in retirement with jobs, et cetera. Rugby league has always been semi-professional (now full-time professional), therefore it attracted more working-class men. Union players called league players "Neanderthals", to which the league players replied that union players were "white-collar, leather-elbow-patch wankers". League is very tribal: in Sydney, you follow your local team, have a second favourite and that's it – you hate every other team. Club games of union are boring, it's not until it gets to the provincial (Super 14) and country level that it gets any good. League players are always in the press for getting pissed, fighting and harassing girls. Union players not so much.'

THE MYTH OF THE SEXUAL ATHLETE

It seems to me that the culture of sporting boys and men indulging themselves in dodgy sexual behaviour towards girls is more an American problem than an Australasian one. It happens in our culture, but it's not endemic. I didn't have any adult experience of sporting men and I loathe sport and the culture that goes with it, so I put my interview cap on and bravely set forth to ask men about this topic. There is plenty of evidence of date rape, pack rape, objectification of girls, intimidation and disrespect in the papers. I have always just assumed the men doing this were the rotten apples – these were the ones we heard about. But, I wondered, were they exceptions or was there actually a culture related to sports that supported and encouraged disrespect of women? And what about the legal system's response? These men often seem to get off charges laid against them and are often granted name suppression. Over the last ten years there have been numerous cases of sporting heroes being charged with violence against women, everything from smacking the wife to raping intoxicated women they pick up in bars. Even when the police actively encourage the victims to press charges, all too often the men, who inevitably get name suppression, are either acquitted or receive light sentences. In some cases the victims are then subjected to unbridled abuse from the public for attempting to discredit a sporting hero.

Locker room sexual conversation revolves around boasting, graphic objectifying of girls, mind-boggling disrespect, even hatred of their sex objects, and joking about the things they force women to do. The men talk about superficial sex and anything that uses, trivialises or debases women. Frank discussions about sexuality that unfold within a loving relationship are taboo. But we all know that even sports jocks need love so there is this terrible split between inner needs and outer appearances – between their desire for a woman's love and their indifference towards them. Men often feel that their masculinity is threatened by the intimacy and commitment a serious relationship with a woman entails. Sexual relationships are games in which women are seen as opponents. Some men view dating as a sport, and 'scoring' or having sex becomes an act of winning, not a sexual act involving emotions and love. Sexual desire is detached from tenderness for a woman. Adolescents internalise the idea that sex is power. 'Scoring' results in 'man points' in the realm of masculinity. Using women for sex is okay, but emotional attachment promotes distraction, draws off energy and erodes team loyalty.

David Horsman

PM 'Can you bear to talk about sports?'

DH 'When I was at boarding school, we'd sneak into the stables at two in the morning with pissy little transistor radios to listen to rugby matches live from South Africa. I went along with it once or twice and then thought, "I don't get this."'

PM 'So you didn't play sport at school at all?'

DH 'Oh yes. I hated rugby because it was so brutish. Having cauliflower ears and a broken nose, somebody grabbing your balls in the scrum, the overt male physical contact in a very rough way. There was no sensitivity. But I loved hockey because you had a weapon; I played basketball because I was tall. I like individual sports like shooting.'

PM 'What about really loner sports like surfing?'

DH 'I thought surfers were wankers, but then I had a Californian girlfriend when I was eighteen or nineteen and she harped on all the time about surfing. Then I tried surfing in Kerala, India and since then I have had nothing but enormous admiration for surfers. It's difficult, dangerous and requires a huge amount of balance and skill. Since then it has fascinated me as a sport.'

SPORTS

> **PM** 'What about bullfighting?'
>
> **DH** 'It's not a sport – it's an art form. Hemingway said you need to see at least thirty bullfights before you can appreciate what they are doing in the ring. Unfortunately, you can't really justify it as it's terribly cruel. I always want the matador to get gored.'
>
> **PM** 'Do you watch sport on TV?'
>
> **DH** 'Occasionally I'll watch a big game and get caught up in it. You know, a really good, open game of rugby is a beautiful thing. I have something embarrassing to tell you – I like watching snooker.'
>
> **PM** 'That is very embarrassing.'
>
> **DH** 'Snooker has a weapon and is a precision sport.'

SADOMASOCHISM

Dr Richard Pringle has published a paper that compares rugby pleasures with sadomasochism to encourage people to question why such an aggressive game has a dominant place in our culture. (Sadomasochism, or S&M, is a sexual practice that combines sadism, the tendency to derive pleasure from inflicting pain, suffering or humiliation on others, and masochism, the enjoyment of such activities.) Richard carried out in-depth interviews with seven adult rugby players. His strategy of defamiliarising rugby pleasures by positing them as being akin to S&M also provides a heuristic (enabling a person to discover or learn something for themselves) framework for understanding broader rugby culture.

Competitive rugby players do not typically 'hate the enemy', but instead respect the opposition for being willing to engage in the pain, fear and excitement of rugby. The players will try to batter the opposition into submission then celebrate together after the match.

Although rugby is supposed to be healthy and character building, one might be forgiven for thinking it has nothing to do with either. In contrast, one can assume that rugby players seek pleasure through physical confrontation – risky pleasures that align well with indulging in alcohol and playing at dubious, 'taboo-breaking' off-field activities. One is reminded of S&M when observing the affectionate names used for things in rugby; for example, stadium – house of pain; wheelchair rugby – murder ball; and players' nicknames such as 'chainsaw', 'bumface', 'le pit bull'. Tee-shirt slogans might say 'Happiness is a good ruck' or 'Always kick ahead – any head'. A billboard will say 'You surround them and we'll put them to the sword'. The fans are also in on this in their position as voyeurs of pain and pleasure. This recognition offers an explanation for why the most violent sporting actions tend to be shown in the media in multiple replays, including slow motion close-ups of the graphic bits.

Richard concluded that the interviewees had to be suitably disciplined in order to gain certain pleasures in rugby. The performance and subsequent enjoyment of the skill involved in rugby playing, for example, takes disciplined training but one also has to be soundly disciplined to *desire* to stand in front of, and attempt to stop (and knock to the ground) a large charging body. The interviewees uniquely highlighted the importance of physical confrontation and the excitement associated with overcoming fear, dominating opponents, avoiding and participating in punishment and, for some, inflicting pain. Without the contextual risk of fear and pain the game loses its thrill. The pleasure of rugby 'violence' transports the players to an edge that necessitates their negotiation of the blurred boundaries between pleasure and pain, confidence and fear, well-being and injury and at the extreme, consciousness and unconsciousness. This intoxicating 'edge work' demands great skill and concentration and proves addictive to some. Richard himself finds the bloody and injurious pleasures of rugby bizarre, but concludes in his paper that it can be understood as a consenting, desexualised form of sadomasochism.

THE TEN MOST BORING SPORTS TO WATCH

All sports are boring but these are the worst offenders:

1. Five day cricket – this is a sport for manic-depressives who should only watch it in their manic phase.
2. Golf – if you want to go for a walk, why let all those balls get in the way?
3. Bowling – I'd rather watch a dog show but quite like the white outfits and would you believe it's becoming fashionable again?
4. Surfing – only good to watch if you're stoned.
5. Ping pong – please. Am I five?
6. Car racing – only interesting when someone crashes and burns and yet walks out without a scratch. We all love a miracle.
7. Snooker or billiards – can be good for five minutes if the camera gets good shots of the players taut buttocks.
8. Sailing – elitist pastime in which you get wet.
9. Tennis – only interesting at the very top end and when the players throw tantrums.
10. Rugby – don't start me again.

SURFING OR USELESS BEAUTY

When I was a child, I went surfing and had a great time falling off the board. And then someone else's board came up, *wham!*, under my chin, and knocked out quite a few of my front teeth. Aside from the shock and my mother screaming at me to stop spitting my teeth out, it put me off surfing forever and ensured years and years of painful, non-anaesthetised dental treatment. Root canals and exposed nerves at the age of twelve with no anaesthetic. The cruelty of this dentist is barely believable by today's standards. My parents told me to stop being so ungrateful, that he was the best dentist in town.

Not really knowing anything about surfing I sought out my friend Jimmy Keogh to tell me about the old days. The first thing he said was, 'Well Peta, you can't put it in the sports chapter – it should go under religion. I don't agree that you can call something a sport if it gets judged by a panel of judges. In surfing, you are alone; nobody wins or loses – you get points.' After our interview Jimmy let me into the inner sanctum of his art studio to show me posters of surfing and a photo of Duke Kahanamoku, the god of Hawaiian surfing. What a specimen – perfect body and stunning, handsome smile. Surfing looks easy to me but to do it you need a strong upper body, good cardiovascular fitness and good balance. It's not true that you need blond hair and white lipstick.

Duke Kahanamoku was born in 1890 and died in 1968. He is not only the patron saint of surfing but was also, along with his brother, an Olympic swimming champion. He grew up on Waikiki with his family and used an old-school, traditional, *olo* surfboard, which he called his 'papa nui'. The olo board was originally only for the *alii*, or ruling class, in the old Kapu system of laws, and could weigh almost 80 kilograms. After the board had been planed, the ancient Hawaiians applied a black stain. When this had dried they rubbed in kukui oil to shine it up. It was blessed before it went into the sea for the first time and after each outing was treated with coconut oil and wrapped in tapa cloth. There was great cultural, symbolic and religious significance; the chiefs used surfing and other sports to sustain their strength, stamina and authority over their subjects.

Petroglyphs of surfers, carved into Hawaiian lava rock and ancient chants from AD 1500 tell stories of surfing feats. In the late 1700s Captain Cook wrote about the amazing sight of naked Hawaiians riding waves on boards – keep in mind sailors of that time couldn't even swim and had trouble understanding why the natives would be doing this. Cook's journals described Hawaiians setting out from shore, diving under the waves and avoiding dangerous rocks to reach beyond the surf. There they would lie down flat on the boards and wait till a big surge came then stand up on the board and ride the gigantic wave at the most terrifyingly rapid pace until they got to shore. Or not. Sometimes they failed to negotiate the rocks near the shore and either they or their boards were smashed to smithereens. The boldness with which the 'natives' executed these difficult manoeuvres was a source of utter astonishment to the sailors. There is no record of maidens performing these tasks – I surmise they were hanging about on the shore braiding their hair, practising hula moves and using berry stains for lipstick.

Obviously this happy, carefree, sensuous state of affairs could not continue, so in 1820 God sent in the missionaries to correct the Hawaiians and explain to them that surfing was a hedonistic waste of time and they were to cease forthwith. By 1890 the missionaries had almost destroyed the culture, religion, eating habits, sensuality and sporting genius of the people. However, thanks to certain staunch sporting kings, like David Kahanamoku, surfing *just* survived in pockets. In 1905 the teenage David (Duke) Kahanamoku and his surfing friends started up a club called *Hui Nalu* – Club of the Waves. They are credited with the rebirth of surfing in Hawaii. After he retired from the Olympics, around 1914, Duke travelled and took surfing to Sydney and Santa Cruz.

Jimmy Keogh

PM 'Did you surf to show off to the girls?'

JK 'Not really and they actually didn't pay much attention to us – they were more interested in sun-bathing and gossiping. The reason we surfed was simply the elation of riding a wave. When we came out of the water there would be serious flirting. Also there was the surf club for socialising. You had to belong to the club if you wanted to surf in any capacity.'

PM 'So one didn't operate as a sole trader?'

JK 'No, but there were gypsies, as we called them – guys who would just turn up on their own from some other part of Sydney. They would catch the waves they wanted then leave.'

PM 'How did you and your brothers learn to surf?'

JK 'We found an old board we called 'The Cigar'. I think it came from Hawaii. God it was hard work – every season you had to sand it off, dry it out and give it umpteen coats of paint to keep the water out. As the

SPORTS

summer progressed it got heavier and heavier. We only stopped surfing for maybe three winter months and then went out almost every day we could. And even if it was freezing we would sometimes go out – we put football jerseys on and never felt the cold. The older surfies were our role models but you can't actually teach someone to surf. It is a very individual, solitary pastime because you have to work it out yourself and it takes a long time – a couple of years at least. You have to put up with a lot of frustration; the movements for controlling those big boards were quite subtle. You had to have the right moves and positions depending on the shape of the wave. Nowadays with the short boards you have more control and you can get off a wave if you choose to.'

PM 'What about sharks and other exciting dangers?'

JK 'Sharks are a very exaggerated danger, although it can make you a bit nervous to see a circle of them – that's when you move to shore. There was much more danger from the actual boards – the Lawson board had me "going down the mine" several times. Once I was knocked unconscious and my friends dragged me in. The most dangerous part of a ride is when the wave peaks which is actually quite close to shore.'

PM 'How did it make you feel when you were surfing?'

JK 'Extreme elation. Once you got it right and took on one of the big ones and survived, there was no feeling quite like it – a mixture of fear and joy – in fact it is the greatest sensation of fear and joy I have had, ever, including sailing. On a perfect day there is nothing like it – hard to describe. When you were out there with mates you talked about politics, cars, gossip, hardly ever work and you never talked about women, never. In the old days – the early 1950s – we used speed to stay alert. You just went to the chemist and bought it over the counter – three and sixpence for a hundred tabs of methedrine, benzedrine or dexedrine. We also used it for long-distance truck drives and the girls used it for dieting. In those days girls didn't want to be skinny – they wanted the rounded, smooth look. I personally was attracted to cheeky girls, the ones who wouldn't take any crap, the funny ones . . . Both my brothers ended up being better surfers than me – and Danny made a very successful business of building surfboards and boats. He made the first fibreglass, foam-core board on the east coast of Australia – he is the inventor of the Keyo board, the short board everyone uses now. He was in a loose partnership with a famous American board- and catamaran-maker called Hobie Alter.

PM 'Are you interested in team sports like rugby and soccer?'

JK 'Not really. I think team sports are like war, tribes fighting. I did play soccer though, because you didn't have to be a certain shape or size to play. The American influence – having to be huge to play football and a freak to play basketball – has ruined the whole noble, gaming aspect of sport. There aren't teams any more,

SPORTS

> there are franchises. I'm not going to get excited by a team called the "Blues", but I might if it was called "Auckland".'
>
> **PM** 'How would you sum up surfing?'
>
> **JK** (Big smile) 'It is a glorious waste of time. It's very reflective – almost Buddhist.'

SEXIEST SPORTSMEN EVER

I asked my friends to help me with this section and this is what we came up with. Some people attached pictures in support of their submissions. These are not in any particular order.

DAN CARTER – who can resist a man in undies? It's so hard to find a sexy New Zealander full stop that Dan comes as a bit of a surprise. New Zealand men usually only take their clothes off if they're drunk, but he did it for money and with class and he's hot. Oh, and I believe he plays rugby.

DAVID BECKHAM – who can resist another man in undies? David is handsome, stylish, kind to children and old ladies, beautiful on the field (they say), but sexy? With that voice? An entire television office described him as a perfectly chiselled specimen. David came high on everybody's list and some seemed to admire his fidelity to his wife!

GEORGE BEST – oh come on! When he was young he was unbelievably sexy and stylish. Go and look at some interviews with him – all that Irish bollocks and magnetic dark flashing eyes. Not to mention his dazzling skill on the field. Pity about the alcoholism. Did you know he talked his doctors into giving him a liver transplant on the understanding he must never drink again and then drank himself to death?

Steve Price – when I asked my radio colleague Alison about this New Zealand Warriors rugby league player she said, 'Where do I begin to tell the story of a love that never ends? Have you ever seen this man with his shirt off? He is hunk personified and a seemingly gorgeous personality to boot – no pun intended.' Steve is a prop and you know what that means – strong thighs.

Roger Federer – this tennis player came up high on everybody's list. My friend Ruth describes him as 'gorgeous but self-effacing, confident but gentle. He married his long-time sweetheart, and she isn't a supermodel. Did I mention rich?'

Michael Bevan – this Australian cricketer induced my colleague Sarah to wax lyrical: 'He is a chiselled, perfect combination of Marlboro and metrosexual man. You look at him and think: "I want you to be playing backyard cricket on my lawn."'

Muhammad Ali – my friend Irene came up with this one and she is so right. In his day Muhammad Ali was sex in boxing boots. He was tall, pretty, cheeky, funny, smart, confident and an unbelievably fast, light fighter. It was he who said, 'Float like a butterfly, sting like a bee.'

BULLFIGHTING

Bullfighting is not an exclusively male domain, but it is a mostly male activity – in terms of the fighting anyway. In the South of France, a lot of women watch the spectacle (**corrida**) and there are some female fighters. Bullfights in Portugal are never fought to the death, but in Spain they are. I was in Evora, Portugal, when I saw my first bullfight on television. I was passing through the lounge of my auberge clutching a glass of Licor Beirao, but such are the vicissitudes of life that I didn't get to my room without

SPORTS

being defiled by the blood spectacle, the ornate sanctioned torture called bullfighting. A well-dressed man was watching. He smiled and stood up as I sat down on the arm of a chair to observe for five minutes. It was October, which is when the fairs are held and the bulls driven through the streets of Vila Franca de Xira, the Mecca of Portuguese bullfighting. The animals are herded by CAMPINOS, wild characters dressed up in green stocking cap with a tassel, white blouson shirt, scarlet waistcoat, green cummerbund and black velvet knee-breeches. Even though the TOREADORS are very splendid in their outfits and have lovely buttocks in their terrifyingly tight pants, the unavoidable fact of the matter is, both the bull and the horse suffer dreadfully.

As it enters the ring the bull is sleek, powerful, alert, leaping and looking for action, the powerful tossing muscle rising between the shoulder blades. Its eyes are bright and virile as it lunges at the toreador's crimson cape. Every so often it thunders into a horse which is blindfolded with a red band and 'protected' by padding, which is of little use, proven by the blood all over it. The horse is incredibly disciplined and stands firm when attacked, even if the horn goes in. When this happens the brave PICADOR slams a PIC (a pike or short lance) into the bull's back, causing terrific pain and weakening it. This goes on until finally only two pics are left, which are stuck into the bull's neck by the toreador on foot, the agony of which drives the animal crazy. At this point I could take no more. The man in the chair was riveted. I went to my cool room and vomited hot indignation. And to think, Ernest Hemingway wrote a whole book on the glory of it.

A week later I was in Seville, Spain. The Maestranza bullring down by the Guadalquiver River is quite fascinating if you've never seen an amphitheatre for brutalising and demeaning animals before. It was built in 1760, is actually a rather lovely building and has a very busy schedule. In Spanish newspapers, you will not find accounts of the bullfights on the sports pages – they are in the arts and culture section.

Bullfighting as entertainment comes from the Romans, who fought bulls on horseback in arenas. In the Middle Ages Spanish noblemen held centre stage on horseback and the **MATADOR** was a minor figure who swiftly plunged the sword in through the neck to the heart at the end. That changed in the seventeenth century when the men on horseback diminished in importance and the toreador, alone and on foot, became the star. The present form of corrida with its pattern, moves and passes originated around 1800. The reality is that more often than not the job is botched, but if he gives a good performance, the toreador is rewarded with the bull's ear, or even two ears, and if he's exceptional, the tail as well. In the past there have been scandals of weak bulls, doped-up bulls and bulls with shaved horns.

When I was there, the mad cow scare was still in full swing and the Spanish government had the jitters, saying it was considering halting sales of meat from bulls killed by matadors. Unbelievably, around 11,000 bulls are killed each season in Spain in about 2000 fights, many held in far-flung villages. Meat from slain bulls accounts for 10 per cent of the revenue taken in by ring owners, who buy animals from breeders. The stew they make from this death-in-the-afternoon is called 'Estofado de Carne de Toro' and is simmered with vegetables in red wine, vinegar, herbs and spices and accompanied by white beans. The meat of this adrenalin-poisoned beast is bitter and tough (can't think why) and needs to cook for many hours. They also grill the enormous cutlets (*chuletas*) make a *Rabo de Toro* (bull's tail stew), and in Andalusia the yummy testicles are served coated in breadcrumbs and fried. In La Mancha the testicles are served together with the brain in scrambled eggs, *Huevos a la Porreta*.

One day I decided to enter the heart of darkness and see what a bullfight was like in real life, rather than on television. I was in that most spellbinding of all French departments, Provence. My friends said, 'Are you mad, why are you doing this to yourself?' 'I am doing it,' I said, 'to know what I am talking about and to analyse my emotional reaction. I want to see if it's as beautiful and honourable and clever as they say.' My friend Gina and I jumped into the Land Rover and made our way to Saint-Rémy-de-Provence for a 10.00 p.m. *Corrida Portugaise* – a Portuguese bullfight.

There are many differences between the Portuguese and the Spanish methods, aside from not putting the bull to death. The Portuguese fight is longer, structurally different and the bull's horns are taped. The small bullring at Saint-Rémy is tiered and full to the gunnels with men, women, grannies, teenagers and tourists; a brass band is playing rousing bullfight standards, the atmosphere is electric – excitement inherited from generations past – and there is a smell of danger. I too am excited and looking forward to the fight, briefly fancying myself as Jacqueline, the last wife of Picasso. In that photo of them at a bullfight, she is sitting very straight and proud; his eyes are burning with intensity and intelligence.

Picadors come into the ring first, followed by the three ornately costumed principal toreadors, one of whom is Frenchwoman Patricia Bellen. On their equally fabulously dressed, plaited and beribboned Lusitanian stallions, the three fighters face the official stand, take their hats off in a flourish, bow their heads then circle the ring slowly with their hats off to the spectators. Everyone claps and cheers. The assistants unfold the cerise, yellow-lined capes and the first bull thunders out of the gate, incandescent with fury. The animal is glossy, black, focused and excited, the huge muscle in its neck standing up. Its eyes are shining and dangerous as it begins its dance with the toreador's pink cape. The men and capes and bulls play this chasing game for a while to warm things up then, like a warrior princess on a minotaur, Patricia quietly enters the ring on her splendid horse.

She is wearing vicious stirrups protected by a hard sort of clog. In her hand she has pics. The bull is fast and smart and goes for them but the pics are wily with their fancy, complicated movements, and dance around the bull like fairies. Because the bull's horns are taped the game is played very close to the horse, which is wearing no protection. Patricia manoeuvres the bull into a position where it is still for a moment, the horse steps back, she sits high in the saddle, raises her pic, yells, the horse gallops forward like lightning and the pic is stuck into the bull's lower neck. This causes pain which is not bad enough to incapacitate but enough to seriously annoy and weaken. The crowd roars and the game continues. Patricia leaps and cavorts around the thundering, enraged bull, which jumps and jack-knifes to get at her. The second pic goes in, the irritation of which ignites the animal. It is now bleeding, moving heavily and panting. Patricia throws her arms up triumphantly to the crowd, she and her fast, disciplined horse smiling with power. The bull is still very dangerous but now clearly at a disadvantage. The third pic goes in. My eyes start to water. The fourth one goes in.

The banderilleros with capes move in and provoke the

exhausted bull, which is looking distractedly from left to right, not seeming to understand what is going on. Now another toreador enters on a fresh horse and he and the bull skid and gallop around each other. His pic goes in and he holds his hand up for applause, the handsome bronzed face glittering with sweat. Patricia re-enters on a fresh horse, the bull charges her and in go two pics at once. It is driven mad by the pain of these pics, now hanging down its side. Gina and I sit there. She is engrossed. Tears are streaming down my face, my body is twisted in anxiety and the band plays gaily on. The bull is roaring and stamping and pawing the dust in rage as the toreadors leave the ring.

But its trial is not yet over for now eight Portuguese campinos, the wild characters, enter. They line up behind each other in a row and the front one talks and calls to the bull, making unfaltering eye contact with it, slowly stepping closer until he is really close. Suddenly the bull thunders straight into him, he puts his arms up and, incredibly, throws himself over the bull's head between the horns and holds on for dear life. This is when you understand why the other seven men are standing closely behind him because they take the impact and concertina into each other. This slows the bull down dramatically, giving them time to surround it and drag their friend off. One of them grabs the bull's tail and skids round and round with it then finally the humiliated, exhausted animal is allowed to exit the ring, blood pouring from its wounds. Gone is the arrogant pride, gone is the power, gone is the beauty. The bull is frothing, its tongue hanging out, the eyes are glassy, the breathing laboured. The toreadors come back and parade slowly around the ring on foot, smiling and accepting things thrown to them by the ecstatic crowd.

A man comes around selling chips, but I need alcohol. I stayed until the bitter end because I kept hoping for an epiphany, to understand the glory of it, to appreciate the beauty and technical perfection of the movements, to be at one with the cultural past, to turn on to the theatricality of it all with the colourful people and emotional music.

When we got home I dived for the cognac and we talked about the corrida. The experience of a bullfight was a phenomenally exciting piece of theatre but also very disturbing. I don't know if I could go through a Spanish one, where the bull is put to death in the arena by a long sword plunged into the neck, piercing the heart. Gina had not attended a Portuguese corrida before and said she would never do it again. In her opinion the mis à mort Spanish style was much better because it was faster and cleaner and the death more honourable. Gina told me the bull is not, as I thought, at a disadvantage – sometimes the toreador and horse can be gored or killed. But I was left with the cruel, humiliating image of the dying bull collapsing three times before slowly but defiantly leaving the ring.

The following year I was once more in the South of France. Gina asked me if I would like to see a Spanish corrida in Nîmes, to compare it with the Portuguese one. I agreed, with trepidation. I felt I had to get back up on the horse, so to speak, to complete my research. We drove to Nîmes and settled into the ancient amphitheatre. Two bulls would fight three teams of horse and toreador each; the entire show would take about two hours.

The first fight ends relatively quickly and cleanly – a famous matador, Mendosa, is on the ticket. He is pitted against a bull called Rincon that is so smart and coiled it jumps every time someone calls out to it. A dance is acted out right to the last, very intimate moments. It is just the bull and the matador on foot,

SPORTS

alone in the arena – they could both kill each other. They are very close now, to the point where the man, such is his power over the bull, can turn his back on it. The man next to me is explaining everything. Suddenly the matador approaches the bull for the moment of truth. I leave nail marks in the man's arm. In a dramatic arc the sword plunges in right to the hilt – this move is called the 'descabello' – and goes straight through the heart. The bull drops almost immediately.

I am confused and sorry to say this, but this fight is absolutely fantastic – the sort of performance all aficionados hope to experience. The passes are beautifully executed by both the man and the bull, the fight isn't too long, and the kill is brilliant. Everyone is hysterical as Mendosa walks over to the dead animal, pats it and quietly speaks to it, thanking it for fighting bravely and dying honourably. He then cuts the two ears and tail off the bull and holds them up triumphantly.

It's all terribly macho. The toreros (the bullfighters on foot supporting the principal one, the matador) with their lithe bodies and handsome, tanned faces are a hundred times more gorgeous than any rugby player. It is breathtakingly theatrical and sexy to see the torero quietly enter the ring, he and his horse dressed like sparkling gods and secure in the knowledge that history, honour and religion are behind them. Good toreros, like Mendosa, are supreme artists and act with unsurpassable technique, intelligence and delicacy. They exercise total domination, which is never gratuitous or misplaced, right from the first cape to the final descabello.

What's happened to me? I have gone from weeping through my first corrida, to enjoying my second, to reading the reviews in *Midi Libre*! The Spanish anthropologist Lorenz Rollhauser described the corrida as, 'a didactic drama, an intimate tragedy which tells of female power, seduction, passion and death. This is the ritualised story of a man and a woman kept apart by fate, a story told from the perspective of the man, who pays for his unquenchable desire with his life.'

There are links, of course, between bullfighting, rugby and surfing – the need to control, the exercise of power, the macho nature of it, the homoeroticism. The bullfight, however, is the most sadomasochistic of all because the price really is death. Yes, well.

Midi Libre newspaper put out a list of the seven different families at the feria – the fair or festival surrounding the bullfight. Here's a loose translation:

Super VIPs – not celebrities and dilettantes but suits, schmoozing their top clients. Everything is paid for; alcohol and bulls are great for team bonding.

VIPs – principally these are Nîmois toffs. They always know someone who can give them a pass to a corrida or bodega.

Aficionados – these are hard-core corrida people. Even if they can't afford to indulge themselves at bullfights they do it anyway – blowing the credit card if necessary – because it is their life.

There to be Seen – these people understand nothing about the corrida but want good seats. They turn up in designer clothes with a strong feria tendency and go to fashionable joints afterwards, but never really get to the soul of the party.

Tribes – these may not even make it to the corrida. They move in packs with cell phones stuck to their ears so they know in advance where the action is. Sometimes tribes party at home,

SPORTS

sometimes in their neighbourhoods – it's not about the bull.

BROKE – these are the most numerous. For them the feria can only be a window. It's not all bad as there are still really cheap bars and improvised bodegas in the back streets of Nîmes.

SUPER BROKE – these teenagers from the poor suburbs don't give a stuff about the cultural significance of the feria and have zero interest in piercing the mysteries of the corrida. They stagger around with a plastic bottle of cheap pastis in one hand and a joint in the other.

LESSONS LEARNED
- None
- It's not true that you need blond hair and white lipstick to be a surfie. You need strength, balance and skill.
- Men need sports to control and channel their inner Conan the Barbarian.
- I have a problem with sports that I probably need counselling for.

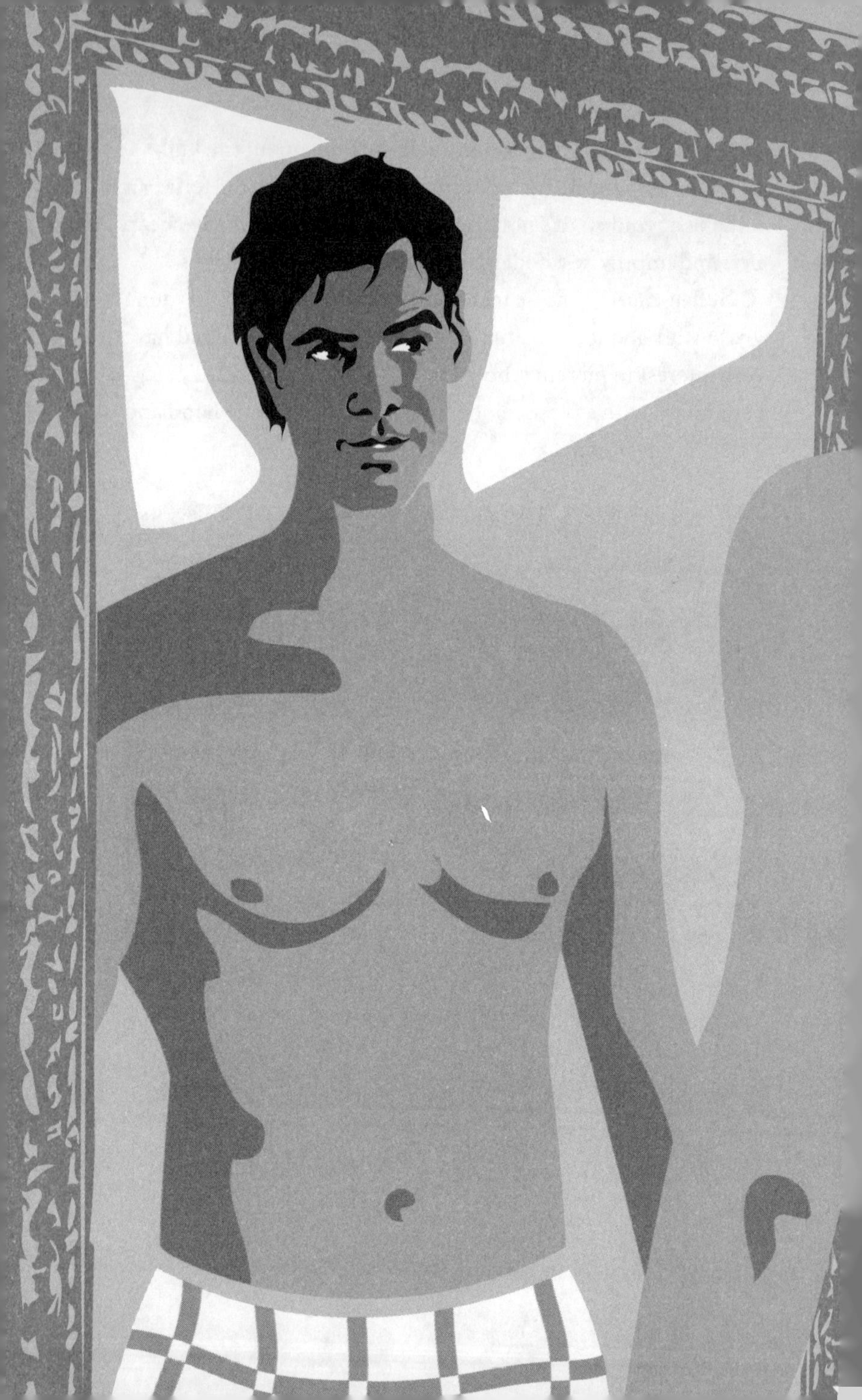

5

Fashion
THE GAME FOR THE YOUNG AND THE DEAD

LA FASHION STORY

I travel a lot and always try to go through cities or countries that lodge my most interesting friends. If I know someone who's an accountant and lives in Dubai – I don't go to that city. If I know someone who used to be an Aussie rock star and lives in Los Angeles – I go to that city. LA airport is so hideous that I need a very strong motivation to subject myself to it. This is where my friends Connie and Andrew come in. Connie strides through the airport to meet me in a look guaranteed to snap anyone out of jet lag: huge black platform boots, tiny slip dress over an hourglass body, white rimmed shades, long black hair with a thick blonde streak, slashes of black eyeliner and white skin (having a tan is losersville among the truly hip in LA).

Connie is a stylist for rock bands. On the way to her place we pick up a flared velvet jacket and $800 faded jeans to deliver to Tom Petty's PA, with whom we have conversations in which the word 'like' appears at least once in every sentence and has nothing to do with her liking anything. 'I'm going, like (deep suck on the fag), what does he take me for? A valley girl, or what? Like, it says in this review here that Tom wore a poofy shirt. I never gave him a poofy shirt. You think that shirt looks poofy? I bet he found that poofy shirt in the back of his wardrobe. I would, like, *never* give him a poofy shirt. I mean, get outta here!'

Inhabitants of the City of Angels spend most of their lives in four-wheel drives on the freeway in the mistaken belief that they have somewhere to go. On one occasion Connie, Andrew and I actually *did* end up somewhere. First, we had dinner on Sunset Boulevard with Gilbert, a producer, and his wife, Ronnie, make-up artist to the stars. In between the steamed artichoke and the crispy ravioli with pea sauce, they freely told me all the top secret goss on the stars. They did this because they knew they would kill me by the application of noise later. With what Connie and Ronnie let slip over dinner I could write a Hollywood gossip column so hot you'd need asbestos gloves to read it. They paid the bill while I choked on the details of Jennifer's latest surgery. Oh and yes, if you tip less than 15 per cent in LA they throw you in prison.

The death by noise turned out to be a concert by heavy metal band RATT (Connie's clients) at Universal Studios. As we approached the concert hall, which seats 2500 people, I became aware of the colour black. It was like a giant Westie funeral: cowboy boots, tattoos, black eye make-up, nails and lips on both sexes, leopard skin and rhinestone cowboy hats (they're not over leopard skin yet in LA), long hair dyed either black or white. There's a certain type of LA fashion that involves a frightening combination of feathers, tassels, beads, crowns of thorns and

FASHION

leather. Enchanted by the complex fashion statements, I briefly considered killing the girl with the 'ROCKER CHICKS RULE' tee-shirt, discarding her white tasselled boots, boiling down her implants for nail polish and wearing the tee-shirt with my Marni skirt, but then decided it would be crueller to let her live.

The concert was grunty, staunch and fantastically degenerate; the backstage party gave new meaning to the term 'superficial'. Like, I can *do* superficial if there's nothing deep around, okay, but do I have to listen to fat old metal-rockers with runny make-up and a collective sperm count of about 100 – due to a lifetime of hermetically sealed jeans – discussing their children's school reports? You call that fashionable? Get outta here.

It was when we drove past the pastry shop on the way back to the airport and I saw Cher's face in icing on a cake that I realised the word 'gastronomy' as I know and love it would have to be redefined. Bad enough we have to listen to her – now we have to eat her. Then I saw the de-alcoholised wine with Jerry Garcia on the label and made a mental note to call Jean-Paul Gaultier. The world needs a nice pinot noir with Jean-Paul smiling rakishly at us. It was then I thought – I'm outta here.

HARDY AMIES

> 'A man should look as if he had bought his clothes with intelligence, put them on with care and then forgotten all about them.'
>
> HARDY AMIES

In his book *The ABC of Men's Fashion,* written in 1964, iconic designer and couturier Hardy Amies gives all sorts of interesting if hilariously snobbish information about men's fashion. He talks about the difference in dressing the 'established classes' and those who 'shop in the high street' and the 'tourist classes', who 'have less trouble with excess baggage'. His advice for someone who is poor is to always wear expensive accessories as they will reflect glory on cheap clothes. (My mother always used to say, buy good clothes when you are rich so when you go through hard times, you will always look fabulous.) He describes American styling as comfortable, lightweight, loose and conservative. Americans have a horror of being different except in casual wear, where they are quite happy to be horrors. The one golden rule for any garment is, if it looks right, it is right – use your mirror. A perfect fit is a combination of good cut, good look and good feel. The natural desire to relax at the beach is absolutely no reason to abandon standards – never wear shorts except at the extreme water's edge (they are inelegant and indecent), never wear short-sleeved shirts – roll long sleeves up, and never wear 'loud'. 'Black is a colour much loved by Italians and Americans, best suited to swarthy Latin types and totally inappropriate to russet-toned Anglo-Saxon gentlemen.'

One wears country clothes to blend into the countryside and not frighten the pheasants (or the peasants). Every man of substance should of course have at least one formal country suit in his wardrobe, preferably tweed.

On being overweight, Amies asks: surely you can be vain enough to make yourself less fat? All hints on dieting lead up to the simple suggestion: 'eat less'.

If you are going to a ball where members of the royal family will be present, you must wear full evening dress, which means white tie, white waistcoat and tails. Get the chambermaid to iron your shirts if you are womanless. Towelling is for towels, not for clothes. The way Italian men dress is very stylish and slightly predatory with that attitude of male supremacy softened with a slightly feminine grace that women love. It has proved rather successful in the sexual attraction game. Underwear should be brief as wit and clean as fun. A boy becomes a man at fourteen and remains one at forty; at twenty-five he starts getting depressed at impending middle age. In fashion there are only the young and the dead.

MEN IN BLACK

In popular culture the term 'Men in Black', or 'MIB', is used to describe men dressed in black suits claiming to be government agents who attempt to harass or threaten witnesses of UFOs into silence. They are usually dark men in dark suits wearing wrap-around sunglasses who drive black Cadillacs. The phrase has been adopted as a tongue-in-cheek term in geek culture for any generic suited government/corporate official. Possibly MIBs are a modern-day manifestation of the same phenomenon that were earlier interpreted as being the devil or fairies – the words 'the black man', referring to his clothes, were used for centuries to indicate the devil. In witchcraft trials this black devil man was accused of having sex with the defendant. Now, gangsters and Italians wear black, so it must be exciting and dangerous. The ultimate man in black, of course, was Johnny Cash, who had a distinctive deep, baritone voice and wore dark clothing. His songs held themes of sorrow, moral tribulation and redemption – he even wrote one called 'Man in Black'.

I feel completely the opposite about men wearing all black to women wearing all black. Women wearing all black is very boring and rarely flattering, unless they are beautifully cut designer clothes. But, inexplicably, a man wearing all black looks sexy and very masculine. Black men wearing all black is so hot it's hardly bearable. The true secret to looking good in black is the fabric – all fabrics that reflect light, like alpaca or mohair, are attractive. Some fabrics hold black dye better than others and some textures look better together than others. Wool is always a deeper black than cotton and holds dye for longer, thus fading more slowly. There is a right and a wrong way to wear all black – you don't want it to look like a uniform; you don't want to look like the parish priest. Shades of black differ (some look brown and some look purple), so when a man is wearing all black he has to be careful with the mix. It's a good idea to pair different fabrics and textures, for example a textured jumper with smooth pants; a smooth wool sweater with patterned black pants; a silk tee-shirt with jeans.

Black cotton fades, which is a shame – I think black cotton garments are fabulous. One way around this is to buy cotton shirts with a little Lycra in them because that holds the dye. Another way is to buy mercerised cotton (cotton that has been treated with sodium hydroxide to shrink it and increase its lustre and affinity for dye) because the blacks are deeper and richer. Given the fading problem, it is best to dry-clean black clothes, but if you insist on washing them at home, throw in a cup of vinegar with the first wash (which must always be cold) – this helps to set the dye. There are also washing products that help keep colour intensity. Finally, when it's time to let go, let go. Don't be shaming yourself by wearing faded, tatty black clothes – say *au revoir* with dignity and throw them away.

FASHION

David Horsman

PM 'Okay, David. Men's fashion.'

DH (Groan) 'Don't start me. At least half a dozen women have said to me in recent years, "Why don't you start your own label? I love the way you dress. I wish my man would dress better." For 130 years men have worn exactly the same kit, which is basically a military uniform. The most individual thing Savile Row tailors can do for you is to put in a pink lining – WOW. You're defined by the fact that you have two buttons on your cuffs or something, or a different tie. This is only marginally less boring than watching paint dry. Women have this huge universe of fashion. You can wear absolutely anything.'

PM 'But lots of men are not remotely interested in clothes or fashion.'

DH 'That's just cultural. Before 1880 men were the peacocks and wore all sorts of things. Every time I wear an Indian shawl people think I'm a weirdo. Women have the enormous advantage of being able to wear clothes that reflect their character and inner essence, and they can change three times a day should they choose. And what leeway do men have? One more button on the cuff! I turned up at the stiff family lawyers once wearing a silk Indian jacket and pants. The whole office from the secretary upwards thought, "What's this then?" Six months later the lawyer said, "Gosh, I love your clothes – I would love to dress like that." Men often say to me, how can I dress like you? Tell me what to do.'

PM 'Why is it important for you to wear beautiful clothes?'

DH 'To express my personality, be comfortable, be free. I would like to do a range of clothing for men that straddles both extremes. I don't look like an ethnic hippy and I don't look straight. It's important for a man's self-respect to dress well and it doesn't have to be a jacket and tie.'

PM 'Look, men don't know how to dress. Most men's wives dress them.'

DH 'So the women are to blame.'

PM 'But men put their wives in the position of having to dress them because they look so appalling otherwise.'

DH 'Most men's casual wear is pretty ghastly. There's a stage you get to when you're more mature where it becomes a mutton-dressed-as-lamb situation, for example the man with the ponytail riding a Harley. It's the same thing as a sixty-year-old woman wearing see-through garments with G-strings. I would like to be as smartly and beautifully dressed with the best fabrics as somebody who spends a thousand quid on a Savile Row suit.'

PM 'Tell me about your relationship with shoes. In my experience men secretly love shoes and would like to express their personalities more than in any other way with shoes.'

DH 'My girlfriend is a shoe designer so I am wearing her sandals a lot at the moment. I like them because they

FASHION

> are comfortable, easy-to-wear, beautifully made and come in great colours. She picked out a pair of shoes for me the other day, which are patent leather. Now anything in patent leather in my youth was considered fast, a womaniser's shoe, so you dressed down.'
>
> **PM** 'Oooh, I'm thinking pointy patent Italian shoes. Would you wear uncomfortable shoes like women do – like stilettos – just because they felt sexy or whatever?'
>
> **DH** 'No, never. Shoes have to be comfortable.'
>
> **PM** 'What about a fabulous pair of brogues?'
>
> **DH** 'Too BCBG [haute bourgeois]. The upper-middle classes in France wear them and dress exactly like English dorks.'
>
> **PM** 'What about undies?'
>
> **DH** 'I remember when the boxer short came in in the eighties and jockeys became naff and you were a bit fast or pornographic or something if you wore them. I now don't wear underwear at all because it's more comfortable that way.'

THE SUIT

As the word 'suit' comes from the French 'suite', which means 'to follow', I assume the expression 'follow suit' originates from this. The reason suits were given their name was because the jacket and pants were made of the same cloth – the pants followed the jacket in both colour and textile. Originally, suits were very expensive, handmade to measure (which is called 'bespoke' in the trade) and only for the toffs. Enter the Industrial Revolution and suits began to be mass produced in factories, which brought the price right down so almost any man could afford one. Although the suit appears rather military to me in its relentless uniformity, its creation was in reality a cry from men for more simplicity and comfort in their formal wear. In the seventeenth century men dressed in a terribly complicated and ornate way with jewels and lace all over the show. They moved on to severe, starchy outfits in Victorian times and then, for better or worse, relaxed into what we now know.

For men who wear them, suits are like a second skin with pockets. When a man is wearing a suit, which fewer and fewer men do these days, he feels he is conveying respectability and good taste. In fact he is conveying unadventurous conformism. This is why men wear suits for job interviews, funerals, court appearances and occasions that demand respect and formality. To call a man 'a suit' is a pejorative term meaning he is part of an unimaginative bureaucracy or corporation, straight and contemptible . . . probably lacking in morals and possibly sleeping with the secretary. Having said this, a man in a beautifully cut suit cannot help but be handsome and impressive and we girls all love a man in a uniform – even if it's only the postman.

There have been many versions of the suit over the years, like the zoot suit. This hilarious suit was originally called the zuit suit or drapes and was invented by slick hipsters in Harlem in the heady jazz era of the 1930s. It was very baggy and loose with broad pants that tapered in to the ankle. The jacket part was also big, hugely padded and longer than a normal suit. The style leaders in the United States of that era were the Black Americans, Italians and Puerto Ricans, who loved fashion and fun. Malcolm X described the zoot suit as 'a killer-diller coat with a drape shape, reet pleats and shoulders padded like a lunatic's cell'.

FASHION

The Beatle suit was derived from Pierre Cardin's collarless jackets. The mod suit of the 1960s had very slim-cut, narrow lapels, three or four buttons and a strongly tapered waist. It was usually single-breasted, the cloth generally consisting in part of mohair.

The safari suit is the most unforgivable suit of all. It derived from soldiers' hot climate uniforms, had short sleeves and sometimes short trousers, was usually made out of synthetic fabric that gave you heat rashes and eczema. The pastel colours were execrable and you wore an open neck shirt under the suit. Particularly criminal behaviour also involved a tie. Meant for the tropics, there was absolutely no excuse for it – my father wore and loved the safari suit until we put a stop to it. Australians have safari suit pub crawls wherein they compete for prizes like wigs, fake handkerchiefs, jungle maps, wall hangings and smart walk socks. They drink cocktails, sherry and eat vol-au-vents and liver paste. Ya gotta love them.

Sadly, the dapper pinstripe suit is dying alongside its best friends the tie, the furled umbrella and the bowler hat. Who would have thought the bowler hat would live to survive on the heads of Bolivian women? The pinstripe lived for almost a century, that thin pale thread running through British suits, symbolising the quintessential public school boy, city types and Savile Row. A man in a pinstripe was decency itself, now he's considered your tragic cousin from down the line – sort of unreconstructed and five minutes ago. Now you really only see a pinstripe suit on a gangster who doesn't know any better or in a low-rent clothing chain. You can get a 'credit crunch' suit in London for £25. Now the toffs wear a plain dark blue suit with Cleverley shoes. Cleverleys are arguably the best shoes in the world, famous for their elegance, comfort and workmanship.

Sharp, modern men on the catwalk wear plain, slick camel, corduroy (believe it or not) and Dolce & Gabbana are doing tartan check. However, stay alert for the new 'underground' pinstripe movement – rock stars are wearing it with trainers just because it's unfashionable. How cool.

THE TIE

The first man who wore a tie was probably a member of the Roman legionnaires. It was a piece of fabric tied around the neck both for warmth and to soak up the sweat of battle – they called it a 'focale'. A few centuries down the line, the French took their hankies out of their pockets, tied them around their necks and called them 'neckerchiefs' or 'cravats'. This word possibly comes from 'croat', as they supposedly stole the idea from Croatian soldiers during the Thirty Years War. Only Louis XIV would get a fashion statement from a mercenary. In 1661, he instituted the position of tie maker for the king, a gentleman who was assigned to help the king arrange and knot his necktie. In 1925, the American tie maker Jesse Langsdorf patented a long tie. It was less crumpled and more stable, sewn from three pieces of fabric and cut to a taper. The modern tie was born. All good ties are cut on the bias, essential for give and to make a good knot; and are lined with silk at the tips. Oscar Wilde, in *The Importance of Being Earnest*, wrote, 'A well-tied tie is the first serious step in life.' The daily gesture of tying the tie assumes a symbolic and nearly magical meaning. In symbolic, masculine iconography the knot represents union, marriage, fertility and therefore life. Tying the knot correctly is a true ritual of elegance. A tie is not just the finishing touch to a suit; it is an indispensable part of it and should always be in contrast (unless you are an MIB) to it. A symbol of elegance and refinement, it expresses the personality of the wearer. Nowadays it mostly symbolises conformity.

THE BELLBOTTOM

The bellbottom is the shape of sailors' trousers where they meet the boot. They were supposedly thus shaped so that sailors could quickly remove their boots in an emergency situation. Hardy Amies predicted that this trouser shape would never catch on in civilian clothing, but he was wrong. In the late 1960s bellbottoms started to be worn by bohemian artists and musicians and by the 1970s they were considered wildly stylish by the counter-culture hippie generation. Related styles included flares, loon pants and boot-leg trousers. I myself wore powder blue bellbottoms with a hairy pink jumper and love beads. Bellbottoms were originally made of denim but were soon fashioned out of just about anything, including the home-made version in which you cut the pants and inserted a wedge of a different fabric. They were a cultural statement of the youth-oriented hippie generation and were a direct reaction to the straight-legged pants worn by their straight parents. They made a big comeback in the mid-1990s, as the Generation X crowd mistakenly copied their parents, who had by then gone back to straight-legged pants.

HOW TO TAKE ADVANTAGE OF MEN – A QUICK WOMEN'S DRESS GUIDE

In terms of dressing, the male population tend to go for comfort and to appeal to the opposite sex, which, bizarrely, is what they think we should do. Women dress to give the message of who they are, to impress themselves and to impress other women, because we know men don't give a stuff what we wear. What men care about in women is the general look: they like a little bit of sexy but not in-your-face, they like a bit of fun and they like femininity. They don't think you're a scrubber if you have sex appeal – they think you're alive and someone they would like to meet. Conversely, if you are too obvious, showing too much skin and looking like the happy hooker, that seems to be a turn-off. If you're wearing black or dowdy clothes, men can't see or hear you. Of course, some men *like* invisible, quiet girls, though I can't think of one right now. Once you have the male shark circling, then you can ask him to focus a little on the neck up. Note: This is only if you're looking to take advantage of a man; if you're not interested in attracting those sexy devils, wear what you like.

French women understand how to be attractive to men – they are very straightforward about flirting and wear stylish clothes, which accentuate their best bits. However, don't exaggerate more than one best bit at a time – even though they are visual creatures, men can't do two things at once and that includes looking at two things. If you have great legs, don't cover them up; if you have Scarlett Johansson breasts, give us all a thrill; if you have a tiny waist get that cinched belt out; if you have toned biceps, a little cute tattoo is hot. If you have beautiful hair, leave it loose. Most women don't realise how much men love their hair, especially if it's long. The wisdom used to be that the older you got the shorter your hair should get. False. Long hair is great on older women. I'm very sorry to say this but in the dating stakes, men will notice sexy way before they will notice sophisticated. Even wolves are just pussies in sheepskin moccasins – most men

FASHION

like women who are approachable and not scary. Wearing pretty clothes is not shallow – it shows pride in your appearance.

Invest in some gorgeous lingerie – thunderpants are not it. It doesn't matter if no one can see them – you can see them, you know you're wearing them and you know how they make you feel. Don't worry about the panty line – this is attractive to men – it's only women who don't like it. High heels make your feet and legs look wonderful and change the gait of your walk, but you have to know how to walk gracefully in them otherwise you look like a duck. Men falling for ducks is quite unusual. The way to cover up lumps and bumps is to wear cotton – it doesn't cling. Stand up straight and put your shoulders back. Men like bums, something most women hate or think are imperfect. Don't wear baggy trousers – they can be flared but have to be fitting around the hips. Wear dresses and skirts that flatter your bum – always turn around and get a good look in the mirror. Having said all this, my friend Johanna met her partner while lying on a couch dressed in old sweatpants and weeping into her soup over another man. So go figure.

Steve Yeoman

PM 'Why do you wear clothes? Are they just to cover you or are they telling a story?'

SY 'Both. Right now I'm wearing a tee-shirt from MOMA (Museum of Modern Art), which shows you that I am a walking work of art. But I am also capable of wearing silly tee-shirts that say 'Port Douglas Singlet Hire'.

PM 'Are you into designer clothes?'

SY 'Armani is like Country Road on speed – always perfect, always safe, always well-stitched. I used to work at Hugh Wright (menswear shop) and was seriously into fashion – the Carnaby Street end. If I was ever to spend money on clothes again it would probably be on a pair of Armani jeans because the fabric is so fantastic. I used to love Paul Smith because he has a brilliant sense of humour. I had a pair of his herringbone jeans. If I had to wear a suit I would always pair it with a top quality, Italian tie – at one stage I had $4000 worth of ties. I collected them by label. I can tell you the very day I lost interest in buying fashion. I was buying trousers in the Armani store in Milan. I suddenly thought, "This is as good as it gets – I'm buying Armani trousers in the Armani flagship in Italy – I can stop now." It finished twenty years of focusing on fashion and I am now a lapsed fashionista.'

PM 'Tell me about shoes.'

SY 'As far as I'm concerned if I never had to wear shoes again, I would be happy.'

PM 'Tell me about shopping.'

SY 'There's shopping and there's buying. At home I just buy what I need – I go there, I buy it and I come home. Unfortunately, men's fashion never changes much. When I'm away I'll do proper shopping and look around because there are different things. There are always other bored men to talk to – Australians are particularly friendly. The guys have that look on

FASHION

their faces of "I'm not even watching television", so if you said to them, "What are you thinking?", and they said, "Nothing", it's absolutely true. In Germany, in shopping malls, they now have crèches for men. One whole wing of the store where the crèche is will be focused on men's stuff like electronics. The wife drops her husband off and he is met by a hostess who takes him over to the bar, introduces him to other men, settles him in...'

PM 'And the men play with their toys.'

SY 'Yes. Ha ha, very funny.'

PM 'Do you think men should dress absolutely the way they wish, whether they look hopeless or not?'

SY 'We have a dress code at work which says "Tidily self-expressive".'

PM 'That's quite good, but why do men dress so desperately – why are they so hopeless?'

SY 'Peer pressure – they don't want to stand out and be the peacock. Most men don't care what they wear and don't think it's anybody else's business. It's about the only gender-specific thing we have. A man might see a stylishly dressed man or woman and think, "Oh, that's nice", but not give it any more thought than that. They are already thinking about fishing or the next coffee. Women see someone coming down the street and analyse their look for ten minutes.'

PM 'Yes but 200 years ago, men were complete peacocks.'

SY 'I bet the rabble weren't. I bet the accountants and clerks were just as drab as they are now – it would

> have been the upper classes who were dressing up to ponce off to the palace. Everyday folk would have just worn the same old sheet turned inside out.'

HOW MEN WENT FROM WEARING THE LOINCLOTH TO GOING COMMANDO

The story of men's underwear and swimwear is very touching and related not only to the changing style of clothes they wore over the centuries but also to hygiene. From prehistory right up to the ancient Egyptians, men wore loincloths because, well, you had to wear something to protect all that exterior gear from wear and tear. The ancient Greek slaves wore them because they had nothing else. The toffs had big togas so didn't really need them but by the Middle Ages, men's clothing had changed to being in two pieces – a top and pants. It was quite uncomfortable to have rough pants against your boy skin so undershirts and big, baggy drawers called braies were invented – they were linen and tied at the waist and knees. Then they became smaller and got a flap in the front, which soon became the exhibitionist codpiece. The codpiece was obviously so you could go to the toilet, but needless to say, six inches became eight with padding in the larger and larger codpieces. Henry VIII was a particularly flamboyant offender in this department. These undies were handmade from flannel, silk, wool, linen and cotton until the Industrial Revolution, when you could actually go to a shop and buy them.

Then in the Victorian era, inexplicably, these perfectly good drawers and undershirts grew together into a one-piece, which went right from the neck to the ankles with a back flap. By World

FASHION

War Two, the one-piece or union suit had become the shorter long johns, named after a famous boxer of the time called John Sullivan. Fortunately, designers came to their senses by the 1930s, long johns went out the window and in came the nifty boxers (also taking their name from boxing) and briefs. They were great because they had an elastic waist which eliminated fussy buttons, snaps and ties. This is when the word underpants was invented and in 1934, Jockey came up with the truly innovative Y-fronts men still wear today. They were sewn from knitted fabric until flash materials like Dacron, Spandex, and Lycra were invented. Now you could get undies in any colour or print you fancied, but interestingly enough, white cotton remained the favourite. By the 1980s, the big designers like Calvin Klein and Tommy Hilfiger had got in on the act and the word 'sexy' was put in the same sentence as undies. Now undies were small, tight, had a fantastic cut and design and were aimed at specific markets, like casual, sexy, warm, romantic, 'figure enhancing' and sports.

These days, flash Italian and French designers make ergonomically designed undies from super-smooth, silky microfibres. But wait! How much further can we go? Less is more and the very latest look is no look at all. Wearing no undies is called freeballing, or going commando. This is not as horrifying as it sounds and some of my interviewees said they indulged in this practice.

You see, in the filthy old days you needed underwear for hygienic reasons, but modern men shower every day so undies are not as necessary. I don't really see why men wear them at all because they just make you infertile – testicles have to be kept cool or the sperm die – that's why they're outside the body and not inside it. Just as it is very sexy for a woman not to wear her knickers, so it is for men. Five million Scotsmen can't be wrong.

THE SEASIDE

The odd habit of going to the beach and jumping in the water was invented in the 1880s – before that only boats and fish were in the sea. Because of the need for modesty, the first men's swimsuits were incredible creations, so heavy (5 kilograms when wet) you almost drowned. If you survived the swim, when you emerged, the swimsuit fell down. Because men couldn't shock the ladies with too much raw male flesh, regulations were drawn up wherein you had to have a sort of skirt around your trunks. Enter the speedsuit, which was sort of rubbery but it was tight, light and had big slashed armholes. You also had to be modest and not show your chest. Men fought for liberation to go topless. Someone thought up the idea of a zip separating the top from the bottom, so you had a choice – thrilling I know, but still dodgy and men were actually arrested for indecency in America. But in naughty France, those Froggies whipped off their tops to give us a bit of the old je ne sais quoi and the rest is history. The 1950s saw the fabulous, unforgettable Cabana Sets – matching boxer shorts with loud Hawaiian shirts favoured at barbecues and pool parties. By the 1960s, the beach world was subjected to Speedos and thongs, but in the 1970s, the hippies saved us from gross-out with cut-off shorts. Now, you can wear anything you want – board shorts seem to be the most popular. Aloha baby!

SHOES

Men let themselves down with their shoes. My careful research, trawling the streets, showed that men don't care about shoes that much – they are not in love with them the way we are. They don't sit around fantasising about them all day. They don't think

FASHION

a fabulous shoe will change their lives. They don't wear uncomfortable ones just because they are fabulous and they don't own three thousand pairs. Interestingly, knock-out women's shoes are completely wasted on men. They couldn't care less about your Robert Clergeries or your Jimmy Choos. They wouldn't even notice that Christian Louboutin shoes all have red soles. Number 1 Shoes is fine with them and they wouldn't know the difference. Possibly excepting the Beatle boot in the 1960s, I can't imagine a male shoe becoming fetishised the world over in the way the Manolo Blahniks and Jimmy Choos Carrie wore in *Sex in the City* were. No.

The shoe scene for men is prosaic and comfortable, not particularly sexy and they don't seem to use shopping as a form of therapy. Although men's shoes appear to all be rather similar in comparison to women's shoes, men actually have quite a lot of choice in makes and styles. Because they don't care, they often buy uncomfortable, cheap, nasty, trendy rubbish. This is a false economy, not only because the shoes fall apart quickly, but because it is bad for your feet and posture to wear ill-fitting shoes. If you can't walk comfortably you end up always being just in time to be too late. If you buy good quality shoes and look after them, you will not only be comfortable but you will have saved money because they last much longer – they will last for years, even generations. Also, you feel fantastic. My mother always used to say, you can judge a man by his shoes – if they are dirty or run-down at heel, that is how he is as a man. You know what no attention to detail means.

Men seem either to think that shoes are unimportant, or that shoes can't be seen. Just like clothing, men's shoes in the past were serious peacock territory. Well, most of the population had no shoes at all, but the toffs were extremely ostentatious with embroidery, make-up, floral kit and high heels. After the French Revolution, businessmen thought they'd better be seen as more sombre and less superficial, and moved towards a sensible and almost austere way of dressing, which included toning down the shoes. Heels got flattened, brilliant buckles were chucked out for ordinary eyelets and eventually men gave up the high boot for the Oxford-style shoe, which came in in 1910. Flash and dazzle for the boys went out the window and never really came back. Because men are really only interested in comfort, it tends to limit manufacturers' creativity. Men's feet get bigger as they age so shoe designers don't put much effort into styles for fear of losing customers over fit problems.

Men should spend more money on shoes because a well-made shoe is obviously extremely comfortable and if they started getting dressed with a good shoe, the rest of the outfit would be more likely to follow the same tone. As men wear ties less and less, sharp shoes and beautiful belts will become more important – that way a fairly ordinary shirt and pants can be spiced up with fab accessories. Here's how it goes with looks: Italian style is sleek; British style is traditional but can be edgy; and American style is conservative and clunky. As with women's shoes, a high-end pair of men's shoes cost a lot, mostly because of the way they are constructed, the quality of the material, the fit and the durability – and they are worth every penny. The colours to go for are black, burgundy, ox-blood, honey and cognac. As the Frank Zappa song says, 'brown shoes just don't make it'.

Some men *do* care deeply about shoes. I have a friend in France who is the Imelda Marcos of Marseilles. He has shelves and shelves of shoes, boots and riding boots. They are all of the same colour palette – beige/ochre/tan – and all perfectly lined up. I know if I changed the place of one pair, he would notice. His room is a fabulous vision of the most beautiful expensive shoes you could imagine – mostly lace-ups, mostly fitted with old-fashioned shoe trees, all shining and all well looked after. There are no rundown heels, no scuffs and no looseness of character showing in these shoes. You never know what is behind a quiet exterior and a pair of glasses.

In the 1960s the commonly worn men's shoe called the low shoe was a short version of the boot worn by army officers. After World War One, the popularity of the boot declined as men associated it with the horrors of trench boots, suffering and destruction. Fascinatingly, after World War Two, two influences created a new type of boot. The crepe-soled, rough suede Dutch *voertreker* boot was introduced into Western Desert Campaign by South African divisions of the Eighth Army. Indian troops on the North-West Frontier wore a sandal called the *chupplee*. Officers from the Western Desert visiting Burma admired this sandal for its comfort. Both these pieces of footwear came together in 1950, when the desert boot was invented by Messrs Clark. This style has a soft upper suede with a two-tie lace-up front and a crepe sole. The soft, floppy, ankle boot stepped into the fashion scene and became an icon.

Chelsea boots – also known as dealer boots, worn for horse riding in the Victorian era and known as paddock or jodhpur boots. They are plain-fronted with elastic sides running from the heel to the top of the boot, which just covers the ankle. They first reappeared in the 1950s, becoming really fashionable in the 1960s mod scene and worn by the Beatles, who in 1961 popularised a derivative called the Beatle boot. Said Beatle boots were tight-fitting, Cuban-heeled, ankle-high boots with a sharpish pointed toe. Sometimes the side was zipped rather than elastic. This is when high heels came back in for men, signalling erotica and virility.

Cowboy boots – cowboy boots refer to a specific style of riding boot, historically worn by American cowboys. They have a high heel, rounded to pointed toe, high shaft, elaborate stitching, cut-outs, embossing and inlays and, traditionally, no lacing. Cowboy boots are normally made from cowhide leather, but are also sometimes made from exotic skins, such as alligator, snake, ostrich, lizard, eel, elephant, sting ray, elk, buffalo and the like. Riding boots have been around for centuries and the cowboy boot seems to have descended from the Hessian boot, a boot style that was common among cavalry in Europe in the eighteenth century. Early American designs were heavily influenced by the vaquero tradition imported from Spain to the Americas, dating back to the early 1500s. In the 1960s the romance and mystique of this work boot suddenly became fashionable among the general public, for both men and women. Urban cowboys can now buy very simple stylish boots for city wear or incredibly decorative, elaborate ones for that special knees-up. The Frye boot company still makes some of the best boots on the planet.

Brogues – a form of decorative punching and serrating of the toe, side and heel of leather shoes, thought of as being typically British. Originally they were stout leather shoes from Scotland or Ireland – the word is derived from the Gaelic for shoe. They have typified the classic office shoe for generations.

Winkle pickers – these boots were worn by rockers from the 1950s and were distinguished by their medieval look of long, sharp, pointed toe. The winkle picker was so called because, in

England, winkles are eaten with a pin or pointed object to get the winkle out of the shell. They were lace-up Oxford-style with a low heel and were also worn by women. There seems also to have been a practice, among increasingly liberated and forward young women, of using the pointed toes of their footwear to surprise and perhaps embarrass their male partners by prodding their private parts under tables in public places. Thus effectively turning the historical tables, as in the fourteenth and fifteenth centuries, long, pointed male footwear called poulaines or Cracowes were allegedly used to do the same to females, a practice that was also allegedly revisited by some winkle-picker wearing males.

Loafers – a loafer is a casual, low, laceless, slip-on shoe, typically with a wide strip across the top with a diamond cut-out, sometimes with a tassel, which a man's foot slides into without any fastening. The loafer was invented by the Norwegians in the 1930s and was subsequently taken up by visiting Americans. It has a moccasin construction, was originally only worn at home in the summer, but soon became mainstream casual wear. In the 1950s American prep school students started inserting a penny into the diamond cut-out as a fashion statement, which is where they got the name penny loafer. In 1966 Italian designer, Gucci, added a metal strip across the front in the shape of a horse bit, which is when they became Gucci loafers.

Moccasin – a sturdy slipper-shaped type of shoe sewn from tanned deer or elk skin. The word moccasin comes from an Algonquian American Indian word, *makasin*. They were originally made of soft leather stitched together with sinew and with buffalo hide soles. One piece of leather is stitched together at the top, sometimes with a vamp (additional panel). Tribal differences included not only the cut of the moccasins but also the extensive embroidery, beadwork, quillwork, and painted designs many Indian people lavished on their shoes. Indian scouts could identify a tribe by its moccasined footmarks on the ground. Moccasins are still worn today and in New Zealand sheep shearers' moccasins are made of synthetic felt with a back seam and gathered at the top of the rounded toe. These moccasins are laced in the front, and the lacing is covered with a flap fastened with a buckle at the shoe's outer side. The fastener arrangement prevents the shearer's comb from catching in the laces. Shearers' moccasins protect the feet, grip wooden floors well, and absorb sweat.

Brothel creepers – these were invented in 1949 and worn by teddy boys and rockabillys. They were worn with drainpipe trousers, pompadour haircuts and electric blue clothes. Malcolm McLaren and Vivienne Westwood sold thousands of them in their famous shop on the King's Road in London. Brothel creepers were so called because a man put them on before a night of debauchery in the brothels of Amsterdam. They have a soft, thick sole and are often made of suede, as you may well imagine.

Sneakers – rubber-soled shoe used by basketball players. The first sneakers, so named because of the stealth and quiet manner in which you could creep up on someone when you wore them, were designed in 1917. They were used by kids for most of their running and walking needs. Before the late 1970s, running shoes were not high-tech items. With rare exceptions, until the middle of the nineteenth century, shoes were made on a single straight last and there was no differentiation between left and right shoes. Today, these shoes are frowned upon by biomechanical experts. Interestingly, Abebe Bikila won the 1960 Olympic

Marathon in Rome *barefoot*, gliding along the cobblestones and not even stubbing a toe. I don't believe he'd heard of biomechanics, energy return systems and ergonomics. Did you know that the initial pairs of Nike soles were cooked up in Bill Bowerman's waffle iron? Today's running shoes, such as Reeboks and Nikes, are designed with an eye toward accommodating various types and shapes of feet.

Note: Flashing lights on your running shoes do not make you run faster.

Sandal – a sandal may have a sole made from rubber, leather, wood, tatami or rope. It may be held to the foot by a narrow thong that generally passes between the first and second toe, or by a strap or lace, variously called a latchet, sabot strap or sandal, that passes over the arch of the foot or around the ankle. A sandal may or may not have a heel strap and leaves most of the foot exposed. The oldest known sandals were discovered in Fort Rock Cave in Oregon, USA. Radiocarbon dating of the sagebrush bark from which they were woven indicates an age of at least 10,000 years. The ancient Greeks and Egyptians wore them. A fashionable sandal derivation is the slide, which is backless and open-toed, essentially an open-toed mule. I really like slides on men – they may cover nearly the entire foot from ankle to toe, or may have only one or two narrow straps.

HOW TO CARE FOR SHOES

Keep shoes on shoe trees to maintain their shape and keep them polished, even if you are not using them. They need polish to preserve the leather and keep it from cracking. Don't let holes develop – get them fixed when they start to wear thin. Don't wear the same shoe two days in a row – they need time to rest and breathe. If your boot zips get stuck, run a lead pencil down the zip and they will run smoothly. Allow wet footwear to dry naturally in a well-ventilated area as this will prevent any damage. Do not dry your footwear using an artificial heat source as this will damage uppers and cause the leather to separate from the bonding. Don't wear them to bed.

THE MODERN MALE SHOPPER

Sam Gray and Linz Ariell started their fashion lives selling vintage clothing at a market. This eventually progressed into owning several menswear shops called Marvel. Linz is the designer and Sam the buyer and seller. Sam is very pretty and exudes an air of charm and openness – quite the opposite of a lot of people in fashion, who specialise in being thrilled with themselves. Linz rolls his own cigarettes, rather heart-warming in this day and age. Their shops are a 'destination', small but perfectly formed, a bit funky and full of innovative and exciting men's clothing. They also stock accessories like vintage tie clips with hidden miniature swords and contemporary bead necklaces with little skulls; stylish men's hats and collectables like Crown Lynn crockery and sixties German ceramics. I have been buying shirts there for the men in my family for years – my father is still wearing a pink and grey geometric number for special occasions and he's in his mid-eighties.

FASHION

Linz Ariell

PM 'Your clothes are very stylish – would you ever do lace and embroidery on men's shirts? I saw an outrageously frilly shirt on a heinous criminal in a James Bond movie and thought it was fabulous.'

LA 'No. We don't do that very often because that European sensibility doesn't really work here. Although we have sold shirts like that, our men like to look masculine.'

PM 'Okay, for example there is a very cool shirt on your rack – black check lined with red check with turned up short sleeves so that the red check is just showing – who buys that? Gay guys?'

LA 'No, you'd be surprised. All sorts of men buy that shirt – older, younger, straight.'

PM 'At the beginning what were you designing, Linz?'

LA 'The shirts were very basic, but the prints we were buying were wild. They weren't fabrics traditionally being put into menswear and that was our immediate point of difference. We were never mainstream. Both Sam I have a real feel for cloth and that comes from working with vintage. We can put our hands in a bin of vintage clothes and just by feel, pull out the best one.'

PM 'When you are buying fabrics, what are you attracted to?'

LA 'The weave and quality of the cloth, the way it feels. We like quirky prints.'

PM 'Is finishing important?'

LA 'Yes, because a garment that has just been overlocked together and not finished properly inside will fall apart in the washing machine. It's the things you can't see which count in a garment.'

PM 'Now, this is one of my favourite topics. Do you think men should wear what suits them, covering up the flaws and emphasising the good bits, or do you think men should just wear what they want and it's nobody's business?'

SG 'Oooh, this is one of my favourite topics too. I like to help men look the best they can but at the same time, if you are happy with an unusual look, people will accept you and that's kind of admirable really. Generally, though, men are more conservative dressers than women, who are more likely to wear something showy. Men prefer to conform, but are still looking for a point of distinction.'

PM 'Maybe that's because men have so little choice.'

LA 'It depends on the person. If a person has a big personality and is outrageous anyway, they can carry off just about anything and it's fun. But if a man is inhibited he won't look good in something that is not tasteful.'

PM 'But what if the man looks absolutely revolting and can't see that – thinks he looks fabulous?'

SG 'Our philosophy in the shop is to gently and politely direct men away from something unsuitable to something flattering. There are different tribes of men – some men love to be looked at, some want you to see the shape of their biceps, some want to hide themselves, some just want to blend in, some are flamboyant. Fashion is much more relaxed than it used to be and men want to be recognised as belonging to their tribe.'

PM 'Sam, you have a teenage boy – tell me about tribes.'

SG 'Teenage boys don't all dress the same – they have sub-tribes they wish to fit into which will have a look. It depends on your tribe what the look is. Some boys are into baggy pants hanging off their bum, some are into tight, skinny jeans. They dress to fit in but also to attract girls and men never stop doing that.'

PM 'Really? Do boys care what girls think?'

SG 'God yes. To the extent that you will attract a like-minded girl who will fit in with your tribe.'

PM 'Do boys use body products like face cream?'

SG 'Yes they do – my son wears more than I do.'

PM 'How have your menswear designs changed over the years?'

LA 'The shape. The shape of the shirt has changed to be a lot more fitted. Even a big guy wants something shaped and fitted – not tight but fitted. Jeans have changed – I am now designing jeans with a slightly higher waist – hipsters are out. Our dress trousers have a fifteen centimetre zip and the jeans have a twelve centimetre one. The shape of the moment is definitely skinny.'

PM 'What about flares?'

LA 'No, so far flares have never really made a comeback – they did briefly for women, but not for men.'

PM 'Are men into accessories like fancy undies?'

LA 'Yes – especially if they are wearing low-cut jeans where the underwear is visible. They might wear fancy underwear if they are going out and think they may get lucky. Cuff links are coming back in so we are now making shirts which can go both ways – links or buttons. Some men wear jewellery, but most don't.'

PM 'Do men put a lot of thought into dressing?'

LA 'Not really. I'm a designer and even I open the wardrobe and decide what I am wearing by what is clean, what is ready and what is easy.'

PM 'Who is your style icon in terms of fashion designers?'

LA 'The Spanish designers and Issey Miyake. For long-standing, great work Miyake is just so so clever. My favourite shirt is probably a Miyake.'

PM 'How do men shop?'

SG 'Very focused. They decide they need to buy a shirt, they go to the shop, buy the shirt and leave. Or they decide to buy four things for summer, then come back in winter and do it again. However, we do have regulars who come in every week just to check out the scene. The age group starts at sixteen and finishes around seventy-five. Also, because our clothes are well-made and have longevity, we have a lot of regular customers.'

PM 'Where is fashion going for men do you think?'

LA 'Well, for this winter we are doing a black and grey

palette with a bit of hot orange. They say fluoro is coming back in, but we're not interested in that – you have to be very young to wear it.'

PM 'Why haven't you taken over the world?

SG 'Because we are control freaks, I think. We like very much the idea of following the garment right from when we buy the fabric, to designing it, sewing it and selling it. We have had the same people working for us for years – it's like a family.'

LESSONS LEARNED

- Men have had fashion and style beaten out of them and need to re-access their inner-peacocks.
- Men dressed all in black are truly, deeply, madly sexy.
- Men should not wear their shoes to bed even if they are commitment-phobic – that is only for cowboys.

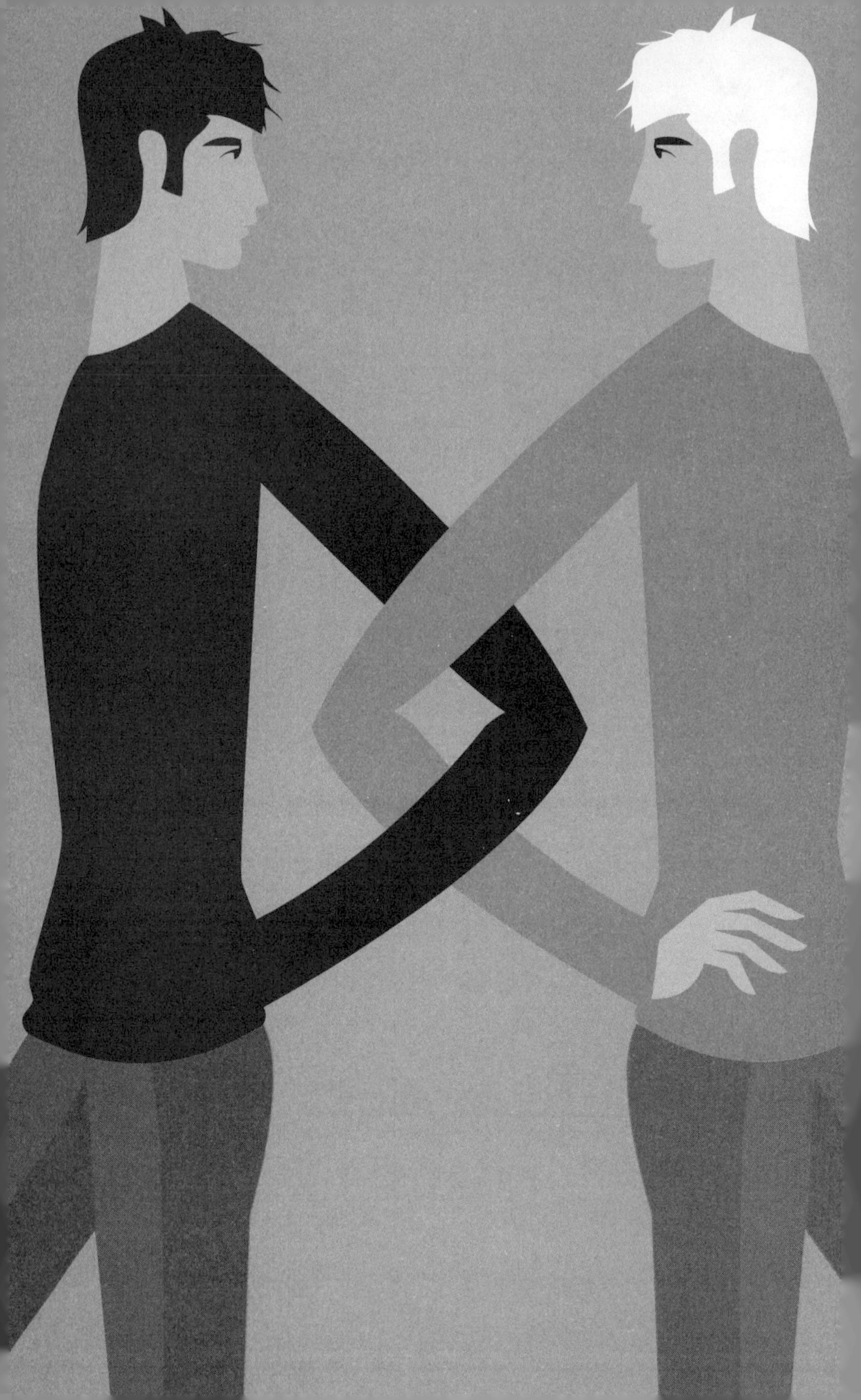

6
GAY MEN
BOYS ON THE PINK EDGE

You may be interested to know that most men do not decide to be gay just to get on their father's nerves, to have a bigger wardrobe, or because they want to go into interior design. People have been heard to ask, 'What *is* this fashion with being gay? Nobody was gay when I was young – how come everyone's gay now? And another thing – where did all these transsexuals and cross-dressers come from?' The answer is you're just in time to be too late, because there have always been lots of gay men, gay women, transsexuals and cross-dressers, but they were hidden, often as priests or married people. Male cross-dressers have always worn their wives' underwear and clothes, and women have always been pretty tolerant about it. You'd be surprised.

Nobody really knows why some men turn out gay, but it can become obvious from quite a young age – as young as eighteen months and certainly long before any sexual experiences. Some men don't realise it themselves until they are adults. It is simply the way a portion of the population expresses human love and sexuality.

THE POWER OF HORMONES

We all start off as 'girls'. The male foetus in the womb is 'female' for the first six to eight weeks, then receives doses of androgens, or male hormones, to turn it into a boy. This is why men have redundant female characteristics, like nipples, which they don't need. It is also why they have mammary glands or breasts, which generally don't work, although sometimes they can produce milk. The first dose of hormones makes the testicles; the second one makes the brain (not in the testicle area, as one might think, but in the cranium). Now, one theory is that sometimes the foetus doesn't receive enough male hormone at six weeks, but keeps growing and the baby boy is born with a male/female brain structure to varying degrees, and he will probably be gay. He never feels completely right with girls and may even marry, but will eventually see the light, sleep with a man and feel hugely 'right' and happy about it.

A little boy who likes dolls, paints his fingernails and requests pink curtains is exhibiting strong gender non-conformity. Not always, but he usually turns out to be gay. Then there is 'the older brother effect', where the more older brothers you have, supposedly the more likely you are to turn out gay. Studies have shown that for every older brother a man has his chances of being gay increase by one-third. Older sisters don't make any difference, and this theory does not apply to lesbians. The idea is that if the mother has already had lots of sons, she may be making antibodies that affect subsequent boy foetuses when she carries them.

Her body may be telling her she has to make more girls.

There are also many people who believe homosexuality is a result of social, parental and environmental experiences after birth (the nurture theory). No one theory or experiment leads to a definitive answer. Perhaps there is no definite answer; perhaps sexual orientation – whether gay, straight, lesbian, or bisexual – are all the result of a complex interaction between environmental, cognitive and anatomical factors that shape the individual at an early age.

A child who is born as a boy with all the physical male equipment, and a completely female brain is transgender or transsexual. This boy can see he is a boy and dresses as a boy, but feels like he's a female. Research has shown that their hypothalamus (the brain structure in which sexual behaviour resides) is more like a woman's. Twenty per cent of transsexuals have gender reassignment surgery, the brilliant writer Jan Morris being the most outstanding one I can think of. A soldier, dare-devil, war correspondent and happily married father of five, James Morris had nevertheless always felt he was a woman in a man's body. In 1972, he underwent a sex change at a clinic in Casablanca, Morocco. He continued to live – as a woman – with his wife Elizabeth, carried on writing travel and history books, and in 2008, at the age of eighty-two, remarried his wife.

Hermaphrodites are people who possess both male and female sexual organs and now prefer to be called intersexuals. It is rare that a child is born with both male and female genitals, one of which may be hidden and will only emerge at puberty. They can look like a girl, feel like a girl, then without warning, develop testes and a penis at puberty. At this point they turn into men because they have a male brain, in spite of the fact that they thought they were girls. The fact that social and behavioural grooming and family expectations ceases to have any effect once the true sexuality kicks in lends credence to the understanding that you are born the way you are. Nature not nurture perhaps. Mummy can dress you as a girl, be controlling, be in love with you, may even, in exceptional circumstances, sexually abuse you; Daddy may have aggressively pushed you to do 'masculine' things and criticised you for not having natural talent in head-banging sports; but generally you won't turn out to be gay unless you were biologically programmed to be. Samoan fa'afafine may be the exception to this; a boy in the family will be chosen to be a girl to help the mother with family work. He may not be gay at all, but accepts his role, sometimes throughout his whole life.

Conversely, parents can bend over backwards to discourage a son who is gay and that has no effect either – it can't, because the boy's brain structure is mostly the reason he is gay, not exterior influences like friends, teachers, the price of fish, et cetera. Some people say to accuse a gay person – male or female – of deliberately making a controversial lifestyle choice is like accusing someone of deliberately being born with dark hair and brown eyes when you would prefer them to be blonde and blue. (Incidentally, red hair and freckles is a genetic combination that happens at the same rate as homosexuality.) Ninety per cent of people are straight, so next time you meet someone who says 'Oh they're just making it up', ask them to try making love to a person of the same sex and see how they feel about it. They will no doubt discover that in spite of having a fabulous beautiful same-sex partner, they didn't enjoy it and are resolutely heterosexual.

People have tried to 'help' homosexuals in all sorts of bizarre ways, including surgery, shock therapy, counselling, exorcism, prayer, psychotherapy and even lobotomy. None of it has worked – the gay person either went back into hiding, lived a lie, committed suicide or restricted their activity. Thank God that people's differences are more accepted now and that gay people are proud of who they are and live openly in the way they wish. Most gay people I know don't want to make an issue of it at all – they don't see how it affects anything or anybody else. Embrace your hormones I say. Be at one with your universe.

SO, IT'S IN THE GENES?

What happens with identical boy twins? The 'nature theorists' say that because the testosterone distribution happens at six weeks in the uterus, they most likely will both be gay, but not always. If they are non-identical twins, they are two individual foetuses with separate sacs who will receive their hormone input individually. Research has shown that if a gay identical twin is separated from his brother at birth, there is a 70 per cent likelihood that his twin will also be gay. Why aren't the other 30 per cent gay? It's because of gene 'penetrance', meaning the ability of a gene to become active and dominant. The penetrance of the gay gene is 50 to 70 per cent, which is why some identical twins are not both gay. Also, homosexuality runs in families (uncles, fathers, cousins, et cetera) and the gene is usually carried by the mother. Why are some gay males very feminine and others very masculine? Simply the amount of testosterone in the brain. The next logical thing to ask is, so if a gay man wants to be straight, why can't we just inject him with testosterone? Well you can, but it's basically too late because human brains are fully formed at birth.

BISEXUALITY

There are lots of men who are heterosexual and quite happily sleep with other men occasionally but don't consider themselves to be gay. They don't consider themselves to be anything except sexual. Moroccan men are an example – in Moroccan culture many men have sexual relationships with both sexes and don't consider themselves gay. It's not talked about much there, but it is very common. They believe that this is the norm and don't really adhere to the idea that they may be part of a minority. They don't get the concept of 'gay' because they think it is completely normal to express sexual interest in both sexes. They consider it masculine to show affection, hold hands and be physically intimate with their male friends. There is also the possibility that Moroccan men go for other men when they are younger, or before marriage, because they are unable to sleep with women before marrying one. Anthropological research has found that in Afghanistan, India, Pakistan, Bangladesh, Sri Lanka, Morocco and elsewhere, men's sexual desire for other men is understood as being mainstream. This thinking predates Western ideas of sexuality and gender, and it has even been suggested that the whole concept of homosexuality is quite recent. Before the mid-nineteenth century, when the words 'homosexual' and 'sexual orientation' began to be used, homosexuality did not exist as a separate notion.

FA'AFAFINE, TAKATAAPUI AND FAKALEITI

In Samoan culture, there are men described as fa'afafine who consider themselves a sort of third gender. Fa'afafine are wonderful people who are biologically male but raised from childhood to assume female gender roles. This is actively encouraged by traditional Samoan society (fa'asamoa). 'Fa'a' means 'in the manner of' and 'fafine' means 'woman'. In Tongan these ladies are called fakafefine, in Maori whakawahine, and in Hawaiian mahu. The ancient Polynesians had an honourable role for takataapui, fa'afafine, fakaleiti, et cetera – they held positions of responsibility, especially in caring for, nurturing, training and protecting children. The missionaries tried to suppress the fa'afafine, as they did all sexuality in the Samoans, and they became socially marginalised, but fa'afafine survived to be prominent in all aspects of Samoan society as workers, administrators, educators, church elders, business people and artists. They are known for their hard work and dedication to the family, and are often the guardians and caretakers to elderly parents, as well as the biological children of their siblings.

Samoa's social acceptance of fa'afafine has evolved from the old tradition of raising some boys as girls. These boys were not necessarily homosexual, or noticeably effeminate, and they may never have felt like dressing as women. They became transvestites because they were born into families that had plenty of boys and not enough girls. In families of all male children (or where the only daughter was too young to assist with the 'womens' work'), parents would often choose one or more of their sons to help the mother. Because these boys would perform tasks that were strictly the work of women, they were raised as if they were female. Although their true gender was widely known, they would usually be dressed as girls. As they grew older, their duties would not change. They would continue performing 'women's work', even if they eventually married (which would be to a woman). Sounds like the dream husband to me.

Modern fa'afafine differ in two fundamental ways from their traditional counterparts. First, they are more likely to have chosen to live as women, and secondly, they are more likely to be homosexual. These days, young Samoan boys who appear effeminate, or enjoy dressing as girls, may be recognised as fa'afafine by their parents. If they are, they will usually be neither encouraged nor discouraged to dress and behave as a woman. They will simply be allowed to follow the path they choose. If it becomes apparent that a boy wants to become a fa'afafine, he will be taught the duties and crafts of women. Coupling those skills with the strengths of Samoan men can make a fa'afafine a valuable member of society.

When they move to the big city they sometimes become drag queens and prostitutes. I used to have an apartment in the red light district and became acquainted with fa'afafines working the beat around my building. They were incredibly tall, strong, beautiful, tough and funny. They would make comments about my clothes, ask me to make them muffins and if business was slow, would sing together from corner to corner in four-part harmony. I often woke up in the middle of the night to opera or hymns or show numbers. They didn't consider themselves to be gay and felt that gay behaviour is different from their own – they considered themselves female and believed that the men who have relations with them also saw them as females. Some fa'afafines believe they are women trapped in a male body. There is a cocktail called a fa'afafine made with vodka shaken with apple and lemon juice, honey, passion fruit syrup and a dash of grenadine. Sounds fruity. Sorry.

HIJRAS

Many cultures have a third gender population. On the streets of India and Pakistan you sometimes see dramatically different-looking women who are actually men – the hijras. Hijras describe themselves as belonging to a unique caste, characterised by their devotion to the mother goddess Bahuchara Mata and Shiva. Like fa'afafine, they identify as being transgender, not gay, and have their own distinct customs, society and reality. They are colourful, loud and entertaining. They wear outrageous make-up and saucy clothes and normally grow their hair long. Despite being over one million strong in India, they are politically invisible and have no identity in the eyes of the rest of the population. Some people hate them, some love them and some don't really care but think they should be left to live their lives the way they wish. Some people are embarrassed by their ostentatious behaviour and begging and fear that they spread sexual diseases.

Because they have no official status and have often been rejected by their families for being different and thus do not receive an education, they have no qualifications for work and have to invent their own ways of making money. These include entertaining at births, weddings and housewarmings, begging and prostitution. Sometimes they gatecrash parties, start singing away and then blackmail the hosts for money by threatening to cast curses that will ensure infertility, bad luck and God only knows what else if they are not paid for their performance. You'd be surprised how many Indians believe in the occult and can be manipulated this way. Supposedly the hijras possess this power because they don't have sex (in the loss of semen sense), and they therefore accumulate sexual energy which they can give to others. If the people who have been gatecrashed do fork out the money, of course blessings, wealth and many children will follow.

Hijras have been around for hundreds of years in India – in the sixteenth century they were entrusted by the kings with looking after the royal ladies, guarding the harem and running the palace. They were respected and often rose to powerful positions within royal households. Things have changed dramatically since those days and along with being chucked out of home, they are generally marginalised and exploited. An exception to this discrimination is that hijras can earn money from the Indian government for collecting taxes in villages and cities. It is the most effective method ever employed by the Indian government for tax collection and is still used in some areas. Hijras are now becoming politically active, some even being elected to high political posts. They have been on screen in Indian cinema since its beginning, but usually as figures of fun, dancing or entertaining.

Note: In Indonesia, transgender or third sex people are known as 'waria'; in Thailand as 'kathoeys' or 'ladyboys'; to North American Indians as 'two-spirit'; and in Oman as 'xanith' or 'khanith'. Among the Gaddhi in the foothills of the Himalayas, some girls adopt a role as a 'sadhin', renouncing marriage, and dressing and working as men, but retaining female names. In the Balkans, women who dress as and do the jobs of men are known as 'sworn virgins'.

LESBIANS

The word 'lesbian' comes from the Greek island of Lesbos, home to the poet Sappho, who wrote beautiful love poems to women and girls. A lesbian is a woman who prefers to make love with another woman. Some are butch, some are fem, some like and some dislike men. A lesbian might possess a great sense of direction, be assertive, self-reliant and have good spatial skills, or she may be just like a heterosexual woman. If you open the bonnet of a car and ask a lesbian and a metrosexual man to point to the ABS braking system, the lesbian is likely to locate it first. For every one lesbian there are, supposedly, ten gay males.

THE ANCIENT GREEKS AND ROMANS

Homosexuality has existed since the beginning of time. In ancient Greece, homosexuality was respected and boys were considered to be the pinnacle of beauty with great sculptures and paintings done to honour them. Older men wrote beautiful love poetry to younger men inspiring them to a higher purpose, to be noble, to become important in society. 'Gay' men made great soldiers and warriors as they fought in unison with courage, love for each other and solidarity in each other's company (bit like rugby really). Apparently Julius Caesar was rampantly bisexual. Men were considered much more important than women, who were basically chattels or property; in fact, some sources even suggest the greatness and beauty of ancient Greece was due to this homosexual culture. The ancient Greeks were the first to describe, study, systematise, and establish pederasty as a social and educational institution. It was an important element in civil life, the military, philosophy and the arts. Men sleeping with men was mostly for the elite aristocracy, not the peasants, who looked down on it as political, and in the case of the young men who were being penetrated, shamefully passive. Men had sex with each other in various ways: they masturbated each other and had anal and intercrural sex (the latter being between the legs – the male partner places his penis between the other partner's thighs and thrusts to create friction). You can see paintings of this activity on ancient Greek vases – they are facing each other and embracing.

Christianity put a stop to open homosexuality when the cities of Sodom (which gave us the word 'sodomy' for anal sex) and Gomorrah (which did not give us the word for 'gonorrhoea') were destroyed by God in an orgy of brimstone and fire. The whole area was completely razed as if a nuclear bomb had been dropped. In the Bible these two cities are associated with sin and sexual deviancy. Some texts say God destroyed Sodom because of general naughtiness like arrogance, gluttony, snobbery, blasphemy, uncharitableness, cruelty, inhospitality and general perversity. Christian texts concentrate more on the fact that these bad, glittering cities were xenophobic and that their inhabitants engaged in sodomy; that they 'knew' men. The naughty men of Sodom and Gomorrah were very interested in getting to know the beautiful male angels who God had sent to negotiate with Lot (supposedly the only good man in the place, but also supposedly having incestuous relationships with his daughters!). Famously, when Lot and his family were running from the city, they had been warned by God not to look back at the destruction. Lot's wife was distraught at leaving her wonderful, rich home and so looked back. She was instantly turned to salt. Cripes – I miss those colourful days. In fact, these cities were probably destroyed by a natural disaster such as an earthquake or electrical storm.

GAY MEN

HOW TO TELL IF YOUR HUSBAND IS GAY

According to some studies, 10 per cent of men and more than 10 per cent of women admit to having had homosexual sex. A lot of this is experimental, but still, there are a lot of men who are married with kids and are driven to have secret homosexual encounters. It's easy to make fun of having a gay husband, but in fact it's no fun at all – it can be a very dark tunnel with much conflict, rejection and pain for the woman. Here are some things which might indicate that your husband is homosexual:

1. There are mysterious absences always explained by 'I was at the supermarket'.
2. He has been using the same sexual positions since 1990 and thinks you are a sex maniac. 'Again?' he screams. 'But we did this last month!' He screams even louder if you ask for oral sex and has a preference for anal sex.
3. He has more shoes than you do.
4. His shirts are always undone one button too far.
5. He cleans up and polishes marble benches *during* dinner parties.
6. He likes shopping.
7. He is excessively homophobic; he mocks and imitates gay men.
8. He keeps humming the following line from Linda Ronstadt's song 'Faithful': 'No I have not always been faithful, I always have been true.'
9. When you say, 'We need to talk', he rolls over and plays dead. Mind you, straight men do that too, so that is not a very reliable sign.
10. He tells you.

THE GREATEST GAY MAN I HAVE EVER KNOWN

In 1980, I went to Paris for three days and stayed for ten years. About a year into my life in the City of Light, I was invited to a 'salon' at Willy Maywald's atelier (artist's studio) in Montparnasse. The salon is an old European tradition, which has unfortunately mostly died out now, where people gather for the express purpose of exchanging ideas and engaging in serious discussion. It's not frivolous like a party, has quite an intellectual tone and doesn't go on indefinitely. It starts at a certain hour, usually around 7.30 p.m., and finishes at a certain hour, usually 11.30 p.m. Wine and snacks are served. It's by invitation and you may bring guests. I was swept into a world of painters, writers, filmmakers, hangers-on, ancient Russian aristocrats and generally remarkable people. I don't know how I got past the front door.

Montparnasse is a chic part of Paris; its wide boulevard is lined with elegant cafés which are frequented by a cosmopolitan mix of writers, rich Yugoslav thieves, urbane prostitutes and American students from the Alliance Française. It's a quarter with a romantic past and an artistic undercurrent.

Willy Maywald was an elderly, gay, German photographer famous for his portraits of painters, notably one of Picasso on the beach at Cannes taken with a child's Brownie camera. It shows Picasso holding a sun umbrella, staring fiercely at the lens. 'Picasso vos a terrible man,' he told me, 'he 'ate vomen, vos very mean and often bad tempered.' In the 1950s Willy specialised in fashion shots, memorably one for Jacques Fath showing a woman in long gloves and wide-brimmed hat, which is now all over Paris in poster form. His photos were the utmost in elegance and refinement and his models adored working with this gracious, cultivated man. He was modest and serene, taking composed photos of subtle opulence even when they were in arcades, footpaths or stairways. He not only photographed models, but also painters and writers like Cocteau, Chagall, Utrillo, Modigliani, Man Ray, Fernand Léger and Simone de Beauvoir.

When I met Willy he was in his late seventies, hosting Tuesday night salons as he had been for the last thirty years. After World War Two he had arrived in Paris with nothing but a camera he had been given and started photographing friends and acquaintances. These friends and acquaintances turned out to be very famous, and so did Willy as a result of photographing them. He held court, surrounded by admiring friends and visitors. He was a tireless and droll storyteller. I remember him so clearly sitting there in navy blue pants, striped shirt, always a tie, navy jacket, a cigarette holder in his long, elegant fingers, legs languidly crossed. Mocking blue eyes smiled out of his handsome aristocratic face and his silver hair was brushed straight back. He always looked impeccable.

When I started going to the salons I was very intimidated and speechless for the first time in my life. Everyone ignored me but I was fascinated and kept going back. Although the grand Willy never paid much attention to me, on his friend's recommendation, he asked me to look after his Paris atelier for the summer, which he spent in Grasse in the South of France. The atelier was a large split-level, open-plan sculpting studio transformed into a living space. The photography studio and darkroom were on the second floor. The walls were white, the Bauhaus furniture was mostly black or white and the place was full of paintings, sculptures, Picasso vases and Willy's photographs.

I spent an idyllic summer having dinner parties in the garden under the chestnut tree. I laid the table with a blue and white tablecloth embroidered by Willy's mother, hand-painted Italian plates and green-stemmed German wine glasses. My friends and I had breakfasts of warm, buttery croissants dipped into steaming bowls of café au lait in the cool, dark, dining room. We had morning tea in a corner of the living room under the enormous, sloping skylight, and afternoon tea upstairs on the balcony while listening to Nino Rota's greatest hits from Fellini movies. Everyone was touched by the beauty and symmetry of the atelier, with the winding staircase going up to the second floor and the extraordinary light that flooded everything. When Willy came home from Grasse at the end of the summer, he was astounded to find the atelier spotlessly clean and exactly as he had left it, down to the last ashtray, and asked me to continue living there with him. Thus commenced a deep friendship that was to last another four years until his death.

We lived together in perfect harmony, with never a harsh word passing between us. Every morning he would rise at exactly 9.00 a.m., make tea and burnt toast, then call from the bottom of the stairs in his heavenly German accent, 'Darling! Your tea eez r-ready.' I would float down the stairs and we would sit in silence and darkness, sipping and crunching. We never talked at this meal. All the talking was done in the evening, usually about his past or his loves. He told me he had always been gay as far as he could remember. We sipped mulled wine and I listened to his stories. His Nordic blue eyes always seemed to be laughing even when he wept describing the war (*'le temps'* he called it) and how his parents had died of grief.

'You know darling, in 1940 ze bastard French put us German artists in an internment camp in ze South of France. Everyvon vos there – Max Ernst, ze writer Hasenclever, ze journalist Alexander Alexander.'

'But what did you eat, how did you live?'

'Ve made bags and shoes out of raffia and sold them in ze village. One day I vos sitting outside a café. Of course ve had no money to buy anyzing but ve liked ze smell of ze coffee. A voman came up to me and said, "Vhy don't you put a coat on, it's so cold?" You know darling she had no idea zat ve vere starving and didn't even have coats. On ze vay home ve collected mossy stones and boiled zem up for soup.'

The conversation could turn from morbid to indiscreet very quickly. Another sip of wine, another Rothmans in the holder and he would launch into the spinster story, gently ridiculing an old friend who had only had one man in her whole life. 'She and our old friends vere gossiping about ze problems of lovers. Suddenly she said slowly and knowingly "*a qui tu le dit!*" in ozer vords – "I know better zan anyvon". Everyvon turned to her. She who had had ze sum total of von man in eighty years, she who had ze experience of an amoeba, she who vould have been so lucky to have had problems viz lovers.' Willy told this story with tears of merriment in his eyes. It became a catch phrase in the house. Whenever someone confided something about which the other knew nothing, we all shouted '*a qui tu le dit!*'

My mother came to visit and stayed chez Willy. He thought she was '*such* a lady', but it didn't stop him from telling her dreadful stories about drag queens, virgins who weren't virgins thanks to their surgeons, and his friend the princess, who, when her house was on fire, removed all her jewels before calling the fire brigade, thereby losing her life.

When it was cold Willy and I installed ourselves in the dining area, cleverly disguised as Spanish widows in shawls and rugs with the heating on full blast, the lit oven open and jugs of hot whisky within arm's reach. The house was always full of flowers. I cooked and Willy ran around muttering, 'A voman's vork iss never done' and singing, 'Wake up to reality'. Sometimes, friends from New York would turn up to stay and one morning I woke in the middle of the night to hear someone crashing and falling around downstairs. I went down and found a woman, apparently drugged, trying to make tea in the dark. She was tall, very beautiful with long blonde hair and had an unusually deep voice. In the morning I asked Willy who she was and he told me the story. She was Nico, singer, model and actress friend of Andy Warhol. Her son Ari, who mostly lived in Paris, visited Willy often and was the lover of my friend Paola. A more beautiful and gentle boy you couldn't imagine; he had been ruined by heroin introduced to him by his mother.

People came and went and we settled into winter in our various ways. For me it meant quiet evenings reading and listening to music. I devoured Lawrence Durrell's *The Alexander Quartet*, Marcel Proust's *Swann in Love*, Paul Bowles' *The Sheltering Sky* and reread Anaïs Nin's diaries. For Willy, winter meant business travel to New York, a city he adored, always returning with layers of stories. He was exhibiting a huge retrospective of his photos at the Fashion Institute of Technology and had left his portfolio, worth thousands and thousands of dollars, in a cheap restaurant on 77th Street. The photos turned up the next day in a garbage can across the road from the restaurant. He loved stories like this and told them over and over again. The part that amused him the most about New York was that anyone could have such a monumental lack of imagination as to give streets numbers instead of names. To Willy's astonishment, photos that he had always considered just the livelihood of a capable craftsman were now being revealed as the work of the brilliant artist he was. I was always horrified that he kept his work in old envelopes in drawers in his office simply marked 'Dior', 'Fath', 'Piguet', et cetera – no security, no temperature-controlled rooms, nothing.

At this time he was finishing writing his memoirs and was having frequent nightmares, little depressions and stomach upsets. Writing about the war was a cathartic experience for him, but he felt he had to get it all out whatever the emotional cost. Sometimes I would sing him mournful Irish songs, which always brightened me up and resulted in Willy asking me something like, 'But vie doss zee girl in zee song wait for zee boy so long. Vie doesn't she find ozer boyfriend?' How do you explain to someone so happy and radiant the exquisite pleasure to be derived from morbid songs of unrequited love?

Willy's health started going downhill. I feared it was the end, but the doctors kept saying he just had hepatitis. Living in the house was like living with a low-register menacing cello note that was all pervasive. There were plausible explanations for his personality changes and general ill health, so we didn't even consider the obvious. I couldn't see that he was dying and no one else in his circle mentioned it. Before long he couldn't get up and down the stairs, so a bed was made up for him in the dining room, and there he stayed, giving orders and being disagreeable. His secretary, Utta, a severe and humourless woman who disliked and envied my friendship with him, was finally persuaded to put him in hospital and cancer of the liver was diagnosed. Every day I called her and every day she said he was too ill to receive visitors. After two weeks his old friends called me, distracted, to see why I hadn't been to see him, and I realised what Utta had done. I flew to the hospital to find his room full of visitors, who were there from all over the world, but he was so sick he didn't care. Willy held my hands and with tears in his eyes said, '*Ma chérie,* I zort you had deserted me. Vere haff you been?'

One day I got the call I had been expecting – the person who had added so much light and depth to my life was no more. I was inconsolable and my life in Paris didn't make sense to me any more. After Willy's death I went to the house on rue de la Grandechaumière to get some things. There was a huge wreath of dead roses on the door and the house was dusty and dirty. I sat down at his desk, where I had seen him so many times smiling at me out of his handsome, aristocratic face, laid my head down on it and wept. I felt for the first time that it was really all over. I know my life would have been less in every way without having known him. I still dream of that atelier and Willy and sometimes when I am in Paris, I sneak in to stand in his garden and breathe in the memories of the greatest gay man I have ever known.

HOW TO MARRY A GAY MAN

Gay men can successfully marry and be happy with women so long as both parties understand what is going on. It gets tricky when one party doesn't have the right dance card, and it is usually the woman. Here's how I ended up marrying a gay man. I was living at Willy's place in Paris and cooking in a restaurant illegally. Soon it became obvious I couldn't continue working in France unless I got a formal work permit. I fell at Willy's adored feet and begged for a solution.

'Vell darling,' he said, fitting a new Rothmans into his ivory holder and smoothing back his long silver hair, 'I know you are a modern girl and all zat but vot about I find you a husband?' This last word was said in a whisper like it wasn't really the husband word at all.

'A husband?' I asked in equally hushed tones.

'Ya darling. You know. Your mozer has von.'

'Merci, Willy, I know what a husband is. That's why I don't have one.'

'But sink of ze advantages. Vee vill find a nice gay boy, maybe vee vill ask my friends if they know somevon suitable, and having a pretend husband vill keep any ozer husbands avay. You vill be safe from making any stupid or dangerous moves ze next time you fall in love. Is perfect no?'

I was horrified at the thought of annexing myself to any of my lovers, so I asked him to introduce me to someone on the other side of the fence. The search for a husband began. One day Willy asked me to come downstairs to meet Alexy. I leaned over the balcony and my eyes fell on a beautiful young man – my future husband. He was polite, gentle and charming, but best of all, he was gay. The three of us sat down over tea and talked. Alexy was the youngest of seven sons of an army family from Toulouse.

'*Très bien élevé,*' said Willy, 'and he'll never cause you any problems, *ma chère.*' Alexy told me he worked part-time as a model and part-time waiting in a restaurant. His manner was almost of another era in its formality and discretion. My proposition was explained to him and he agreed to give it some thought. There I was, asking someone a lot younger than me who I hardly knew to marry me, with thoughts going through my head of the first time I had been proposed marriage. I was nineteen and threw my head back and laughed. At least Alexy had kept a straight face. Over the next few months we saw a lot of each other, but there really wasn't much more to discuss. He wasn't interested in money – he would marry me because he liked me and wanted to help me, but also because his papa was starting to ask difficult questions about girlfriends. Obviously his true self was hidden from his conservative bourgeois family.

Willy was thrilled there was going to be a wedding party *chez lui* and we all threw ourselves into the preparations. Nobody wanted to be the one who wore the white dress so we all wore black. Willy and Alexy wore smoking jackets, bow ties and white silk scarves and I wore a black, Italian, designer dress, topped with a red veil and red flowers in my hair. We travelled on the métro from Montparnasse to Saint Sulpice, accompanied by a group of imaginatively dressed friends including my boss, who turned up with tassels everywhere and a cowboy hat. Our photographer in a feather jacket arrived at the Mairie of the 6th Arrondissement. The mayor, to his credit, was nothing if not civilised and amiable when faced with this Felliniesque scene. After we had exchanged vows, Willy said it was traditional to kiss my new husband. This I did and God forgive me I even managed to blush. I then invited everyone else to kiss him, which they did with just a shade more enthusiasm than the occasion demanded. When the deed was done we returned to chez Willy on the métro, threw ourselves on the Champagne and put more lipstick on for the wedding party.

At least a hundred people crowded into the atelier, dancing, singing, falling up and down the stairs, shouting, screaming and clapping. The whole house from top to bottom was overflowing with the eclectic mix of people only Paris can produce – the gay fashion scene, old Russian royalty, artists, chefs, babies, dogs and embassy friends. Willy was radiant and this was the last time I saw him dancing. Alexy and I spent all day whipping up finger food. His friends created a wedding cake from ladyfinger biscuits and whipped cream that either resembled the Eiffel Tower or a phallic symbol, depending on your orientation. There was a bunch of penniless old Russians in the dark corner of the dining room, trying to get the samovar to work. Lying all over the white couch in the living room was one of my friends in her white wedding gown (women had permission to wear their wedding gowns if they could still fit them) and her wild Albanian artist husband dressed in tails. I could see why she was attracted to him, but to marry him? He had a big head of yellow curls, devastating cornflower blue eyes and a very macho attitude. I know it's sick but my friend found the man very sexy. Anyway, who was I, a happily married woman, to judge? In the space of a few hours I became the equivalent of the reformed whore, the strumpet brought to heel, the spitfire doused – there are none so sanctimonious as those who have sinned. Alexy was very calm and relaxed at the wedding party, taking care of business, changing the music from Bruce Springsteen to Les Rita Mitsouko to Les Négresses Verts to Sting.

The wedding festivities went on and on and people arrived with presents and money for Alexy and me, just like a real wedding. We said no, no, no, we can't accept them, but people love a do and love getting into the ceremony of things. For our friends, it was a happy occasion, a celebration; it didn't matter a jot whether it was a farce or not. My boss gave me her sapphire engagement ring, there was a toast, I slugged back some more whiskey, said 'Thank you' and fell off my chair. This prompted me to check that the food department was under control. Food and cooking for people I love is a big part of my life and probably the only thing Alexy and I had in common. If food has the ability to transport us back to our origins, to our very essence, then it has the ability also to cement certain rituals. Imagine no food at a wedding? It's like taking communion at Mass – you share something of your very soul by sharing food with loved ones.

At three in the morning there were still about thirty die-hards left. I was deep in conversation about the incredible detail required for food styling in photography. Alexy shouted over the music, which was now Arab rock, 'Peta, it's time to make the soup.'

'The soup?'

'It's traditional to serve onion soup at five in the morning after a party. You can't let people go away hungry. With all the alcohol they've consumed, they'll never make it home on the first métro and we'll have them forever.'

I looked at him in disbelief.

'It's true. You're the bride. You have to do it. It has to be made with your hands,' he laughed.

Believe it or not, we lurched into the kitchen, I put the big white apron on over my black finery, dragged out the onions and started peeling. It didn't take long at all and everybody was thrilled to have the delicious, warm onion soup to slurp up. This filling of stomachs prompted the diehards to suddenly feel sleepy. Some of them went upstairs to various beds and couches and the rest wandered off up the garden path just as the first soft suggestion of the Parisian morning was dawning. Willy, the most senior member of the wedding, was the last to go to bed. Alexy kissed me good night and went off with his young man. I wandered around the house switching the lights off, sat down at the dining room table, poured a whiskey and thought, so now I am married. *Et vogue le navire*.

For a little while there were people in my head talking to me: family members saying I was immoral and dishonest and had slippery values; the nuns from my childhood reminding me I was on the fast track to hell; the French secret service saying, you have broken the law because you are not in love, you are not going to populate Mother France with your little babies and for this you will go to prison or worse. They soon went away. It's only in the last two hundred years that people have married for love anyway. Modern marriage was originally a property relationship, which passed the ownership of women and their chattels from father to husband. A woman married for protection, financial security, social position and political, business and religious alliances. Who did we harm? Certainly not Mother France, who benefited from my income and expertise. Certainly not each other – we had a good friendship, which would last until Alexy's death. Certainly not the church whose portals we hadn't even darkened. I rest the case for the Defence.

My new husband, Alexy, carried his slim frame and medium height as if he was modelling an Yves St Laurent suit, which he probably was in his head. He walked in that slightly stylised, stiff but liquid way some models do. Certain of his friends threw themselves all over the catwalk dancing, shoving their pelvises in your face, behaving like strippers at some puke-inducing ladies night out show, but not him. Alexy was too discreet and fundamentally shy for overt displays of sexuality. His rigid Catholic private school upbringing had seen to it that he never expressed himself openly. He never really recovered from his mother's death in his early childhood, always felt an outcast even in his own family. Being the youngest of seven boys was bad enough, but having been ripped away from the breast at such a vulnerable age, he remained vulnerable into adulthood. His homosexuality effectively alienated him from his straight siblings, strict father and unsympathetic step-mother, cementing his profound insecurity. Nature had blessed him with a handsome face. Everything had fallen into place on this face as it had never done in life – full lips, large eyes like black rivers at night, high cheek bones and a classic square jaw. He thought if he was polite, moved quietly without taking up much space and didn't rock the boat, someone would love him eventually for something other than his beautiful face.

Alexy and I remained friends and then a terrible day dawned and he discovered he was HIV positive. I couldn't believe he wasn't having safe sex, but in those days the French thought AIDS wouldn't pass the border. I went back to New Zealand to live and we kept in touch by letters and telephone. Eventually, Alexy went to live in a hospice because it was obvious he was too fragile to survive. In 1995, after a few months' silence from him, I received a very kind letter from his brother, Jacques, saying the family didn't know Alexy was married and had found letters from me in his possessions. Alexy had died and his brother was inviting me to come to France and meet him and his wife, Aline.

I flew to the village of Cordes-sur-Ciel, near Toulouse, in the south-west. Aline and Jacques bent over backwards to be hospitable from the moment I walked into their lives until the moment I walked out four days later. They opened their home, their hearts, their pain and their joy to me in a way that was deeply engaging. It was to be a stay of gormandising, drinking good wines, dancing and much talking about Alexy and the family. Like a lot of French people, they were very open and self-disclosing, talking about relatively private things like politics, relationships and personal philosophies right from the start. The French are not superficial people. They talk about the meaning of life and history and food the way we talk about cricket or sailing. They lost Alexy in 1995 and Jacques lost his only son in a motorbike accident in 1996. Bizarrely, there was to be another family death during my stay. They decided to work through their pain by never wasting a moment of their lives, by living the good times to the full and by being a lot more open with family and friends.

We started with Champagne and pistachios and the dragging out of family photos. I saw the severe father and the seven sons, who in fact all looked very different — Jacques and Alexy were the only two who resembled each other. Alexy wrote a lot of poems in the years he was ill and Jacques put them all together into a book. With tears of ink Alexy accuses and condemns his inflexible father and the insidious society that won't tolerate difference. I read the sad, joyous, painful poems and was surprised to find a fantasy love poem to me called 'Chevelure de Feu' (Flaming Hair). I knew my husband liked me, but I didn't know he had been in love with me. The poem spoke of his desire for us to be a proper man and wife, and of how good that would have been, in another world. These bittersweet revelations came as a total shock to me.

Towards the end of my stay I realised something was wrong with Jacques and I couldn't put my finger on it; he seemed sombre and reflective and I assumed he was tired. The next morning we said our fond goodbyes and Aline drove me to the train

JUST IN TIME TO BE TOO LATE

station at Toulouse. On the way she told me Jacques' father had died the day before. He got the news as he was preparing our dinner and he continued without saying anything. The father, who in life had alienated Alexy, not even seeing him before he died, wished to be buried next to him. What you can't achieve in life you try to achieve in death. There's nothing like being just in time to be too late.

LESSONS LEARNED

- There is nothing mysterious about being gay – it is simply the way a portion of the population expresses human love and sexuality.
- The story of the destruction of Sodom and Gomorrah is very dramatic and is often used to point out how naughty homosexuals are, but in fact these towns were destroyed by an electrical storm or earthquake.
- If your little boy is showing gender non-conformity, give him the pink nail polish and thank God you've got a man with good taste in your family.

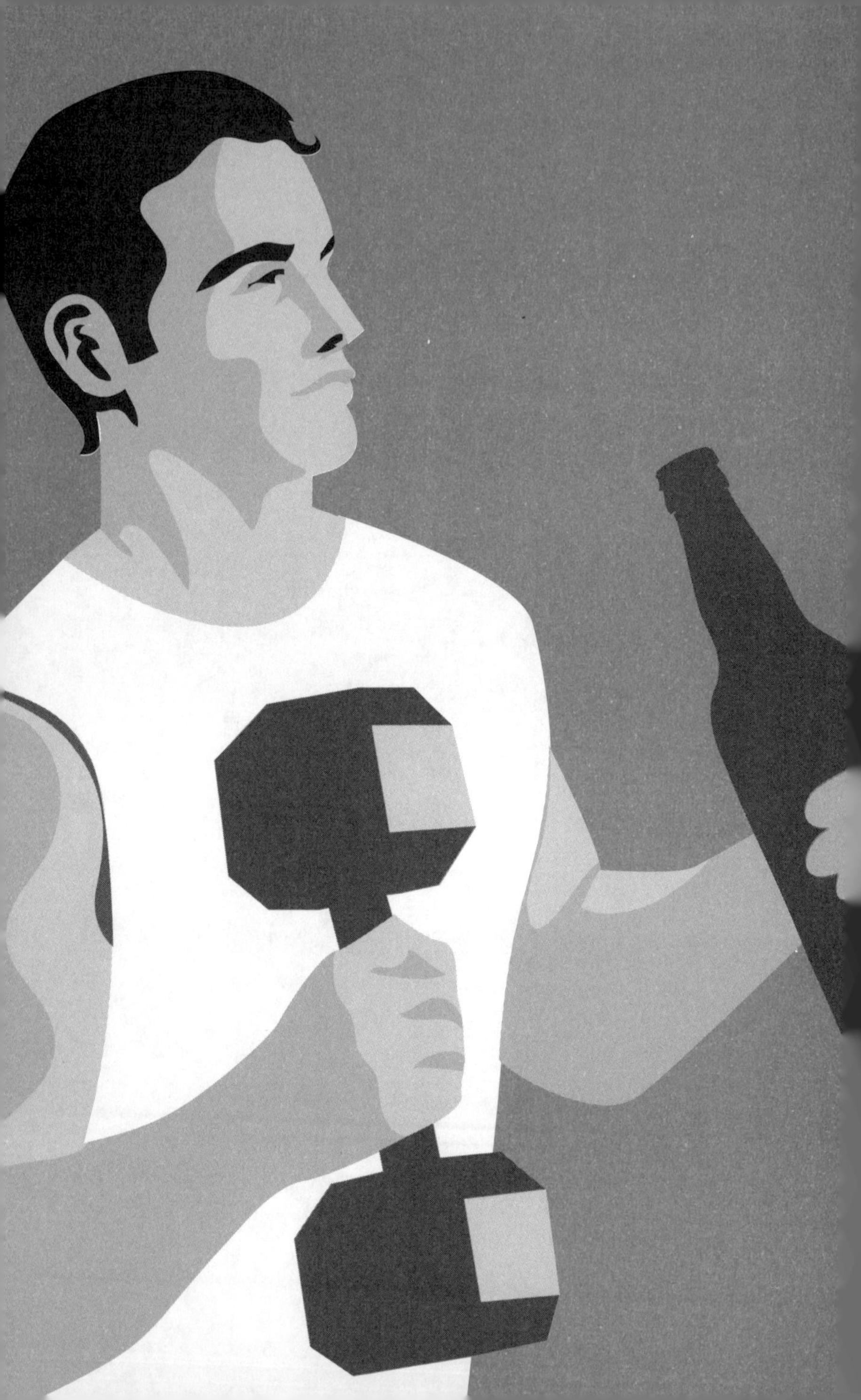

7
Health & eating
THE ROAD TO SELF-RIGHTEOUSNESS

WARRANT OF FITNESS

Men hate thinking about or dealing with their health. You say 'Check-up', they say 'Check out'. You say 'Doctor', they say 'See ya'. You say 'Colonoscopy', they say 'Don't be dirty'. Their mantra is treat it the same as a wild dog – ignore it and it'll go away. I admit I find this way of thinking very tempting and mostly use it myself. I use the same system with my car – my mechanic calls it benign neglect. The other thing about men's health is that they are not really encouraged to look after themselves and take advantage of health services the way women are, therefore they rarely build up a trusting relationship with a doctor.

Naturally, they are afraid of what they might find out. It's true – if your head is in the sand, you can't see anything, but it's also true that if your head is in the sand, where is your bum? Don't ask. My brother David says all this is rubbish. The reason why men don't like going to the doctor is the total, infuriating waste of time in waiting for your turn. If you could see the doctor at the allotted time, they would do it, no problem. You don't have to wait at the dentist – why are you made to wait for an hour at the doctor? The trouble is, if you put it off, you may be just in time to be too late.

If I had one, I would probably ignore my prostate talking to me in the language of urinary problems. I would let it go until blood appeared. There's the diagnostic fun – doctors going where, in most cases, no man has gone before: finger up your bum, ultrasound up your bum, needle into your prostate gland via your bum, needle biopsy via the perineum (the area between the base of the penis and the anus). This is the man's opportunity to say to the doctor whose hand is up his bum, 'Could you tell my wife my head isn't up there?' Prostate cancer is slow-moving, so for a low-grade one, the doctor may do nothing but keep an eye on the man. Depending on the severity, prostate cancer can be treated with surgery, radiotherapy, hormone (testosterone) therapy and chemotherapy. If all this sounds terrifying, think of the alternative. The upside is, this information leaves lots of room for prostate and bottom jokes, men enjoy being the 'butt' of jokes. They laugh, which makes them relax, which makes them think: 'Maybe I'll go get a check-up.'

Prostate cancer is the most commonly diagnosed cancer in men and the third most common cause of cancer deaths, but don't worry – it doesn't usually happen until a man's over sixty. The prostate is a walnut-shaped gland that surrounds the neck of the bladder and the beginning of the urethra (the tube connecting the bladder to the penis). Its main function is to produce semen, a fluid that protects and enriches sperm. Nobody knows the cause of prostate cancer; however, it is thought to be related to factors such as age, hormones and environmental influences (such as exposure to certain chemicals). Smoking and a diet high in saturated fats don't help much and there may also be a genetic link – the condition is more common in men who have a history of prostate cancer in their family.

WHAT MIGHT HAPPEN TO THE MALE, DECADE BY DECADE

1. Up until twenty years old, bar a few hundred pimples, the inability to communicate except by grunting, excessive wanking into socks which he leaves under the bed, and feeling that no one understands him (he's right), it's pretty much plain sailing health-wise. Teenage indulgences such as smoking, drinking, drugging, eating complete and utter rubbish, self-inflicted sporting injuries and treating girls as target practice will put future health at risk.
2. The twenties are similar to the teens health-wise, but risk-taking behaviour such as sporting injuries increase, often coupled with the stress of first marriage, children and serious job. The twenties are pretty full-on – he may need counselling as his heart will be broken, possibly for the first time, and while body-building he may become addicted to protein drinks, resulting in 'power pimples'.
3. In his thirties, because of his twenties, the male has the beginnings of cardiovascular disease, heart disease, high blood pressure, diabetes and a few thousand dead brain cells thanks to all those joints and six packs. His testosterone poisoning is killing people on the roads and seriously pissing the girls off.

4. Thanks to intelligent lifestyle choices, the forties boys now have protruding bellies, skin cancers, can't quite keep up on the sports front the way they used to and may have the beginnings of lung disease as they almost but never did give up the fags. Possibly sexual problems are starting to show up now and late onset, Type-2 diabetes may rear its ugly head.
5. The fabulous fifties herald prostate problems, often ignored until walking gets difficult. Anything to do with bottoms, colons or bowels is similarly ignored – only poofters would volunteer for a colonoscopy. Heart attacks drop out of the sky like meteorites, he can't see a thing without glasses and impotence drives him to mad things like Viagra. Male hormones leach away, not suddenly like women's, but slowly and inexorably, like memory.
6. Dementia can start in the sixties. A wife suddenly starts having to be very patient and treat her husband as kindly as a mental patient because he is no longer playing with a full deck. Cholesterol problems ensure he can't enjoy fat on his meat and yolks in his omelettes (which actually has no connection with cholesterol).
7. From seventy on, life can't get any worse and he finally stops making a fool of himself with younger trophy wives, chooses easier sports like golf, accepts the hair, hearing, eyesight situation and starts enjoying himself again. He has nothing to lose so develops a relationship with his doctor (who turns out to be quite interesting because he's from some exotic country), gets things fixed when they go wrong and thanks God that he's alive. Women are attracted to him for his charm, wisdom and wit. Think Clint Eastwood.

HEALTH & EATING

What most men do about all these health changes is ignore them, refuse to talk about them and assume their wives/girlfriends will deal with everything. If they get diabetes, they continue drinking and sometimes their wives find them in a coma in the middle of the night; if they have had a triple bypass, they continue smoking; if they suffer from impotence, they continue seducing women with empty promises. They would rather die happy after a life of indulgence (I can relate to that). But even if they *do* take care of business all along, men generally just don't last as long as women.

David Horsman

PM 'Why won't men go to the doctor?'

DH 'It's a stiff upper lip thing. My mother was always very careful about health and I have inherited that so have regular check-ups. However, I don't look after my body as I should because I smoke and drink. Why do men in the West live eight to ten years less than women? A lot of it is because of the trials and tribulations of life.'

PM 'Do you think men sacrifice themselves to keep the world going?'

DH 'Yes we do and to a large extent it is very unfair. Warren Farrell wrote about it in *The Myth of Male Power*. When push comes to shove, it is invariably the male who is in the firing line, be it war, finance, health, just walking on the outside of the footpath – we are the sex that is able to be sacrificed. This is called gallantry and I subscribe to some of it, but there is a limit.

> From the point of view of forty years of feminism, which achieved so-called equality, it is bloody unfair. Women have improved their lives and have a greater range of life options, but men seem to have carried on in the same vein. The fact of the matter is men don't have the same range of options that women do. If you say that in company, people call you a male chauvinist pig, which I certainly am not; in fact, I'm very in touch with my feminine side. If women want to be equal then let's be equal in all ways. If they don't, then let's go back to the forties, but you can't have it both ways.'
>
> **PM** 'But we do want it both ways.'
>
> **DH** 'Actually, I would like to have it both ways too. I would like to sometimes be able to say, "Okay, I'm feeling really feeble right now, I'd like to be looked after", and I'd like to let my guard down. Women criticise men for being rather closed and stoic, but men are mostly like that because they are taught from day one that's the way they should be.'

IRRITABLE MALE SYNDROME

Andropause (this is just a pop term – not a scientific one), or male menopause happens when the production of testosterone and DHEA (dehydroepiandrosterone) goes down. It is different from menopause in that although men leach hormones, they leach them slowly over a longer period of time and can continue to reproduce. Menopause is dramatic and it happens all at once, so it's rather noticeable, but men just go downhill like a slow stream. What may happen, just as with women, is a loss of libido, nervousness, depression, impaired memory, the inability to concentrate, fatigue, insomnia, hot flushes and sweating.

Of course, the man can be given testosterone pills or injections, but sometimes the result of that is that he can't tell if he is horny or a hat rack. Women have always thought they were the only ones who feel invisible over fifty, but men feel it too and are very vulnerable to it. Because women's power is their beauty and men's is their money, nobody even thinks about how desperately dreadful it is for an older, handsome man to be ignored by a younger woman when he puts the moves on one. The only way they escape this cruelty is if they are famous – the ugliest broadcasters in the world have all the production assistants jumping all over them. Believe me – I am in the industry. The women get younger and younger until the men are practically dating sperm.

What not to do about these symptoms – hide, pretend it's not happening and refuse to talk about it because it becomes toxic. What to do – find out about it, understand it and do something about it. It happens slowly, so men have lots of time to do something helpful should they wish to. Quite soon it may even be preventable, or at least correctable. Most urologists focus on declining testosterone as the main cause of impotence and scientists believe research will uncover a biological explanation for it in older men. I'm not even talking about that old – my GP tells me it can start any time after forty. Testosterone supplements also prevent bone loss, depression and other symptoms. The emphasis on performance is endemic in our society and it's a great way to ruin your sex life. We are far too obsessed with penetration, forgetting all the other erotic pastimes in our repertoires. Impotence can be related to stress, tiredness and medication, and it happens from time to time for most men anyway. The trick is to not let it upset you and not let it prevent you from being intimate. Don't stop hugging, don't stop holding hands. Men say women keep score on them. We don't. Men are the ones keeping score on themselves.

Andropause doesn't even affect some men and lots of them can function robustly well into their seventies and much further – look at Picasso. Forty per cent of healthy, normal men remain completely 'potent' at age seventy. While impotence in older men is a physical problem, in young men it is psychological – in other words stress, which can be caused by childhood problems, overwork, alcohol, fear of women, to name a few. Stress constricts the blood vessels that allow the penis to become engorged. Although andropause symptoms are physical, it's not that simple. Other things come into play like his health, both mental and physical; his cultural context, that is, living in a society which does not value older people; these economically depressed times; those bloody feminists ruining everything and spoiling his comfortable position of superiority. To a man, impotence *is* a loss of power and a source of great shame.

In terms of physical health, here's the impotent man's profile: over forty, unfit, stressed out, smoking, over-worked, attitude problems, over-weight, high blood pressure and a defeatist mindset. None of this can be fixed with a testosterone injection or Viagra. If the man with this profile did something about the other stuff in his life, he would probably get the lead back in his pencil – smoking, high cholesterol and high blood pressure all constrict the flow of blood, and you know where that leads. Smoking is devastating as it damages the tiny blood vessels in the penis, high cholesterol clogs arteries and alcohol abuse actually kills the nerves in the penis. The big mistake doctors made with Viagra was in not considering the whole man (that's because a man invented it). A very important part of getting over impotence is communication between wife and husband, or if there is no wife or girlfriend, the doctor. A lot of women blame themselves or think the man is sleeping with someone else when terror strikes in the bedroom.

Sometimes the doctor will prescribe testosterone, but only if the man is actually seriously lacking in it. Now studies have shown that it is really human growth hormone that is lacking. When you give growth hormone to a patient who genuinely lacks it, their excess body fat disappears, muscle mass returns, bones become firmer, skin thickens and sex drive returns. But this drug is very expensive, and anyway you can produce growth hormone yourself by doing regular, vigorous exercise. Old age is just hormones disappearing and if you replace them you slow the process – that's why I take HRT and probably always will, because it's about well-being, about feeling well.

The most important group of hormones as we age are growth hormones, which we all needed in order to grow when we were younger. DHEA (mentioned above) is a sex hormone that revives the growth hormone. If it is given to andropausal men and menopausal women it restores general and sexual energy and bolsters the immune system. DHEA improves sleep, calms and controls stress – what's not to love about it?

Most therapists tell their patients to chill out, stop seeing sex as a goal-oriented activity and see it more like surfing – riding waves of pleasure, stopping when you feel like it, cuddling, whispering sweet nothings, then up onto the next wave. Forget about the penis and remember the magic of the tongue! These are simple, perhaps obvious techniques, like exercises for back pain, but most of us can't be bothered doing them. The other thing is that the man has to let go of what a machine he was in his youth – those days are over. Now you do something different. The upside is that once the man retires and doesn't have that stress any more, quite often 'potency' returns and with it a new intimacy, trust and better loving.

JOINING ENERGY

One of my interviewees told me about a sexual practice he has been using for years and which he believes will protect his sexual potency. It is a Taoist practice called HeQi, or Joining Energy. The basis of all Taoist thinking is that 'qi' (life-force) is part of everything that exists. It is related to another energetic substance contained in the human body known as 'jing' and once all this has been expended, you will die. Jing can be lost from the body in various ways, mostly through bodily fluids, especially semen. Loss of it results in premature ageing, illness and general fatigue. To conserve semen and therefore vital life-force they believe men should either not ejaculate when having sex or should do it infrequently.

How do you have sex without ejaculating? You can pull out immediately before orgasm, or you could use the well-known method of applying pressure on the area between the scrotum and the anus, causing ejaculation into the bladder. Ancient Taoists believed this ejaculate would then travel up to the head and nourish the brain, but modern practitioners say this method should not be used because of potential complications and dangers. I'll say. The real trick is to have an orgasm without ejaculating by training yourself to separate the impulses of ejaculation and orgasmic contraction (this is the pelvic muscles pumping the prostate and the ejaculate). By separating these impulses at the point of orgasm, the man can halt ejaculation, but remain inside his partner and forcibly clench his pelvic floor, stunting the initial prostate contractions. Simultaneously, he adopts a meditation-like intention, which Taoists believe redirects not the actual sperm, but the life energy contained within it, up the back (spine) and to the brain. This way the man will not ejaculate but will still have an orgasm and most importantly, will not lose his erection. Once you learn how to do this properly, there should be no pain in the testes, no semen in the urine and increased good health. Another advantage is that the man can keep having orgasms and not lose his erection.

This is not just about pleasing the man – the woman also has to be stimulated and pleased in order to benefit from Joining Energy. Having sex like this, the woman creates more jing and the man can absorb her jing to increase his qi.

How my interviewee applies this to his life is a bit less complicated. He believes there is way too much focus on the orgasm in our world. 'If you think about it, the orgasm is only the little second or two at the end of the event – in the man's case probably shorter than the woman's. Once a man has had this very short moment at the end of sex he has not only given away all this life-force that the Tao people talk about, but in the very short term he is out of action. This is not good. Not good for the woman and not good actually for his head either. I'm sure you know, Peta, the French call it "le petit mort". It's way better to "pass" on the orgasm and open up the possibility of sex continuing as long as the woman wants it, which will end up being a lot longer than any guy who comes all the time will have experienced before. When I read or hear about someone being too drunk or tired or whatever to come, I think it's ridiculous. HeQi, or something like it, is what they should be aiming to achieve. Women need to be educated about this as well. Sex without the man orgasming concerns *them* initially and very quickly they realise the benefit to them. An interesting side effect of this is that when you have a woman who has difficulty orgasming in a particular way or at all, if you say to her, "Well I'm not going to come, I don't care so why should you care?", it definitely takes the pressure out of the whole situation. I don't do any of that internal ejaculation stuff – I think it's more of a head thing – you just learn how to hold on . . . mostly it works.'

FAST FOOD

Strangely enough, in my experience men rise to the fore when it comes to food, wine and cooking, even though Nigel Slater once said, 'There is no light so perfect as that which shines from an open fridge door at 2.00 a.m.' A huge number of men are really good cooks, know a lot about nutrition and go to great lengths to find ingredients and increase their knowledge. One can no longer be condescending to them. My father always did a lot of cooking when we were children, his specialty being anything sweet – cakes, scones, puddings, desserts, chocolates, jokes, smiles. My mother did the preserving and savoury cooking. My three brothers were taught to cook alongside the girls – to this day they are all interested in good food and wine. Two of them still cook but the third, Jonathan, has become recalcitrant. His wife, Sharyn, has tried to teach him recipes, but he wanders off to watch rugby on TV in the middle of the sauce.

Every so often Sharyn gets it into her head to take off on a holiday and do what *she* wants to do, rather than what he and the kids want to do. Gastronomically speaking, this is like saying to my brother, 'I am going to disconnect your dialysis tube now and go to the beach – see you in a week.' Being a lawyer, he remains outwardly calm and starts speaking slowly and clearly, leaves the back door open for air and tries not to blink. Sharyn recognises these early signs of culinary psychosis and also starts speaking clearly and slowly and making good eye contact. Her dialogue goes something like this: 'Now Jonnie, I am making up six dinners for the freezer. All you have to do is take one out in the morning, leave it in the fridge and then microwave it when you get home. The wine is here, this is a knife and fork and if you suspect you're not alone, it's the home-stay student who will also want to be fed. Please nod if you understand this.' He nods, but it's fake. Inwardly, he's thinking, 'My sister can cook – maybe she'll microwave the food for me and we can crack a bottle of pinot and it'll all be okay.'

Jonnie has three sisters, I'm the only one who lives nearby and I am the least likely to interrupt my fabulous life to feed him. However, I have given him helpful advice for fast food that a guy who is not a great cook could put together for his significant other in thanks for twenty-five years or so of culinary ecstasy and service. Folk these days are very fond of dinners that are fast to put together but taste divine and are satisfying. You can't make a silk purse out of a sow's ear and the same goes for an elegant meal, but if you've got top-quality ingredients you can compose a meal fast and make it look like you've got half a gastronomic brain. My advice is get in the car and drive to a flash delicatessen. The downside is, of course, that you do actually have to get in the car. Buy some really good pasta, eggplant sauce, Parmesan and duck breasts. If a man can cook a steak he can cook a duck breast. Then buy some Spanish peaches, dark chocolate, mascarpone and vincotto, which is like thick, sweet vinegar. When he gets home, the man should remain calm and remember that cooking is a pleasure not a chore.

Incidentally, in case you're wondering how Jonnie managed, I called him after the first day of Sharyn's absence to check if he was taking fluids. This is what I got:

'God, Pete, this is really hard. I'm so exhausted when I get home from work.'

'What?' I gasped, 'all you have to do is take one out of the freezer that's labelled lasagne and nuke it. What's hard?'

'She hasn't labelled them with the days.'

FLAT WHITE

Coffee is the second most traded commodity in the world after oil and all men know this. While supermarket sales of instant coffee are still about five times those of fresh coffee, there is no doubt our preference for the fresh stuff is on the rise. New Zealanders make very good espresso coffee – they learned how to do it from the Australians, who learnt it from the Italians. Thank God they didn't learn it from the French, because they haven't a clue. Men have started to replace beer with coffee in cultural and social terms and take it just as seriously. Now men are experts in grind, crema and length of flavour. God, what they don't know about length of flavour... Parents give their children fluffies in tiny coffee cups and the kids ask for a set of coffee making equipment when they turn five. (If you ask me, there are far too many babies and children in adult's cafés. Do we gate crash their day care centres and demand coffee? No. So they have no place in our cafés breaking the sound barrier and grinding porridge into the floor. Mark my words – next thing they will be expecting us to talk to them.)

The story of coffee reads like an archetypal mythical tale – it has heroes, adventures, travel, subterfuge, ordeals and finally the return of the magic elixir. Coffee so invigorated Mohammed that he was able to 'unhorse forty men and make forty women happy'. Like sex, coffee is very exciting – people have tried to ban it, they turn to criminal activity if they can't get it, and they think they've understood the meaning of life when they do get it. Coffee is good for you and makes you feel better than you already feel as it stimulates digestion, regulates the cardiovascular system, increases awareness, improves concentration, memory and mood. Of course, caffeine is bad for you if you have too much, just like wine, but if you figure out how much you can drink, you will only experience the benefits. Coffee should stain your tongue for half an hour after drinking and should taste a little bitter, a little sweet, with slight acidity and big flavour. You may be aware of tastes and smells like toasted bread, flowers, chocolate and fruit.

Recently, I was sitting in a café in Uzès in the South of France with some coffee-expert friends, Michael and Carolyn, moaning about the indifferent coffee in France. They've got the roasters and the flash machines, but the wrong beans and they overextract when making espresso. Why can some nationalities make fabulous coffee? Michael thinks the difference is that French people primarily drink coffee for the rush, while Italians are more interested in taste and flavour. To get this you have to buy the world's best 'specialty grade' coffee and pay strict attention to exact preparation methods. Generally, the French seem to buy poor-quality beans.

Carolyn believes that people get habitual in their coffee drinking and they need to stop and ask what they really feel like. 'Don't always order the same thing,' she advises. 'Be discerning and more appropriate in your choice. You drink different kinds of coffee at different times of the day. For example, historically coffee with milk was drunk in the morning with bread, be it toast, a croissant or plain fresh bread. You would never drink a cappuccino or a latte with or after lunch or dinner because all that milk just fills you up. You would have a short black at the end of the meal, like a digestive; never before or with, as caffeine is an appetite suppressant.'

My friends are so enamoured of good coffee that they travel with a drip cone and filters and buy the best, freshest coffee they can find wherever they are. They only buy as much as they need for the next few days and don't keep it in the fridge because it absorbs moisture and odours. Michael, in fact, has always been mad about coffee. As a child he stayed up all night playing mahjong and drinking milky coffee with his mother's friends. He ground the beans then steeped the powder in hot milk and strained it – the original latte kid. He slept through school the next day, but seems to have caught up.

As we sat in the sun and watched the world go by, Carolyn and I thought up some enchanting sweets to melt in our mouths with coffee. I was swooning for chocolate and hazelnut baklava, which she thought would be worthy of a cup of smooth, chocolaty Guatemalan coffee. Carolyn imagined aniseed and lemon rind (which we changed to orange rind) shortbread to be eaten with a light and fruity Kenyan coffee. Because we were in the South of France, I thought of fougasse, that delicious holey flat bread. In my area, it is made with flaky pastry, so Michael dreamed up a pistachio and rose water fougasse to be drunk with spicy Ethiopian Yirgacheffe coffee. Yirgacheffe is expensive, but probably the most delicious, complex coffee you will ever drink. Before they jumped in the car to continue their journey, Michael and Carolyn bequeathed me their cone and filters, so I spent the next few hours searching for Triple-A grade, single origin, Arabica, perfectly fresh, perfectly roasted coffee.

To be the king of coffee in your very own home, Michael suggests you buy whole beans, keep them in a sealed container in the fridge, not the freezer, grind in a high-quality grinder and then brew with a filter apparatus using unbleached filters. In terms of strength, if a coffee is of high quality, you can drink it stronger than you think without there being any bitterness, so be generous with your amount – a heaped tablespoon for a large cup of coffee is about right. Don't buy more than you need – coffee only stays fresh for about ten days. Michael also says that a little sugar with coffee is a good idea because it enhances the caramels. Men are particularly mad about making good coffee and it is they who will buy expensive home espresso machines. Because a huge amount of pressure is necessary to produce an espresso with a good crema and to froth milk to the correct velvetiness, it is basically pointless buying a small domestic espresso machine. The best place to enjoy espresso made with a big, grunty machine is at an espresso bar. With a newspaper and without babies. Thank you.

THE BBQ

The word 'barbecue' comes from the Spanish 'barbacoa', which most likely came from an Arawak word for the framework on which meat could be dried or roasted. In fact, it means the framework on which all summer socialising is hung. What we mean by a BBQ in the antipodes is food cooked fast on a high heat; in America what they mean is slow, enclosed cooking at a gentle temperature. A shoulder of pork could take twelve hours and ribs five or six. In New Zealand we grill our food to medium-rare and juicy; there it must be very well done, melting and moist. At my cooking school in the South of France, my business partner David once cooked a Moroccan mechoui on his new, shiny, covered BBQ, which was approximately three centimetres smaller than your average cruise ship. He rubbed my spice mixture into a forequarter of lamb, threw the beast into the machine, closed the lid and walked away. Four hours later we ate the best lamb I have tasted in my life. How he achieved this I'll never know, but there were black carcinogens all over the grill and rendered fat all over the terrace tiles – the place looked like a barbarian sacrifice.

Men love accessing their inner caveman around burning meat, love wearing stupid aprons and love doing nothing else like prep, clean-up or making anything you might eat with blackened meat. There are a few rules to a successful barbie – let the wood or coals burn right down to embers – you can't cook over a naked flame. Gas is for amateurs. Stand back from the marinades – if you must use them, don't leave the food in for more than an hour. Step up to the sauce challenge – yoghurt with mint, cucumber and garlic; honey, vinegar and chili; BBQ sauce; fresh tomato and coriander salsas. This is also the opportunity to make a really good crisp coleslaw with cabbage, red onions, fennel and finely julienned carrots. Cook the food in a long symphony, not all at once – start with longest cooking things, like sausages and double-thick lamb chops, and finish with vegetables and fish. Eat as much as you can with your fingers – it tastes better and allows you to access your inner caveperson, just like the boys.

Our cooking confidence has been stripped from us by a detachment from primary produce, an over-dependence on too much recipe detail and outrageously perfect photos of dishes we cannot possibly reproduce. Why are we like this? Here's my take on it – cooking is one of the few things we can control in our lives. The kids say, 'You can't be my mother – I must have been adopted', the husband says, 'When I married you, you were a sexually voracious style goddess', and the housekeeper says, 'I don't do windows, dishes or anything above my armpit.' Instead of telling them all to get fucked, which is the only morally correct reaction, you invent this perfect world where the soufflé rises, the meringue is crunchy outside and gooey inside and the steak is bloody yet not bloody. This is how you control your universe. If the soufflé rises then you don't have to strangle your significant other. I invited a guest chef to teach a class at my cooking school in Uzès. This was his method: arrive two hours late, speed around like a maniac teaching six dishes simultaneously having done zero prep, no written recipes, dance, sing and throw half the world's known supply of cream into every sauce. I stood by with a face like a cat's arse and thought, 'I want a recipe NOW! I don't want to be like the boys. I don't want to be free range.'

IMPORTANT HEALTH MESSAGES

1. The quality of men's sperm has halved in two decades – very dramatic. It's still mostly above the average sperm density level of 20 million sperm per millilitre, but it's not very flash. Theories abound – it's the mother's fault (of course), the male baby was exposed to something nasty in the womb, bad diet, dodgy lifestyle (drugs, alcohol, smoking, obesity), chemicals in the environment, cell phones. If a man wants to have babies, he should stop wearing tight undies while talking on the mobile with a fag hanging out of his mouth.

2. There are no advantages to structured exercise for men – it's just replacing organised religion – get over it and stand on your own two feet. The correct philosophy is no pain, good. Sit-ups are the worst – they just give you back pain. Humans were not made to eat regular meals or take regular exercise – our ancestors were on the move, so the message is incidental exercise like walking to work and to the bar and not being afraid of missing a meal occasionally.

3. Swimming is not good for your shape – look at whales. Going for a run to 'get in shape' when you're not accustomed to it will kill you. You think if you drive your car faster it will last longer? Still not listening to me? Round is a shape. Your heart is only good for so many beats – don't waste them on exercise – everything wears out eventually.

4. A man should eat fat, meat, fish, veggies, nuts and fruit because they raise sperm count, increase sexual performance and will keep him handsome. Don't eat carbs or processed or junk food – you know what the punishment is – fat, forty and finished. Carbohydrates stop you from burning fat,

which ends up hanging around your middle. Throw away the bun and just eat the burger.

5. Ingest lots of extra virgin olive oil (any other grade is a waste of time). Jeanne Calment died at the age of 120, having smoked and drunk all her life. When asked the secret to her longevity, she replied, 'Olive oil. I have eaten olive oil every day of my life and rubbed it all over my body, the result of which is I have only one wrinkle and I'm sitting on it.'

COHABITING BOOSTS MEN'S MENTAL HEALTH

Everyone knows men don't like living alone but women love it. Men in partnerships do well mentally and do especially well if they stick with their first enduring relationship. It has been known for a long time that married men are healthier, have a longer life expectancy, lower death rates and better mental well-being (not surprising if you've had a woman looking after you all your life). Studies at Queen Mary University of London, showed that if a relationship does split up, men recover faster than women (probably because they have invested less and don't have so much to lose either financially or emotionally). And they recover well from serial split-ups, unlike women, whose mental health progressively deteriorates with each heartbreak. A split-up for a woman commonly erodes security, both of property and love. They are the ones who have the babies and have strong nurturing and protective instincts. A relationship break-up is like a death in terms of grief – it takes at least three years to recover.

Here is the conclusion: true happiness and good mental health for men is in being married or co-habiting and for women it is in being single or not living with their partner. In fact, the ideal for women's mental health is to have stayed single and never loved and lost at all. Go figure.

> ### LESSONS LEARNED
> - Men can orgasm without ejaculating.
> - Swimming is not good for your shape – look at whales.
> - Prostate does not mean lying down.
> - Forget about the penis and remember the magic of the tongue.

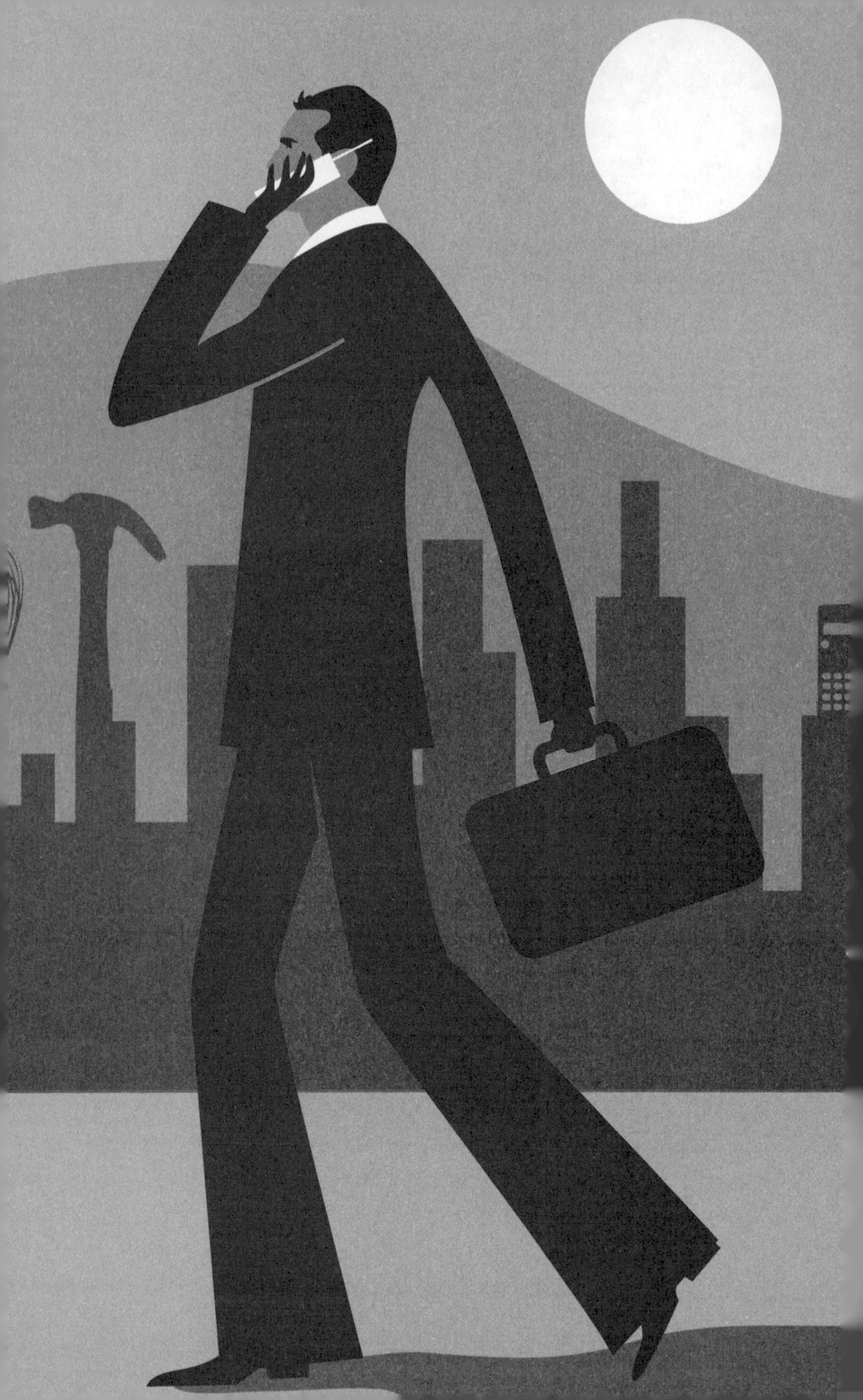

8
Work
AGE ONLY MATTERS IF YOU ARE A CHEESE

THE CHANGING WORKPLACE

Many people think working hard and loving it is natural and normal for men. Before the Industrial Revolution boys worked with their fathers on the farms, in mines and shops. Men and boys knew what their roles were; they liked working together, got to know each other, forged strong bonds and got a lot of satisfaction from being breadwinners. Then, instead of working with their fathers, boys started going to school, where they were instructed that working menial tasks was shameful and with a bit of education they could do much better. School effectively removed boys from their fathers forever. It became good to be clean, wear a tie, be inactive and be surgically attached to desks doing dreary jobs – to demonstrate a strong 'work ethic'.

What does 'work ethic' mean and where did it come from? I would feel worthless without my work. I derive enormous satisfaction from it and feel that by working I am contributing to society – that I am not a waste of space. Has this been culturally imposed on me or is it innate? According to some studies, the whole concept of work having moral or intrinsic value is culturally imposed and quite recent. In ancient times the toffs didn't work as such, while the great unwashed toiled away thanklessly and in great degradation. Working hard without being forced to was not the norm for Hebrew, classical, or medieval cultures. In fact, by our standards, they were a bunch of slackers. The Hebrews thought of work as a curse devised as punishment for Adam and Eve's transgressions and ingratitude. The Greek word for work was 'ponos' – the name of the god of sorrow. For the Romans, work was done by slaves, and free men engaged in either agriculture or big business. For medieval people work still held no intrinsic value. The function of work was to meet the needs of one's family and community and also to avoid idleness, which would lead to sin. Work was 'ordered' by God.

In the sixteenth century Martin Luther believed that each person should earn an income to meet his basic needs, but that building and hoarding wealth was sinful. During the Protestant Reformation work came to be viewed as a calling and it was okay to make a profit if you invested it back into the business. Medieval people had a lot of free time and holidays and would be utterly astounded by the long hours we now work. While the Catholics were still indulging in corruption, indulgence and the concept of purgatory (which wasn't as bad as hell), the reforming Protestants were all about honesty, abstaining from self-indulgence and deserving rather than buying your position, thus earning respect.

What we now call a work ethic really came about with the rise of capitalism. With capitalism we started to believe that all occupations had dignity, work was good and one had the right to choose what one did. Hard work became respected and people who didn't work were considered lazy and purposeless. In the late 1950s there were fundamental changes in employer–employee relationships. It was discovered that factors such as achievement, recognition, responsibility, advancement, and personal growth tended to motivate workers to perform better than the old paternalistic, domineering, controlled system. By the 1960s a 'participatory' style of management was the favoured mode. You could describe the modern work ethic as a cultural expectation that your job should be valuable and meaningful. Parents who have a strong work ethic tend to pass it on to their children.

Women entering the workforce was pretty dramatic, the cell phone was pretty dramatic, word processors were pretty dramatic, but the internet really did it. Email makes the fax, which was invented in the late 1980s, seem like writing on stone. Email and laptop computers meant that no one had to be any particular place to work any more – you could live in a wired-up tree and still get the work done. This unfortunately contributed to the death of the tea lady. A lot of men miss tea ladies and thank God we still have hairdressers otherwise who would we confide in?

Now men don't have meetings in the workplace – they are the flat white groovers. Now entire business proposals and deals are done in cafés over a double, decaffeinated, trim flat white, or a spirulina smoothie. There used to be employees and bosses and you didn't ask any questions – now anybody can ask a question. There used to be memos – now there is email and you are expected to answer immediately. Sometimes the wrong people get cc-ed. The speed of all these new communications means men work faster and do more in a shorter time (otherwise known as stress). It seems unbelievable now but women in my mother's generation stopped working the day they married and devoted themselves to the house. Men didn't bring work home, didn't work weekends and you didn't live beyond your means.

Of course email and text are a dream world for men – now they have whole relationships by internet. You can not only fake orgasms by text, you can have love affairs and never touch the person. (This is not good for men – if they want to succeed in the workplace and the loveplace of the future they will need to talk a lot more.)

Many men now work from home. The office and the home have fused because most people's homes have everything an office has (telephone, computer, broadband, printer) and most offices have everything a home has (fabulous kitchen and dining room, stylish sitting room, plants). Men who turn their mobiles off after work are considered eccentric.

FLEXIBLE, CREATIVE AND GOOD WITH PEOPLE?

If a man possesses all of the above he will have no problem finding work in today's work market. Here are some helpful hints for the male worker:

1. If you are a control freak and authoritarian you will be laughed out of the job, even if you are self-employed. Unlearn these backward ways immediately.
2. Don't scratch your bum or rearrange your testicles or admire your dick every time you think of it. All these things will still be there when you get home – leave them alone.
3. I know your hair is the second most important thing in your

WORK

life after your dick but the office mirrors are for women to put their lipstick on, not for you to try one more way to disguise the creeping grey bits. The office windows are to separate work spaces, not to look in to check the Hugh Grant flop while you are talking to an important female member of staff.

4. Gather up all your ties and give them to your grandmother to make into a floor mat. Ties say that you are a slave and willing to submit and fit in. The only person you should submit to is your wife or your girlfriend. Dress in stylish, well-cut clothes and do not hand your spirit over to the company. That is the route to powerlessness.

5. When women put you down in the workplace, laugh. They are usually doing it for fun and fortunately you know how sexy, brainy and confident you are in your masculinity and that you are the master of your destiny.

6. There's nothing wrong with being competitive at work – that's why you get out of bed in the morning (after you've checked your dick) and head to the office (after leaving all the wet towels from the shower on the floor). Healthy competitiveness is necessary for a business to progress and it is inspiring and motivating.

7. If you were a brainy little boy who refused to cut your hair and play rugby, don't worry – you could turn into a brilliant design engineer with long hair and a great line in Hawaiian shirts, like my brother David.

8. Conversation topics not suitable for the office include how you got coked out of your brain at the weekend; how you are shagging your boss; criticising what your co-workers have dragged in for lunch.

9. If you suspect the compulsive pursuit of money and possessions is a personality disorder, you're right.
10. Read the chapter on lying closely and you will understand why lying at work is *so* five minutes ago.

David Horsman

PM 'Why do you work – is it just a means to an end or is it a vocation?'

DH 'I think all my work has been completely vocational. I decided pretty early on in life that I wanted to do something I wanted to do. When I was seventeen my uncle, who was a very successful stockbroker, took me to the stock exchange in London and we had lunch but it wasn't for me. It fitted into a mould which didn't interest me – the idea of wearing a suit, going into work every day, commuting.'

PM 'I can't imagine why it interests anyone.'

DH 'Money. Ambition. I think by and large men don't think about it that much. They inherit a lot from their parents and then just get on and do it. I can think of a couple of friends who I was at university with who smoked dope, had lots of fun then completely reverted to type and now come home to slippers by the fire, a whiskey and television. As a kid coming from a farm, I remember not wanting to farm.'

PM 'What did you think your parents' expectations were for you as a boy, for work and for your future?'

DH 'I was always told by my parents that I could do

anything but it was a mixed message because of course they didn't really want me to do *anything*. At high school I wanted to do art and geography, but my father said I must do something which prepared me for a proper job – like economics. The idea of doing something remotely artistic was not considered. I used to love dressing up and doing magic shows and theatre but that was not encouraged beyond childhood, so I bowed to the pressure to do something straight and started university with economics and politics.'

PM 'Do you think that men feel trapped on an employment wheel they can't get off?'

DH 'Yes, I think a vast majority of men still feel trapped in the sense that, no matter how liberated a world we live in, the bottom line is that the male has to go out and provide.'

PM 'Do you think men feel used as workhorses?'

DH 'Well I'm not a good person to ask as I've never subscribed to typical male behaviour in any area. Possibly they feel used but they feel a sense of responsibility. They feel they have to fulfil a defined role, the same way as women do.'

PM 'How many career changes have you had?'

DH 'Four. It is the standard now to have several different jobs through your life because of the increasingly fragmented world we live in, and there is no job security, especially when there's an economic crisis. I think it's a great thing to be able to chop and change – very creative – maybe have two or three different jobs at the same time with income streaming in from different areas. My first job was making television commercials and I remember very clearly why I packed it in. I worked very hard and earned a lot of money getting the shoot fee plus a percentage of the profits. Then I realised the profit I was getting was 5 per cent and the people I was working for were getting the other 95 per cent. I understood then it was prostitution and walked.'

PM 'So men *will* walk away from jobs they are unhappy in?'

DH 'Yes, especially if they don't have responsibilities, which I didn't. And I've always liked putting myself in danger; I'm fascinated by the unknown. There is a type of male who always seeks insecurity in order to have a frisson and not be bored. My father was not able to go into the family business in India so went out to New Zealand from England to do something different and became a farmer. People like that who will go off and forge another life for themselves are not the majority. Most men seem to fit into three categories: the ones approaching retirement who have knuckled down and made a fortune; the ones who feel completely stuck in a rut (they might be making good money but they're rowing); and then there are the precious few who have done what they really wanted. It's very hard for a man to admit he hasn't been a success. An unemployed man feels inconsolably awful because it is so beaten into men to achieve or at least to support. Men and women are hard-wired, going back millions of years, to take particular roles. One obvious example is men having tunnel vision because they need to be able to see prey at a long distance and women have peripheral vision because they need to keep their eye on lots of different things going on around them like kids, fires et cetera.'

PM 'Does money make you happy?'

DH 'Yes and no. If you're travelling on a budget airline, you will do anything not to repeat that experience. We have been sold a very commercial way of looking at life but I have spent a lot of time looking into spiritual understanding in which happiness comes from a completely different area. I am convinced you can live with virtually nothing, very happily.'

PM 'Millions of people do it.'

DH 'Most people do it. That success is defined by money, which does give a certain amount of comfort, is ingrained in us. However, getting rid of personal possessions gives one a lot of freedom.'

PM 'Do you think your father would have wanted your working life?'

DH 'Actually I said to him once that he was a frustrated hippy in the wrong era because one side of him would love to have broken out and questioned things, but the other side kept him in place being responsible. In his day you didn't seek professional

JUST IN TIME TO BE TOO LATE

> help and only went to a psychologist if you were completely bonkers. And even if you weren't already bonkers, one visit to a shrink would be the fast road to the looney bin. For sixty years our model for mental health was behaviourism. Your mind was a black box and you didn't go there. Men are still afraid to even *start* delving into what makes us tick – it's the last frontier.'
>
> **PM** 'I've noticed when people come on our culinary tours they often have cathartic experiences.'
>
> **DH** 'Oh yes – travel is a great way to open you up in many areas and force you to look differently at things.'

BANNED WORDS

There are certain words and phrases I never want to hear again in the workplace or anywhere else. These include:

- At the end of the day
- Issue
- Roadmap
- Empower
- Optimum outcome
- Absolutely (the word you're looking for is 'yes')
- Accountability
- Hidden agenda
- Any word a man speaks to me while his eyes are scanning the room looking for someone more 'dynamic'
- Any words (especially business negotiations) spoken on cell phones in enclosed spaces like airport lounges, cars, movie theatres, bedrooms, public toilets

- God, I'm just so busy (the response to this is, 'Like me, you mean?')
- I got 100 emails today (the response to this is, 'Fuck off')
- I just want to get on with my life.

MENTORS

It's now rather fashionable to have a mentor, but I think you have to be careful with them. You have to choose someone who can relate to you; someone who has worked in your field and is close to your age. Things change so fast now – a mentor's advice might be out of date before you even get into action. What worked for them in another era, may not work for you. When I decided to move to Paris and become a chef in 1980 at the age of thirty, my betters were touching in their encouragement: 'You're too old', 'You don't speak French', 'You're a woman trying to operate in a male profession – can't be done'. When I wrote my first book in 1994 it was refused by every publisher I sent it to bar one. Even magazine editors refused it: 'We don't need another food book. Who cares that a nurse went to Paris and opened a restaurant? There's no market for this.' When I put my first proposal together in 1993 for a television food show, television companies threw it in the rubbish: 'There is no market for cooking shows. No one would watch it.' This is why I don't believe in mentors, or at least think they should be used with caution. I have had two restaurants, have now written ten books and been presenting prime time television food shows since 1996. This is not to show you how fabulous I am – it is to show you that you must always follow your own lead, not someone else's. The way to do something is to *do* it, as Janet Street-Porter said in her fabulous book – *Life's Too F***ing Short*. My television company producer went through a few mentors before she got to the right one – a successful charming woman close to her age who knew how to market. This mentor actually comes to events we do to help us – this is an example of mentoring working.

RUNNING-OFF-WITH-THE-OFFICE-MANAGER SYNDROME

Some people think this syndrome is a myth. My friend Suzanna's husband ran off with the office manager, a woman his age. They both left their families. My friend Minni's husband ran off with the office manager, who Minni described as fat, fifty and finished. I met a girl in Australia who was a younger office manager and got her boss to leave his wife, describing the wife as desperate and manipulative. (Can't think why?) An acquaintance of mine had an affair with the pretty secretary just after his wife had given birth, thus driving her into a despair that changed her personality and reduced her to a stick.

I could give you hundreds of examples and it's really easy to explain. There are two reasons why the man runs off with the office manager and not someone else: men have no imagination, so they just turn to the person standing next to them and say, 'Hi'; the office manager actually knows them better than their wife. The man usually says, 'My wife doesn't understand me any more.' Of course she doesn't! She never sees him. The office manager spends all day with him, sometimes socialises with him and knows all his secrets. A man may work long hours. Now add to that commuting, taking work home, playing sports with the boys, doing stuff with the kids on the weekend and there isn't much quality time for his wife.

An office manager or secretary does not behave like a wife and for once in his life, the man is in a position of superiority – you can tell her what to do and she obeys. She makes you coffee, knows her place, they get to know each other without any pressure, she is well-dressed, she can converse intelligently with him about his job. Also, sometimes the man feels his wife is not paying enough attention, so he starts playing around at work to make her sit up. This is why he falls for the office manager, but why does she fall for him? She has an inferiority complex, is jealous of the wife and thinks if she steals her man, she will be better than the wife. She also has no imagination and to fulfil her emotional needs just turns to the man sitting in front of her. Quite often the office manager develops an intimate, trusting relationship with her boss before he really knows what's happened.

RETIREMENT? GET OUTTA HERE!

Men are not particularly tied to retiring these days. If they are healthy and wish to keep working then they should. Being retired can be boring if you've worked hard and enjoyed it all your life. Only twenty years ago, men in their fifties dreamed of the heaven of retirement spent on the golf course or doing some mad thing like sailing the world. Now 'retirement' is almost a swear word. The number of workers of retirement age is estimated to have risen by almost a quarter in the past three years. Half of all male lawyers over sixty-five now hold practicing certificates (a huge increase in the past ten years) and the number of accountants and doctors working past retirement age is rising fast. The current world economic downturn will affect older workers for sure, but it is only a blip and the future trend lies in men in good health continuing to contribute in the workplace. There has been a fundamental and permanent shift in the workforce and this has to be accepted. Work is good for the soul and necessary for the pocket. This is very favourable because in the old days, an older person couldn't get a job even if they wanted one. Pension age will rise and it is predicted that working until you're seventy-five or more will become the norm with retirement delayed till the eighties. Cripes – when are you supposed to do that trip down memory lane to Rhodes?

Specialists in pension economics argue that going from 100 per cent employed one day to zero per cent employed the next is foolish for both workers and employers. The whole idea of retirement needs to be rethought, moving away from the concept of it being a destination toward it being a journey or a process. The actual word should be dropped from the language. The ideal would be to stop full-time work at a certain stage, but continue to remain economically active, working on your own terms with flexible hours and control over what you do. What's very fashionable now is to set up your own business, possibly run from home, or open up a consultancy. This way you can enjoy a degree of autonomy you never had during the years of corporate struggle, ensuring that retirement is positively liberating. But of course none of this applies to the people who have 'Fullered' all their lives, rather than working. A friend of mine in Paris who studied the philosopher and designer Buckminster Fuller also believed, like Fuller, that if you do a job you enjoy, you never have to do a day's 'work' in your life. To that end he called working 'Fullering'. These fortunate people don't really understand the concept of retirement because they don't recognise work as work. They have removed themselves from, or never were in, wage labour; they enjoy themselves and will continue to do so forever. I belong to this group. I have a pitifully inadequate pension plan, no work insurance and no medical insurance. My plan, which my accountant completely agrees with, is to keep working creatively.

If you are unafraid of risk, you have no fear of future unemployment. Look at farmers, look at jazz musicians, look at wine makers, look at fishermen – they all 'Fuller' well into old age. The idea of giving up would be ludicrous to them. It is only if you have chosen to enslave yourself that you need to escape into retirement. Interestingly enough, your brain has something to do with the way you work as you age. Scientists, mathematicians and criminals all do their best work early – usually by thirty-five. Not so with writers, musicians and philosophers. Their best work comes later. Music, writing, and (sometimes) philosophy all reach into our emotions and bear an opportunity for the growth of wisdom. What this means is, if you are artistic, you have a greater chance of working well and productively for longer. If you're a safe-breaker, diversify, or you will find you're just in time to be too late.

One thing that came up quite a lot when I interviewed men who had retired was that they missed the kudos afforded by work. A loss of status and a shrinking social network came as a shock to them. John said, 'When you have worked hard all your life in an important job and you have had a lot of power, you get validation in the form of compliments, bonuses, promotions, et cetera. When you retire, you get a big party and thanks and then it all stops overnight and you never get that kind of validation that you have contributed and that you count, again – ever. In my case it was compounded by the collapse of my marriage. So I was retired, should have been happy, but had a lot of trouble adjusting. Now things are really good, I met a lady on the internet, I am not bored and I travel a lot.' Evidence points to the fact that work as a social act is very positive for men's health. Sometimes retirement makes you think that life is a featureless desert and you realise how important your work actually was. Another man who has always worked as a management consultant said he saw colleagues retire at sixty-five and most of them were dead by seventy. On Friday they had a responsible, stimulating job and on Monday they had nothing. He vowed that no one was going to tell him when to retire – he's seventy-four, still working and might think about retirement around ninety-three. He firmly believes if you are healthy and still doing the job well, it should be illegal to force you to retire. Employment is employment – age should be irrelevant.

Asda (a British supermarket chain which retails food, clothing, toys and general merchandise) has many employees over the age of sixty-five, has no official retirement age, no age limit for recruitment and no longer even asks people applying for jobs to give their date of birth on their application forms. They also encourage flexible hours, leave, job-sharing and shift-swapping. In the chapter on work in my book *Can We Help it if We're Fabulous*, I talked about Generation Y workers (people born after 1980) who are young, want to be head of department within a year, earn big bucks and have no commitment beyond three years. Employers are becoming disenchanted with this lot and now welcome older workers who are not only more stable and realistic but healthy and have different expectations about life. They demand respect and ethical behaviour, and value people more than money. They provide continuity. It used to be that energetic youth were considered the saviours of the world, but putting all your belief in assertiveness, dynamism and positive attitude can be problematic when you don't have the balance of maturity, level-headedness and wisdom. Older workers who have been through the wringer and had ups and downs are actually being dragged out of retirement – there are lots of examples of people going back to part-time work or consulting and earning top dollar. Employers also consider it valuable to pair older staff with younger so they can both benefit from each other. Contrary to what you might expect, there is hardly any absenteeism with older workers because they don't have as many hangovers, mental health days or broken hearts. However, this doesn't work everywhere – some countries have more success with recruiting oldsters than others. Many places are still backward in realising the potential, mainly because they're too busy being fabulous and groovy.

Baby boomers (born in the middle of the twentieth century) have broken all the moulds – in my mind they are the lucky ones. If you were born in 1949, by the time you hit twenty many huge social revolutions had happened: feminism, the pill, television, the hippy movement, face cream, full employment and the sexual revolution. Nobody had ever heard of an alfalfa sprout before 1970 – now everyone acts like they're normal. Nobody accessed their inner self before 1964; nobody knew what a feeling was; and if a man lost his job he just went down the road and got another one. Now men have got feelings coming out their wazoos – it's exhausting for them (and us). Also, around 1974, at about the same time we all agreed on who would open the door, pull the chair out, orgasm first and which children got to use the toy guns, we also agreed that women wanted and needed to work. This was the first generation where both partners worked, so the baby boomers ended up having a much higher standard of living than their parents had. Any men who said stuff like, 'When women started going to work we developed traumatic stress syndrome. We experienced it as a great loss and believed we would never recover from the blow of not being needed to care for women and look after them', were quickly defenestrated by their wives who said, 'Thanks, love, but keeping us dependent on you will not be in your interest in the long term, we need to work to feel fulfilled and happy and please pick up your undies from the bathroom floor.'

Ant Grayson

PM 'Has the workplace changed?'

AG 'Oh yes – enormously. In my bank there is no hierarchy, no offices, an incredibly diverse workforce in terms of nationality; equal rights reign along with flexible working hours. The male domain in terms of financial markets doesn't apply any more and people work together with more of a shared purpose than before.'

PM 'What about older workers?'

AG 'One of my guys who's been with us for twenty years, sixty-two years old, is leaving to go teaching. That is fantastic. No one retires now because it's like giving up. In my father's day you had to retire at sixty-five, but actually mostly you were dead from overwork and pressure before then. People work more sensibly now.'

TAKE A BABY-BOOMER MAN, PLEASE

The world is now awash with divorced middle-aged men in bars trawling for women – preferably younger women. In days gone by they would be at home teaching the grandchildren how to make balsa wood planes; now they're out on the streets and clogging up the spas, getting shaves in places God has never even heard of. A happily married middle-aged man dresses completely differently from a divorced one. The ones in bars wear jeans, pointy boots or shoes, tastefully striped (or in especially confident cases, flowery) shirts *not tucked in*; have product in their hair; are fit and are scanning. I always want to ask, 'Do you have a permit for that shirt, honey?' They have that you-would-be-*so*-lucky-to-get-me look on their faces and long scraggy necks from scanning as they heat up the room with their devastating animal magnetism. How I know this is I am a woman and have eyes in the back of my head.

They are not worried about retirement, health, their house or the job. When people tell them they should be more concerned, that they have to live a safe life, act their age and prepare for the second half of their lives, they are not listening. Women are already way ahead in this arrogant attitude and men are catching up. They took a while to think about it but now they're feeling the fear and doing it. When people ask, 'Who is going to support all you baby boomers when you are old – how are we going to pay for it?' They say, 'We are the baby boomers, we are invincible, we have three thousand times more confidence than you'll ever have, sucker, even on Saturday night. We'll support ourselves, thanks – we'll still be working and liking it.'

Because of his extraordinary circumstances of high knowledge, technical aids, physical and mental versatility, open-mindedness and ability to live in the present, the baby boomer man can roll with the punches in a way his father never could.

He realised, just in time, that he is not doing his children favours by supporting them past the age of twenty, by bailing them out, by arranging their divorces, by letting them live at home till they're thirty-five, by coughing up the deposit for the house – they can work for it the way he did, the spoiled layabouts. Now, he's spending the inheritance on low-life floozies, holidays, face-lifts and expensive restaurants.

Steve Yeoman

PM 'Why do you work?'

SY 'I work for money. But I have failed miserably to stay in jobs I don't like or don't do well, so in that sense work is more a vocation. I need to be doing what I like and if I'm doing it badly I run away.'

PM 'What if you had a family to support – would you still have made that decision?'

SY 'In my case it was more or less irrelevant as my wife went out to work and I stayed at home looking after the children. Even in those days that was unusual – I was the only play centre Dad. After that I would say I changed careers about eight times. I think it's a good idea except that everything I have done has been very different, so it's like starting from the beginning every time instead of building up in one direction. Once I get to a certain point with a job and have achieved creative satisfaction, I tend to lose interest.

WORK

      The scary thing is I never know what I'm going to do next so you wouldn't call me a focused career mover. I don't make a good employee because, as I have no ambition, I can't be manipulated.'

PM 'I get tired of things too, but I usually already know what I want to do next.'

SY 'Yes, but you are incredibly focused. I remember when you said you wanted to do a television cooking show years ago and you didn't let go of that vision till you got it. You were determined to write books despite all the setbacks and you still are.'

PM 'It's tricky, though, because to be a television presenter you have to be an extrovert and to be a writer you have to be an introvert.'

SY 'Same with me. I like people so it's natural that I sold books and had a café, but I also like to be alone so am good at web design. I could be on my own for days at a stretch and be perfectly happy.'

PM 'Me too. Too happy – we're called sociable loners.'

SY 'Are we bipolar?'

PM 'I don't think so – I think a lot of people are like that.'

SY 'I like the label of sociable loner.'

PM 'Why did your father work?'

SY 'Because he had to – there was no option. He came out of the war, went into the valuation department and stayed there till he retired. He seemed happy doing this, looking after the family and doing the right thing.'

PM 'Do you think men feel used as workers to support

243

> women and children and that the pressure becomes intolerable?'
>
> **SY** 'Not really. In my life the women have always earned more than me and I think that whoever is the breadwinner feels a certain amount of pressure, be it a man or a woman. I think the idea of the man being driven into the ground is a myth these days – not in my artistic circle anyway – maybe businessmen in offices feel trapped – I would.'
>
> **PM** 'Do your male friends ever talk to you about work?'
>
> **SY** 'No. Men don't talk to each other about anything.'
>
> **PM** 'Does money make you happy?'
>
> **SY** 'Yes. You can buy stuff. Without money you are unhappy to a degree because it makes you nervous and makes you concentrate on money all the time. Extremely wealthy people also think about money all the time. The trick is to be in the middle – in a position where you stop thinking about it. I could fly business class but wouldn't as I'd rather spend all that money on something else, like family.'

HOW IT'S GOING TO LOOK IN THE FUTURE

Eighty-seven per cent of men today say work is the most important thing of all, which hasn't changed much over the centuries and probably won't change in the near future. There will be very few retirement homes, thank goodness, because old people don't want to live with a whole bunch of old people – they want to be surrounded by folk of all ages. They want to be able to explain to the youngsters that line dancing doesn't mean snorting coke, that a hip replacement doesn't mean an awareness implant, that a poofter isn't a blowfish and prostate does not mean lying down. Modern man will be healthier longer and if he's not living with a partner he may be living with friends in a large house, in an extended family situation or in a mixed community. Work, school and home communications will meld. No one will have to be in any place at any time to do their work – they will have a task which has to be completed and that will be done however it suits them, so long as it gets done. A lot of work will be outsourced. Because today's children were born into families who have had to struggle with unemployment, property downturns, world financial crises and education debt, they will have a different attitude to work. They may well have to be frugal and tough like their great-grandparents were after the war.

The present generation, called generation Y, are brash, confident, fearless, well-educated and not interested in waiting in line to get the promotion. They don't see working in the same job for forty years as something to be proud of – they see it as a monumental lack of imagination. They have no responsibilities as they are still at home with their comfortably off, tolerant and reasonable baby boomer parents. The main reason baby boomers left home so young was because their parents were from another planet, they wanted to have sex, and they were expected to make their own way by frugal parents who were brought up in hardship. The qualities the present generation of workers have is the ability to have good relationships, to think outside the square, be fair, be flexible and casually ambitious. They don't experience large generational differences and are comfortable working and negotiating with all ages. Relationship-driven skills are very important today and it will be interesting in the future to see how generation Y's children manage economic downturn and work. They might have to go back to the old days of strictness and answerability.

Generation Y don't mind doing menial tasks but not blindly – they like to know why they are being asked to chop onions for three months or deliver chicken to a client or photocopy endless pages. There has to be a point, a connection and an end game in sight. Baby boomers tend to be workaholics but their children are too bright, too worldly and have had life too easy for that. They don't expect seniors to bark orders at them – they just don't respond to it – they expect intelligent conversations and to work together.

When I was doing my nursing training there was a notoriously violent and abusive ward sister who terrified us all. It never entered anyone's head to confront or stop her. These days, a young nurse would say, 'You are hurting my feelings. Could you engage with me in a more friendly manner please?' It's our fault Generation Y, and their immediate predecessors, Generation X, have feelings – their parents, the baby boomers, who were not allowed to express feelings, told their children they were special, lovable, wonderful and brilliant just for breathing, doing poo-poo and passing an exam. In days gone by these things were taken for granted – you didn't get a medal for them. We made them addicted to praise.

WORK

LESSONS LEARNED

- It is not true that you need a double decaffeinated trim flat white to make a decision in an office.
- Gather up all your ties and give them to your grandmother to make into a floor mat. Ties signify you are a slave and willing to submit and fit in. The only people you should be submitting to are your wives and girlfriends.
- Men who think outside the square and learn 'feminine' skills like communication and sharing are the ones who will survive in the future.

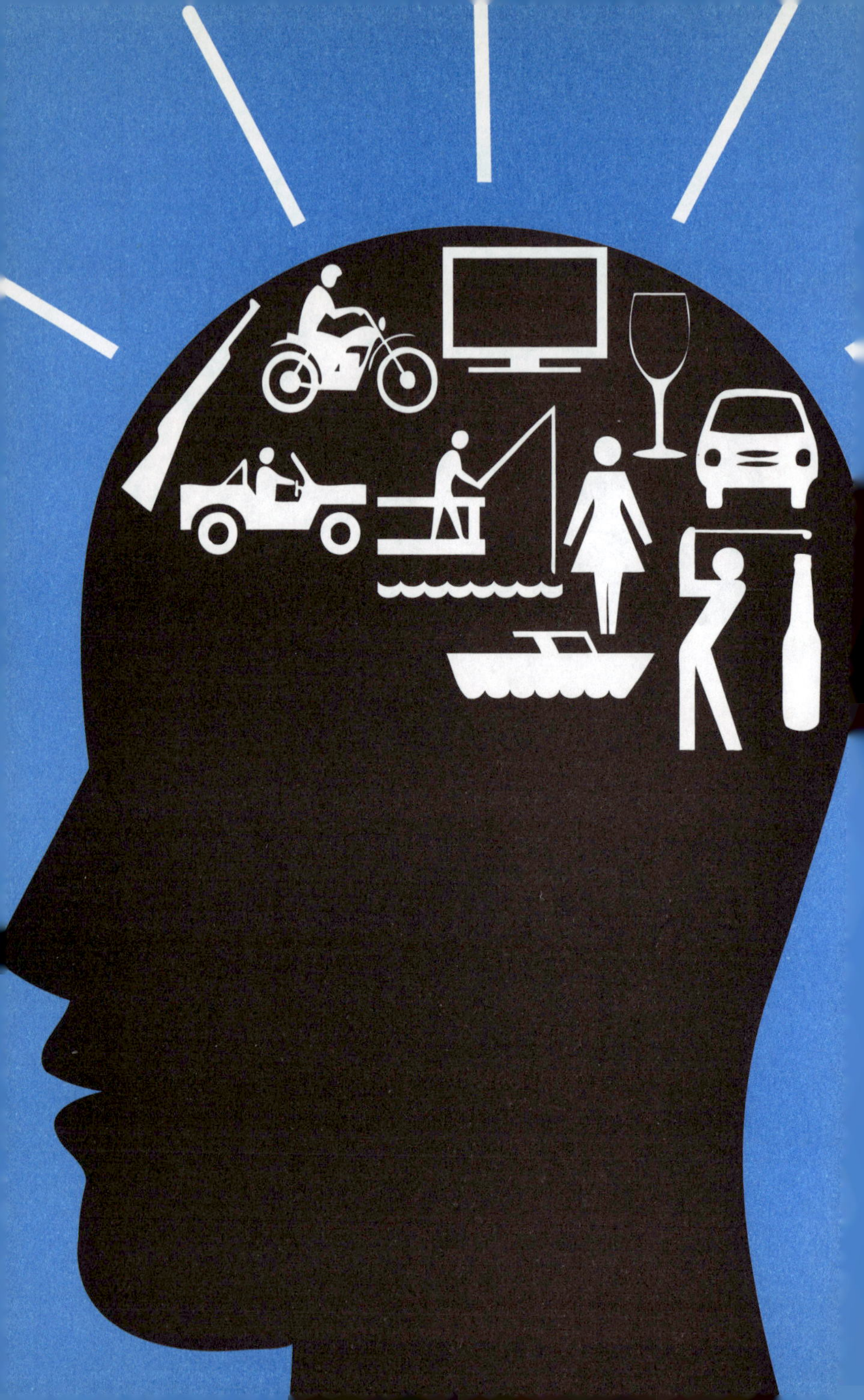

9
Happiness
DON'T OVERDO IT

EMPATHETIC MIMICRY

Happiness is catching, just like beauty – if you feel beautiful you are beautiful. Some people are born happy, while the rest of us learn how to be. Some people are born beautiful while most of us learn how to fake it. Grumpiness is also catching and can spread through networks of friends and family. Moods have a ripple effect, like pebbles in a pond – you can even be affected by someone you have never met. We are far more influenced by other people than we think: our health, whether we turn out to vote, our taste in music and food, our tendency to suicide can all be influenced by friends. How could this be? Social influence operates at a subconscious level – do we have so little control over our lives? Fortunately, social influence is, by and large, a positive thing. How else would I have known at the age of fifteen that it was appropriate to wear tight bellbottoms and pale pink lipstick? Peer pressure. It's great that we are so social and that most of us don't draw tight circles around ourselves. If we are aware of negative social influences then we can control them or use them to our benefit. Susceptibility to a friend's happiness apparently depends on your relationship with them – a close friend can affect your mood by 60 per cent, but a cohabiting partner only by 10 per cent. Interestingly, happiness spreads more effectively via friends of the same sex.

Some researchers think the cause of this phenomenon is the mechanism of empathetic mimicry. People unconsciously copy the facial expressions, manner of speech, posture, body language and other mannerisms of people around them, sometimes immediately. This then makes you actually feel the same way as the person you are copying. Try it. If someone is speaking too loudly to you, speak to them quietly. You'll see that he will lower his voice without realising that you have instructed him. The one behaviour I find hard to change is when a person is standing too close while talking to you, not understanding personal space. When I step back to make it clear they are in my face and I'm going cross-eyed, they step forward. This gives me a nose bleed. It is really hard for me not to put my hand on their chest and say, 'Get off me.'

WHAT MAKES MEN HAPPY AND ARE THEY HAPPIER THAN WOMEN?

Fay Weldon says women can't be happy for more than ten minutes at a stretch. Australian research has shown that men are happy on a week-to-week basis. This is what makes a man happy (in alphabetical order):

- Being with his family

HAPPINESS

- Drinking with his friends
- Driving, tinkering with and fantasising about cars
- Eating food with his friends (or on the sofa alone)
- Making the women in his life happy
- Professional success in a demanding environment
- Rest and recreation – this is a big one
- Sex – 48 per cent of men report that intimate relationships make them happy
- Surfing the internet, playing online games, watching porn (this is a big one)
- Work (within reason).

Men are also happy when they are visiting their parents because it usually involves lying around watching sports and being waited on hand and foot by their mother. Women tend to see visiting the parents as work – sorting out their bills, helping with medical problems, organising family get-togethers. They enjoy it about as much as repeatedly banging their head on a doorframe.

Men and women never seem to be happy at the same time, possibly because happiness is cyclical and depends on your aspirations and the events of your life. There is new research showing men in 2009 might be a bit happier than women, and it's related to age. In 1970 women were happier (no wonder – the pill was invented). Today, men have cut down on activities they don't like doing – they work fewer hours and relax more (on the phone and in front of television). At the same time women's workload has increased. They have replaced housework with paid work. They now have two jobs – one at the office and the other, unpaid, at home. Women feel they are doing neither job properly and so always feel a little dissatisfied and guilty. Boys in high school are happier than girls – they goof-off and are more relaxed. But high-achieving girls (who get better grades than boys, work to excel in sports and music, organise school activities, look spunky and run student newspapers) for some reason feel a little pressured. They are likely to have nails bitten to the quick.

Once girls become women and start working they are very happy and intent on achieving goals, contributing to the world and having adorable babies. At the same time the boys get hit with all the big responsibilities of financial goals, building up a career, supporting families, not letting the kids drive them nuts, and they are miserable. By middle age, men have often achieved those goals and are feeling brighter. Also, most men are single in their twenties and most women are alone in middle age. I think it's great to be single and free in middle age, so I can have exciting adventures – the middle-aged old codgers can have the younger women if they want them. They are well-matched anyway because neither of them are at their sexual peak, which leaves the younger, peaking men for the older, peaking women who are!

A STORY OF THREE BRAINS

It's very fashionable to say we humans haven't evolved much from the cave man, that we are still wired in the same way they were, but evolutionary psychologists like Gary Marcus, who wrote *Kluge: the Haphazard Construction of the Human Mind*, think that's too simple. Do you think your brain is this magical thing and that perhaps, like your computer, you probably only use 10 per cent of it? If so, you are absolutely right. This is okay because what you mostly need your brain to do is execute quite ordinary, uncomplicated jobs, such as remembering who your husband is, counting how many shoes you have and making everyday decisions like whether to eat chocolate now or a bit later. Of course, your brain is actually a stupefyingly complex organ, but that's not because it expects you to be a brain surgeon. It's because it is very, very old and unlike a computer, which can have its hard and software replaced, over millions of years our brains have just had more and more functions dumped into them. To complicate matters, we don't have just one brain. We have three 'brains' stacked on top of each other which are all still functioning – in a raggedy kind of way.

Evolution is slow and conservative. We have sharp eyesight, but suffer from blind spots (even in hindsight); we now walk upright, but were not designed to do so and therefore need chiropractors and osteopaths. The eccentric evolution of our brains has resulted in limited and unreliable memory, hopeless willpower and nutty, unreasonable behaviour. I'm sure you know the feeling of doing something irrational, knowing you're doing it and being unable to stop yourself. This is why we keep making mistakes; otherwise we would learn the first time around. It's almost like we are being driven by something else – how can this happen with such a sophisticated brain? Read on.

This is what happened: the first brain to ever develop was in a lizard a couple of hundred million years ago and is called the lizard or hind brain. It was little, uncomplicated and allowed creatures to see, breathe and move around. It could also generate a few primitive emotions like sex drive, predatory instinct and anger. So the lizard could defend the home base, be bossy and have enthusiastic sex. Humans still have this primitive brain at the base of the neck, just where the spinal cord starts.

Then around a million years ago, dogs developed a better brain than the lizard one. They kept the lizard brain and on top of it came the dog or mid-brain, in which the limbic system is housed. Keep reading. So now there are two brains in the mix. This new brain was a whole other story and, by comparison, desperately clever with complex wiring – it could experience a wealth of feelings like attachment, love and fidelity.

A few hundred thousand years ago, apes (early humans) appeared and developed a third or fore-brain called the neo-cortex. In the human ape this huge brain, by comparison with the others, was stupendously, outrageously advanced and put humans way ahead of any other animal. This is where most of us have stayed. Because of our big brain, humans have outwitted most predators. The powerful neocortex is not only the home of language, music, maths, art, religion and poetry, but also of deception, politics, racism and homophobia. It is the true seat of good and evil – it is responsible for the Holocaust, greed, Gandhi and Mozart.

We humans have the lizard, the dog and on top of that the neocortex. The oldest brains should have been decommissioned and the new human brain rewritten and updated, but in fact the inside of a human head looks like an archaic, multi-layered holograph. All the very old stuff still there, hidden in behind. Since the beginning of time, we have kept every bit of 'information' – evolution has just utilised the same, original genes repeatedly. Sometimes it works out; sometimes it doesn't.

Although the neocortex sits on top of the lizard and dog brains, it functions more or less independently of them. I mentioned before the bizarre experience of doing something you know is not right. Here's the explanation: emotion lies in the lizard and dog brains, while language is in the neocortex. There is a separation of functions into two completely different 'worlds'. Some psychologists say if you don't have the words for an emotion then you probably don't feel it. Logic and thought are running their programs in the neocortex brain while simultaneously trying to run alongside emotion in the dog brain and really, they have nothing to do with each other. You may have noticed this when you scream at your significant other, 'You don't have any feelings you bastard, say something!'

Another example is dieting and completely explains why diets don't and can't work. You are on a diet but you eat a fatty lamb chop anyway, knowing perfectly well this will sabotage your weight loss. You are able to do this because the flash modern brain has said 'Don't eat fat or you'll look like an amoeba', but the lizard is saying, 'Are you mad? Who knows when the next kill will come – eat it and store it!' The old brains just act and feel and this is why we flawed humans display so much inconsistent behaviour.

Take the extraordinary ability we have of being in love with someone but capable of being insanely unfaithful to them. Why do we do this? It's the bloody lizard and dog fouling the pitch again. The lizard is about lust, the dog is about affection and loyalty, and the neocortex has all sorts of fancy ideas like romance and morals (alongside less glamorous ones like deliberately inflicting pain). Animals don't deliberately hurt each other but humans do. So here our male is, away from home on a work trip. He's sitting at the bar feeling hip and groovy and independent despite the fact he is none of these things. A sexy trollop moves up to the bar and right into his pure, unsullied personal space. A few Black Russians later and the naughty lizard is saying, 'Go ahead, put the moves on.' He does. This feels great for about twenty minutes – until he has orgasmed – then the faithful dog speaks up and says, 'You ridiculous creep, look what you have done – I hope you now feel miserable and guilty.' He experiences these feelings very profoundly but is saved from suffering too much guilt at his philandering by, ta-da!, the clever, manipulative human brain, which is already thinking up excuses and justifications that it can spin out effortlessly. So when men say those famous words, 'But you're the one I really love', it's true. But what is also true is the human brain, the neocortex, is more powerful than the other two and can supersede them, so the man can just as easily say, 'You're the one I really love, so I will not listen to the lizard.'

And that's not all. We have more than one memory system. Both the neocortex and the limbic system, or dog brain, have separate memories. Intellectual memory of facts and figures is in the neocortex, which is fast but a bit unreliable; and emotional memory is in the limbic brain, which is slower but lasts longer. Old or senile people remember childhood experiences and feelings in detail, but can't remember their own phone number or what they did five minutes ago.

In fact, the limbic brain never forgets anything. As we age, the neocortical memory degrades and we have senior moments. This doesn't happen to the limbic brain. So it's really true – an elephant, especially a matriarch, never forgets. My friend Kay knows about elephants. She has told me that if you breathe into an elephant's trunk, it will never forget you. If you kill a member of an elephant's family or herd, it will come back and try and kill you. Possibly it is the dog brain memory that is responsible for wisdom as we age – I'm becoming more and more fond of the dog as I write this. This might be the explanation for what a man said to me when I had to sell my restaurant in Paris and was weeping into my bitter soup of exhaustion spiced with failure: 'Peta, this will never happen to you again. We never learn in love but we always learn in business.'

Memory relies on context. How many times have you walked into a room in your house to get something and when you get there you can't remember what you went there for? And if you go back into the first room, it comes back to you because you see something that provokes you to remember. That's context. The reason that happens is that our ancestors didn't need to remember things – you were either in the cave or out of it, and there were no supermarkets. If you're in the kitchen you remember you need more sugar; if you're somewhere else you forget it because there's no relationship. Cave men lived almost entirely in the present and didn't live long – didn't have to remember things. Trying to live only in the here and now in this century is an appealing and powerful idea – it certainly reduces stress and worry, but it's hard to do because our lives are so complicated and we are expected to retain and learn so much more information.

Gary Marcus is of the opinion that *natural selection* probably doesn't exist to any great extent any more because of birth control and medical advances. People now have a lot of sex, but there are no longer consequences for the distribution of genes in the population. Because they are so reckless, humans remove themselves from the gene pool by ending their lives in asinine, foolhardy ways like speeding on a bike with no helmet or going on hunger strikes. What then happens is modern medicine will put them back together again so that *too* changes the dynamics of natural selection. Because humans are so limited physically (we can't fly, we aren't particularly strong, we can't read thoughts

– except for my mother – we can't breathe under water) and therefore our brain is by far our greatest asset, Marcus thinks what will happen in future is *synthetic selection*. Synthetic selection could help us to upload memory better, upload information and knowledge, rather than having to memorise it, and upload artificial impulse control. The downside of all this, as Marcus would agree, is that without our mad impulses and spontaneity, we would have less fun and we would remember we told grandma to fuck off when we were drunk. And too much knowledge can be a terrible thing.

SELF-AWARENESS

Evolution has not had time to integrate our three brains, but there are ways we can help. The most effective one is by *meditation*, which helps to rewire and harmonise our little lives. It allows us to slowly and patiently see through the complications and falsity of the world and in a little way, its gentle ministrations help evolution. Also, although *music, singing, art* and *writing* are part of the neocortex, they also touch on the emotion in the dog brain, so indulging in these occupations is very good for you. But good old *self-awareness* seems to be an everyday thing we can indulge in to outwit our brains. We should set realistic goals. If your man is on a diet (because they all are, after a certain age), is slumped in front of the telly and eyeing the chips, just ask him how he thinks he will look in five years time when he thinks he's too good for you and tries to seduce the much younger sushi waitress.

With the advent of *long-term thought* in the human brain came the emotions of regret, chagrin and humiliation – something you experience when you have made a long-term plan and failed. You have squandered a moment. But we never feel bad for long because the justifying and rationalising kicks in to make it all okay. We don't seem to be able to get through even a day without either lying or justifying – it's like an addiction. How many times have you said, 'It isn't my fault I'm late – it was the traffic'? A sub-species of the skilled rationaliser is the bloke who trains others to do something for him so he never has to be aware of his actions. People who are able to look into themselves, who strive for insight and are curious about the way they go about things and why they came to such and such a conclusion, have a much better chance of outwitting the mistakes the brain makes and doing well in life.

Letting yourself get away with the mad things you do in life like eating and drinking too much by blaming the lizard is, to a certain extent, a habit. You can *train yourself* out of it and also train your children not to do it. Say to your kids: 'When you become a teenager you will want to jump on everything that moves and this is why. When you get very angry you will want to kill someone – here's what you will have to know to control that. When you get older you will forget things – don't worry about it – just make lists.' All those men who end up in prison for assault and murders of passion should have been taught anger management long before they got into trouble. Lashing out physically is just the lizard playing up. It has been proven in psychological experiments (Walter Mischel) that little children who can delay eating something absolutely delicious (like a lollypop sitting right in front of them) for 15 minutes, will become high-achievers later in life, because they can resist instant gratification and wait to get what they really want. Heroin addicts, for example, are instant gratification freaks – they can't wait the normal time to be happy and feel good so they take a short-cut.

HOW TO ACCESS YOUR INNER DOG AND DO THE LIMBIC ROCK – TEN HELPFUL RESOLUTIONS FOR HAPPINESS

1. Smile – it saves energy because it takes fewer muscles to smile than to frown. Don't smile too much – it's annoying and makes you look stupid.
2. It's fashionable now for happiness experts to tell us to be grateful. Your mother was possibly right – gratitude leads to people liking you which is all anyone wants anyway. Saying thank you increases the level of immunoglobulin A in your throat and nose, increasing your ability to resist viral infections. An example of a grateful mind is someone who really notices and enjoys the smell of fresh coffee in the morning.
3. Do exercise – it fosters sanctimoniousness which is next to Godliness. The complication is that it only makes you happy once you stop.
4. Sleep is very helpful if you can manage it – long, sound and refreshing. Lack of sleep makes you grumpy and fat and you die earlier.
5. Be true to yourself and your values. If you don't know what your values are, imagine you are free and loved with no worries, then imagine what you would do with your life.
6. Stop complaining so much – you only need to complain a little to let steam off. This is quite a good one and I highly recommend it. In fact, ask family and friends to pull you up

HAPPINESS

when you do it. Experts say you should keep daily note of all the good things that have happened to you. How ridiculous, but if you want to be so dorky, go ahead.

7. Embrace the pain. You'll never be happy if you avoid pain, loss and disappointment – without darkness there can be no light. You need to have a few unsatisfactory jobs to help you realise what you should be doing. When you lose someone you love it makes you realise how much they meant to you. You need to endure the pain of a McDonald's hamburger to appreciate how delicious real, fresh meat is. Life is hard – too hard for some people. They say those who have mental breakdowns are the ones who are really experiencing reality – the rest of us are pretending that everything is okay.

8. Try and live in the present and in what psychologists call a state of 'mindfulness'. A mindful person is eager to learn, receptive and available both intellectually and emotionally. Don't judge yourself when you are being negative or down in the dumps, just observe you are doing it and the impact seems to lessen, allowing you to move forward.

9. Make sure you have good friends and look after those friendships.

10. Make money, but not too much – once you have enough to make you comfortable and not worry, stop obsessing. More of it does not increase happiness. This is the point where, like Bill Gates, you should start giving it away and helping others. 'Status anxiety' is similar to making money – leave the Joneses alone. The size of your house is not related to the size of your dick.

CRAZED AND COMPULSIVE HOPEFULNESS

In the year 2000 fifty books were published on happiness. Last year, in 2008, 4000 books were published on happiness. The most popular classes in universities are on positive psychology – no wonder – 15 per cent of students are supposedly clinically depressed. We have 'happiness' workshops and 'lifestyle coaches' coming out our wazoos. Suddenly everyone has a half-baked theory on how to walk on the sunny side of the street (it's a bit like the chicken crossing the road – it crossed the road because it chose to); suddenly everyone's saying 'have a nice day' – the most annoying phrase in history; suddenly the kitchen table has become the oracle. What a scam – I'm in the wrong business.

Psychological research put forward the classical premise that people always make rational choices that increase their well-being. Then behavioural economists came along and said, 'What rubbish.' We're useless at predicting what makes us happy, either economically or financially. Even worse than that, we deliberately do things we know will make us unhappy. Look at all the hopeless men we have let drift into our nets – talk about slow learners.

We are now encouraged to desist from worry, boredom, stress and sadness, but guess what? In spite of the huge happiness industry, we are getting sadder and more anxious. A friend of mine used to smile a big smile when I asked him how he was and say, 'Oh, living my life of quiet desperation.' Keats talked about 'the wakeful anguish of the soul'.

It's the fault of nutty Americans who are so superficial, all they can think about is being chirpy all day – it's enough to give you a nose bleed. Remember *The Power of Positive Thinking*? Well even Americans are sick of it – Professor Eric Wilson, who wrote

HAPPINESS

Against Happiness: In Praise of Melancholy, puts forward the idea that we are so preoccupied with happiness that it has come at the cost of sadness, an important feeling we have tried to throw out of our emotional hymn book. He says that the greatest tragedy is to live without tragedy, that to hug happiness is to hate life, that to love peace is to loathe the self, the blues are clues to the sublime, the embrace of gloom stokes the heart. I'm half Irish, so all this dark stuff is like coming home to me, but I can see how not everyone wants to embrace gloominess. Miserable whiskey-soaked Irish writers formed my personality. In my book on women I wrote about the bliss of sad songs. In fact I wanted to write a whole book on sad songs in every culture – I was in ecstasy, which unfortunately my publisher didn't share. See? Ahead of my time in the sadness boom. Eric Wilson himself is blissfully gloomy and says the road to hell is paved with happy plans and incompleteness is the call to life. What's not to love about the guy? The terrible danger of being happy all the time is that we won't face the world's complexity, its uncertainty, its sinister beauties. Everyone would accept the status quo and would become placid Pollyannas embracing the living death of mediocrity. Negative emotions evolved for a reason – fear tips us off to the presence of danger, for example. The backlash is starting now!

Don't medicate yourself (it's chemically silencing the heart) when you have a split with the boyfriend – cry, work through it, feel like three kinds of shite and move on. All comedians are depressives or have had a tough childhood (look at Woody Allen); some of the greatest art works have been produced out of deep melancholy. Melancholia is the wellspring of creativity – look at Patti Smith. In my mother's day, everyone took Valium and was opiated by religion; now everyone is on Prozac. If you're eating too much, drinking too much, doing too much A-class, buying too much stuff you don't need, without maybe being aware of it, you may be depressed and these quick fixes are the rocky road to ruin. They work briefly and should be used occasionally but in the long term make you more miserable and you never learn the necessary skills to get yourself out of trouble.

You don't have to be happy all the time – it's counter-productive and not your right – that is an invention of the twentieth century. When you are sad, don't pour a couple of whiskeys – be sad and experience it. Learn something. Okay, so pour one whiskey then STOP. Happiness is not about smiling all the time – if you're happy all the time you're probably obnoxious, boring or bipolar. Real happiness comes and goes, is more like contentment or satisfaction and is profound and intentional, not impulsive. If your life has meaning, you are following your path, using your God-given talents and not lying around being a purposeless wastrel, then you're probably happy. The old expression 'seize the day' might be appropriate here. These days we have too many options and too many choices – our parents didn't suffer from this. We are almost suffering from a grass-is-greener syndrome, which can make us permanently dissatisfied and always feeling we are just in time to be too late. They say the best way to predict a person's behaviour is by looking at their past behaviour. I find this a bit depressing because although it's probably true, it doesn't allow for the possibility of change. If I were to predict my own future behaviour on that premise, I'd jump in the lake right now.

One good way to be happy is to set goals and achieve them. Research has shown that winning Lotto or getting the job of your dreams or marrying your sweetheart are huge highs but once you have achieved that, you settle back into the pre-achievement level of happiness. If you're a miserable git and win Lotto, you will go back to being who you really are quite quickly. Conversely, if you suffer a huge loss like the death of a spouse or unexpected job loss, you may never recover your previous level of happiness – you will always be down a notch. Humans are incredibly adaptable in both adjusting to achievement and to big knocks. When bush fires destroyed whole towns in Australia in February 2009, they ruined people's lives – exploded their houses and incinerated their families. Many of the devastated people were interviewed on television. Some said, 'I am in shock. I have lost everything. I don't know what to do or where to go.' Others said, 'I have lost everything. The anguish is suffocating, but I will just start over again. I am alive.' By the time we have conquered one challenge, we are already feeling something is missing and are looking around for the next mountain to climb. To stop this becoming addictive, don't turn this into money-making and acquisition of worldly possessions; rather, look out for activities that are progressive, stimulating and meaningful.

Greg Blake

PM 'What makes men happy?'

GB 'Men like tasks. They are really happy tinkering on the boat or on the car. Sex and the chase also makes them happy. Children make them happy – men talk about their children a lot. Work makes me happy, sometimes. I enjoy my job now more than I ever have. As I'm a sailor, naturally I like the gypsy aspect of the job. Adventure makes me happy. Not eating four-legged animals makes me happy. Sitting off an island on my boat fishing and enjoying the peace and quiet makes me happy. I really like being away from everybody from time to time, but also like being surrounded by hundreds of partying people. Most of the time I'm happy but some days are better than others.'

PM 'What do you think makes men sad?'

GB 'I had a Spanish friend visiting recently. It was a beautiful day and he read in the paper about teenage boys committing suicide. He said, "In this beautiful country with this great life, how can they do that?" In Spain, as in Brazil, young people stay living with their families until they get married and even then they might move the new spouse in. There is much more family closeness, communication and unity than in our culture – maybe that partially explains why people feel isolated and depressed. We're expected to be independent and living our own lives relatively young.'

PM 'Do you think men are happy with their changing role in society?'

GB 'Yeah, they seem okay to me and of course, every relationship you are in with a woman is different. In previous relationships we have played it fifty-fifty with both partners working and both looking after the house, et cetera. In my marriage, it has turned out to be more traditional with me earning more and her looking after the home, but that is only because that's the way it worked out and we are happy with that

HAPPINESS

arrangement. Happiness is really about being happy with yourself and seizing the moment. I don't live for some future time, like a holiday, when I will be happy. I enjoy the trip, not the destination. Also, happiness is fleeting and uncontrollable in the sense that I can be really unhappy in my job and a few years later, doing exactly the same thing, I am happy – it's the mindset that has changed. If I can't control my happiness with all the advantages I have, how the hell is some confused teenager supposed to?'

PM 'Does money make you happy?'

GB 'It hasn't. You know the saying – a man who earns twenty pounds and spends nineteen pounds six shillings has a life of happiness. A man who earns twenty pounds and spends twenty pounds and six shillings has a life of misery. So it doesn't matter how much you earn so long as you don't spend more than you earn and you'll always be happy.'

PM 'Who would you come back as in your next life?'

GB 'Me. I know that might sound conceited but I don't mean it that way. In spite of everything I have no regrets really. I might change some aspects, but not everything. I have always said that I don't want to be on my deathbed with regrets and thinking I have wasted my life.'

PM 'When you were young, how did you think your life was going to go?'

GB 'I didn't think about anything really beyond chasing girls. If I had led a straight, settled life, I would certainly

> be wealthier but you can't have it both ways.'
> **PM** 'What makes women happy?'
> **GB** 'The four s's – security, safe sex and shoes. And of course women are responsible for their own happiness. A man can only go so far to make them happy then it's up to them. Some women perhaps prefer to be unhappy.'

EVEN LOCUSTS NEED FRIENDS

Have you ever wondered why locusts, who are shy loners, spontaneously form gigantic, extrovert swarms and set out to eat the world? It's because being with their mates makes them deliriously ecstatic due to being drugged out of their minds on serotonin (mood neurotransmitter). When they form a swarm, which can number a billion locusts, they devour their own body weight in food every day. One-tenth of the world's population are affected by crop destruction from locusts. It has been discovered that serotonin builds up in the nerves in the parts that control the legs and wings, and in a few hours the locust turns from Mr Jekyll into Mr Hyde. The transformation usually happens after a big rain, which causes an explosion in numbers. The drought follows and the normally introverted locusts are forced closer together on smaller bits of vegetation not killed by the drought. When they are forced together and are starving, something weird happens which triggers the swarming and it's all due to serotonin. Serotonin profoundly influences how humans behave and interact. Here's my analysis of this research: if you've got a man who won't talk, give him serotonin injections but be sure to keep him fed.

Ant Grayson

PM 'What makes you happy?'

AG 'Being at ease and comfortable with myself, being independent and I love relationships – family, friendship and business ones. If they're working well, I'm happy. Success makes me happy, both my own and someone else's. I come from a family where performing at the top of your game is a given.'

PM 'Does money make you happy?'

AG 'It is not one of my major motivators and that probably comes from my father. In his day surgeons didn't make a huge amount of money as they do now – sometimes people paid my father with a sheep. My real happiness comes from relationships.'

PM 'What would happen if you lost your job?'

AG 'I'd find another one. Because I have been through some tough experiences. If you've lost your marriage, losing a job is nothing next to that. If I couldn't get another job in my field, I'd do my own thing and start something else up. Losing your self-esteem is horrible, but it's a motivator too. You use it to move on.'

THE SPORTS HERO: A CONTRADICTION IN TERMS

Good role models for girls and young women are a dime a dozen – Hillary Clinton, Michelle Obama, Helen Clark, Kylie Minogue, Nigella Lawson, Meryl Streep, Sophie Dahl and our own mothers. Role models for boys are harder to come by, which is how the 'sports hero' slipped in the door. There used to be James Bond and Clark Gable – tall, dark, handsome and awfully good with a cocktail. These 'sporting heroes' are not real heroes – they are just people who are agile, have great spatial skills and work very hard at one thing. Since the beginning of time, there have been *real* sporting heroes – the prehistoric archers, the Greek Olympians, the valiant runners. They demonstrated strength, beauty, skill and honour. Sadly, the sporting 'heroes' of today are paid obscenely large amounts of money to kick a ball, throw something, treat women like receptacles for their sperm and start fights in bars.

Many boys' fathers are not around much, most teachers are women, and a lot of boys are brought up by single mothers. They have absolutely no idea who to model themselves on or what being a male is supposed to be like. My gorgeous father and brothers open doors, stand up when a woman walks into the room and help them on with their coats. Obviously, no woman needs a door opened or their arm guided into their sleeve, but I personally like it because it is common politeness and I also open doors and stand back for people I respect. These days if a man opens a door for a woman he could be put in prison for condescending, sexist, chauvinist behaviour. If a man pulled a chair out for a woman now, she would end up on the floor – she wouldn't even know what he was doing.

ROLE MODELS

The Nobel Prize-winning scientist Sir Harold Kroto says nano-science (the science of extremely, unimaginably tiny things) is nothing new; the idea of God doesn't make any sense; patriotism

HAPPINESS

and nationalism should be restricted to the cricket pitch; and there is so much lunacy, ignorance and stupidity in the world that our only hope is education. Kroto and two colleagues discovered the carbon 60 molecule, which they call Buckminsterfullerene. It is one nanometre in diameter and looks like Buckminster's geodesic dome or a soccer ball, hence the nickname Buckyballs. Nanomaterials can be very light and very strong, which would be quite helpful if an aeroplane were made of them – if the engines failed, the craft would just glide back to earth. For Kroto, the road to happiness is in sustainability, science with social responsibility and a humanist position. He dislikes Rupert Murdoch for his lack of ethics and social responsibility; Calvin Klein for the ridiculously expensive wristwatches that cost about $3 to make; and Louis Vuitton for a $1000 briefcase. How can you pay $1000 for a bag when half the world lives in abject poverty? He is upset that people pay ten times what an object is worth and hopes the present economic crisis will bring people to their senses and encourage them to take a look at their values. Our children need to have responsible, admirable people as role models, not celebrities or sportspeople. Kroto admires people like Joseph Rotblat, the Polish physicist who stopped work on the Manhattan Project (the atom bomb) on the grounds of conscience and became a tireless campaigner against nuclear weapons. Here are some suggestions for male role models:

- Your father, grandfathers, uncles, brothers
- Trusted friends, male and female – these days a lot of boys have friends who are girls
- Barack Obama – President of America, spunky, has done a lot of community work, is a civil rights lawyer
- Jamie Oliver – chef, spunky, campaigns against processed

foods in British schools, does a huge amount for charity, has an MBE and made a great TV show called *Jamie Saves Our Bacon*, where he showed the true horrors of pig farming
- Al Gore – environmental activist, Nobel Laureate, won an Academy Award for *An Inconvenient Truth*, his documentary about global warming
- Bart Simpson – for his mischievousness, rebelliousness and disrespect for authority
- Chris Martin – handsome lead vocalist of Coldplay, outspoken on issues of fair trade, better than Bono.

WHY MEN FEEL SUICIDAL AT CHRISTMAS

1. They have time off so they lie on the couch sucking back beers and watching movies like *Star Trek: The Wrath of Kahn*, *Brokeback Mountain*, *Armageddon*, *Life is Beautiful* and *Cyrano de Bergerac*. I mean, if you watched *Brokeback Mountain*, for example, you would die a natural, tear-stained death of grief right there on the couch. These movies involve death, angst, and unresolved issues. If you watch them three times over, death follows.
2. They can't face receiving the usual Christmas gifts of 37,000 pairs of socks, ten copies of *How To Make a Million Before You're Thirty*, trick sex toys which don't work, a porn movie that is so ridiculous even the donkey laughs, and handkerchiefs, when everyone knows perfectly well that the last man who blew his nose on a hankie died in 1949. They have no choice but to look around then kill themselves.
3. They know they have to descend into the dark bog of a family Christmas dinner with the very people who turned

them into homicidal manic-depressives in the first place. The entire point of a family holiday is to reduce you to a monosyllabic alcoholic.
4. The family is going to ask them why they're not married yet, wait to hear what they say then give each other meaningful looks. Out of earshot they say, 'I told you it wasn't normal that he would buy seven pink shirts.'
5. If they have children every family member is going to develop a cat's arse mouth at the bad way they bring up their children.

LAUGHTER IS THE BEST MEDICINE

Happy people have healthier levels of important body chemicals, like the stress hormone cortisol, than their sad cousins do. This means they have healthier hearts and cardiovascular systems, which cuts the risk of attracting diseases like diabetes. Cortisol is often linked to Type-2 diabetes and hypertension. The happier a man is, the lower his cortisol levels are during the day and the lower his heartbeat. Also, he has lower levels of a blood protein called fibrinogen, which makes blood sticky and is important for clotting. Lower levels of this mean a healthy heart. The way the brain functions during states of happiness makes life's ordinary upsets and stresses less irritating and you react in a calmer, more manageable way. Happiness even overrides other factors, such as socioeconomic position, age and gender when it comes to health. This is, of course, in stark contrast to all the miserable 80-year-old bastards you know who have smoked and drunk whiskey all their lives and never done a stroke of exercise.

Now what about socioeconomics and happiness – surely

being important and fabulous makes you happy and healthy. We know money doesn't, but high social status does. The status syndrome varies wildly, however. For example, you have the rich American with an average life expectancy of 76.9 years, but you have the poor Cuban with the same lifespan. The reason people of low status are less healthy is mostly lack of control and less opportunity to engage and participate socially, which produces stress and illness. Those at the top may have a lot of responsibility and stress, but it is predictable stress that has an end. Also, they get more support and outlets for their stress, for example they can afford psychologists, yoga retreats and great holidays. Men in general suffer from stress more than women because they go into fight-and-flight mode as a response; women go into tend-and-befriend mode, band together and share the problem.

LESSONS LEARNED

- To be truly happy and well-matched, a younger man should choose an older woman as they are both at their natural sexual peaks.
- Meditation and yoga harmonise and rewire your life.
- Act as if and you will become (a Zen saying). The interpretation of this is what my mother always said: smile and the world smiles with you; weep and you weep alone.

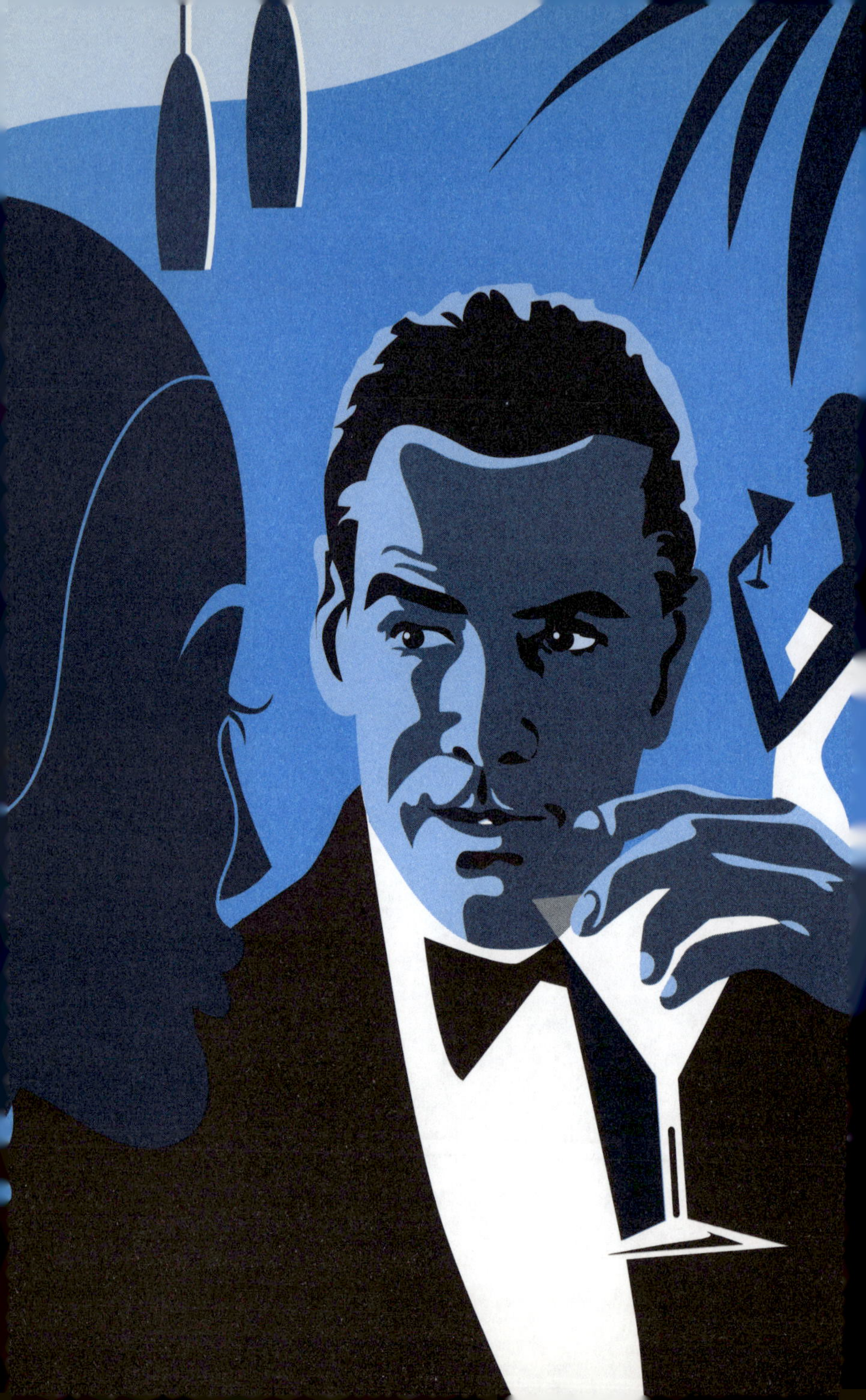

10

Why men lie
FEEL FREE TO KISS MY ASS ON THE WAY OUT, HONEY

One of the things about men that really annoys women is their compulsive lying. What's even more annoying is that they are so bad at it. Why can't they learn from us, who have practised from birth and seem to have superior lying strategies? Not only are our lying strategies superior, so too are our abilities to detect lies. Here's how it happens: in body language research, results have shown that in face-to-face communication, non-verbal signals account for 60 to 80 per cent of information given, sounds (like shrieking) account for 20 to 30 per cent and a tiny 7 to 10 per cent is verbal; that is, the words you say. So, in fact, there is absolutely no point in talking to men at all – best to use sign language. The police department should throw out all their lie-detecting equipment and just get a few women in – our superior sensory abilities would ensure accurate analysis of communication clues.

The brain has two hemispheres which have different functions. Joining the two is a white band of fibres called the 'corpus callosum'. The corpus callosum allows us to bring to bear information from both hemispheres. A man's corpus callosum is on average 40 per cent smaller than a woman's, and it shrinks as he ages. Because women have a stronger corpus callosum, we are far better able to rapidly transfer information between each brain hemisphere to integrate and analyse verbal, visual and auditory signals.

A problem for us is a man saying one thing while his body language is telling us another. Men are always amazed when we know they are lying – the best way for them to get away with it is to lie by email or letter or hide under the bed clothes – these disadvantage us. Some women say you can tell by looking at his lips – if they're moving, he's lying. Because men have a less well-developed corpus callosum, they have limited ability to lie to women face-to-face; they can't think fast enough to cover it up or make sure the body language matches the words. Also, they are not interested enough to remember what they have lied about and when, so they almost always get caught out. Women are much more devious and find it easy to lie to men because men do not have the necessary sensitivity to spot any incongruencies between verbal and non-verbal message sending. Women might set up a lie in a very sophisticated way, ensuring back-up from friends (there must be 37,000 examples in your neighbourhood of men saying they spent the night at Fred's house when he forgot to tell Fred – duh), a correct history, flawless follow-up and plausibility and, of course, Plan B. Women are SO clever that we can lie without even opening our mouths – we use our eyes, our sex appeal, the hairdresser, the plastic surgeon, make-up and the way we walk to trick men into believing we are something we are not. But men are catching up and learning from us – they now use plastic surgeons, rip their lovely body hair off (why?), dye their hair or use implants and try to trick us with their eyes.

Also, women can read between the lines. Men ask, 'What lines?' Women have more sensitivity in spotting tone changes in voice volume and pitch – they 'hear' emotional changes in people, especially their children, because they have sharper hearing. Women are more likely to sing in tune than men and are more likely to say 'Don't speak to me in that tone of voice'. A man is less likely to pick up on tone of voice and this is one of the many reasons why they are at a disadvantage in an argument. In an argument, a woman can think much faster than a man, which is why men often give in – not because they have got somewhere, but because they do not have sharp or sophisticated enough verbal skills. Men tell me they give in during an argument because they would rather talk about something more important. Really – like what? World peace, brain surgery, rocket science? However, they have night vision, a great sense of direction, superior physical strength, and a strong immune system – none of which is very helpful in an argument, actually. Their principal weapon is to walk away, which drives women insane. They love being just in time to be too late.

WHY MEN LIE

But all this is beside the point. The real question is: 'Why do men lie and can they be cured of it?' As a child, I lied like a trooper because I was afraid of my mother. It became obvious to me when I was very young that the punishment for the crime was much worse than the punishment for lying, so I took the lying route to minimise drama. Men lie for the same reason, except they make you the mother. One day I grew up, got tired of lying and became honest, which is what most normal people do. Here's my theory – men don't grow up and become honest because they never get over the fact that their mother has withdrawn the breast from them, which is why they (a) are obsessed with breasts; and (b) never grow up and have truly adult relationships with their women, other men, anybody really. There are many more male fraudsters than female ones and I think they just miss Mummy. A lot of men I interviewed said they lied to their friends as well as their girlfriends. Watch children who do something wrong or make a mistake and admit to it – they don't fear – they know the adult will teach them something and forgive rather than punish them.

MEN LIE TO WOMEN FOR THESE REASONS

1. Believe it or not, most men lie to avoid causing pain and preserve the relationship.
2. They are afraid of women (Mummy). In my opinion, really big fibbers currently have or have had bad relationships with their mothers – either the mother was controlling, domineering, or let them down in some way (like leaving home or getting divorced). Like children, they find it easier to lie than face the truth and prefer to take the path of least resistance.
3. An Alpha Male will consider he is beyond the rules because he's top ape in the tribe.
4. Men resent controlling, mistrustful women and perceive this lack of trust as criticism, so become sulky, evasive and defensive.

5. They are colour blind and get the blue house mixed up with the pink house.
6. To get sex or attention, whichever comes first. Of course you know the story of the homeless man on the street with a signboard saying: 'Will work for food. Will beg for sex.'
7. A lot of men are a little insecure so lie to feel better about themselves – fibs of exaggeration.
8. Lies of omission are not considered lies by men.
9. They are afraid of the explosive emotionality of some women – they almost experience it as life-threatening.

THE TEN BIGGEST LIES IN THE WORLD

1. But you're the one I really love.
2. Being gay and not coming out.
3. No you don't look fat in that.
4. There was no Holocaust.
5. This will not hurt.
6. I did not have sex with that woman.
7. This hurts me more than it will hurt you.
8. I'm not married but my wife is.
9. Size doesn't matter.
10. I've been busy. (Can we get clear on this here? Nobody is too busy to call/visit a person they like/love.)

All men are the same. Shall I repeat that? All men are the same – they are genetically programmed to hunt the woman until they bring the prey down. They may be tempered by upbringing, nationality, education or status, but the hard-wiring is identical. You cannot change men – women have been trying for a million years (talk about slow learners). The best idea is to understand the male–female dynamic and change the way *you* think about it. This is very empowering and gives you a lot of freedom. This way, you see them coming before they see you coming, which is much more enjoyable. Once you have done that, you can change them into a good mate or husband. This doesn't just work for the day you meet the Bad Boy – you will have to be on your toes and stick up for yourself for years, if necessary (but you'll have a lot of fun). Men cannot think like women so there is no point expecting them to. We can't think like them but we can learn to read them, we can become translators, we can channel. You don't even need to mind-read; you just need to lip read and if all else fails, actually listen (should they speak).

BAD BOYS

A **Bad Boy**, as if you didn't know perfectly well, walks into a room and inhabits it with their confidence, sex appeal and charisma. They are often good-looking, though not necessarily, and immediately pay a lot of attention to women. They don't come across as arseholes; they come across as charming, open, easy to be with and usually have lots of women friends. Like child molesters, they are nice, make you feel relaxed and you walk willingly into their trap, they don't talk you into it. Women love them, not only for their raw sex appeal, but for the fact that they are likable and witty like your brother/gay friend/neighbour. They would never be so crass as to make a huge effort but at the same time there is electricity everywhere. This comes from their absolute confidence that they can have any woman in the room, whether they can or not. They enjoy being naughty and we enjoy their naughtiness. What also makes them irresistible is that they don't need anything aside from their personality to seduce you – their success is not dependent on money, position or power.

A friend of mine, Michel, is a perfect example of a Bad Boy – good-looking, intelligent, glamorous job, very funny, generous, self-disclosing and completely adorable. He has slept with, had relationships with, been friends with hundreds and hundreds of women. I met him in Morocco at a party – he looked like shit because he had just trekked the desert and hadn't slept. He had rented a huge riad in the medina for two weeks for the express purpose of partying, having invited friends from all over the world to join him. Over a tagine, during which he almost fell asleep, we became friends. His parties always had amazing food and recreational substances and the friends were very diverse, for example old friends from home, new friends he had met the day before at the shop, children of his friends who were hitch-hiking and passing through . . . one nice young man who we called Cliff Richard, because he was so good and we were all so naughty, went around tidying up, doing dishes, fishing people out of the pool and being polite and well brought up. While he didn't wish to participate in the general debauchery, cooking of outrageous dishes and telling of tall tales, he wasn't remotely fazed by what was going on around him and everyone loved him.

This ability to relate to just about anyone is the hallmark of the Bad Boy. Michel and I have had many discussions about relationships, women, sex and work. Last year he told me about a fantastic Moroccan beauty he suspected he was in love with. No sooner had I adjusted to this than I received a photo of the two of them at their Hawaiian wedding.

Just in case there's a man reading this and saying, 'This doesn't

JUST IN TIME TO BE TOO LATE

apply to me, I'm not a Bad Boy, I'm a SNAG/metrosexual/insecure dork, whatever.' Spare me. You are all Bad Boys underneath and the nicest guys are the worst because we never see you coming. Real Bad Boys are easy to spot and we love them, but wolves in sheep's clothing are the really dangerous ones. An example of a wolf in sheep's clothing is a stay-at-home dad (probably schtooping the housekeeper), a sensitive harp player (ever watched their fingers?), a shy guy (100 per cent success rate), an ugly or fat guy (they get all the mercy lays).

Another complication is the **Faux Bad Boy**, who looks and acts just like a real Bad Boy but doesn't come up with the goods. He plays a very sexy game, but it leads nowhere usually because he is either impotent, unavailable or stupid. You'd be amazed how many stupid men cover it up with good looks and charm. It's only when you ask them what six inches is that you realise they can't count.

A sub-species of the Faux Bad Boy is what used to be called a **Playboy** and he is exactly that – it's only a game, he is a predator, not genuinely interested in women and in fact doesn't even like them very much. It's only about the kill and he is usually a shallow person with whom it is difficult to have an interesting conversation. A Playboy is a predator in every sense – he will pick vulnerable women (drunk, lonely, older, poor or naive). A real Bad Boy will talk to women for hours, days, months if he's into it. A Playboy won't and you always have the feeling you are just providing a service and he should be paying for it in that case. Women who have been the victim of a Playboy or a Faux Bad Boy wish the man would fall into a vat of boiling oil. Ex-girlfriends of real Bad Boys remain friends with them usually. The Playboy often has lots of expensive toys, such as flash cars, vicious dogs and ridiculous jewellery. He lies a lot and makes promises he doesn't keep, he advances sexually at an inappropriate speed. If you are a Playgirl and wish to use him for sex, fine – if you're not, run.

Then there is the **Misogynist**. This is a person, usually a man, who hates women. Fortunately these people are not that numerous; they usually have dysfunctional backgrounds, maybe sexual, physical or emotional childhood abuse, maybe a father who also disliked and disrespected women, maybe a cold mother. If a man doesn't get on with his mother or his sisters, beware – this is a very bad sign. Be careful and watch the body language closely – it's likely to be slightly creepy.

Okay, so there are some good guys too – my father and brothers and brother-in-law – but that's only five people, and even *they* will have strains of Bad Boy in their DNA.

Women never read instructions, so I don't expect anyone to listen to anything I say, but here are some handy hints in reading men:

- Shut up and listen to what a man is saying. He will say what he's feeling whether it's emotional or physical. If he doesn't say he loves you, he doesn't love you. If he says he has a girlfriend *and* a mad sexual passion for you then that is what he means.
- Don't assume things he isn't saying. Gut feelings are due to indigestion, not intuitiveness.
- If the actions don't match the words, for example, he says, 'You're the one, baby,' but only ever calls you at midnight, you can be absolutely sure you are not the one, baby. This is called a booty call. A man who really wants you will kick the door down to get you into his life.
- Good eye contact can easily be faked but it is generally a positive sign if a man looks you in the eye. If he doesn't make good eye contact, he is not being clear with you.

- Is he a good kisser? If yes, none of the above matters. A good kiss is practically a deal-maker.

Unfortunately, in some Anglo-Saxon countries the male has been culturally socialised out of understanding his role and so has the female – the female has to do his job and she learns this young. I can't tell you how many times my brothers and sisters have told me stories of little girls aged six upwards calling their little sons for dates. I myself was shamelessly in love with Marcel, a six-year-old at my primary school, who if he could have ignored me any more, would have lost consciousness and fallen off the edge of the world.

'I'M OVER BAD BOYS – I WANT A NICE ONE'

No you're not and no you don't – that's crap. We like edgy men and slightly dangerous men can be very nice and polite, don't forget. Bad Boys can be all the things you want and admire – they are quite capable of being kind, caring, communicative and reliable, but you have to appreciate the exciting side of them that makes you want to rip their clothes off and them rip yours off. You just don't want one who will rip your heart out before you even realise there is a cavity in your chest wall. You don't have to go for entirely bad; you can have a bit of bad – enough to be tasty and interesting. You can sleep with them quite quickly into the relationship if you want to, but don't get too involved too quickly and don't be too available. Women don't like men who are all over them – well, men don't like it either. I hear some of my long-term happily married friends saying, 'You're wrong, I don't like Bad Boys, my husband isn't a Bad Boy and I love him for his tenderness and kindness. Women who are attracted to Bad Boys have low self-esteem. It's like women who somehow end up with men who hit them. A Bad Boy is emotionally abusive.' I can see their point.

MEN WHO HIT WOMEN

Most women have never been hit by a man. I was beaten once by a man and walked away very quickly because a man never hits a woman once – if he does it once he will do it again. This type of man is extremely primitive and has no other tools to resolve conflict. If a man hits you, you don't even think about it – you go to the police immediately. Men who hit are often Jekyll and Hyde characters – passionate people who can be just as wonderful as they can be hideous. They will weep and gnash their teeth and apologise when they see what they have done, but trust me, they will do it again. This man is not always from the shallow end of the gene pool – he can be highly educated, intelligent, charming and hard to pick until he strikes. It may come a few years into a relationship even. This is a huge flaw in his character and can usually only be fixed by therapy. Men know that they can overpower a woman physically any time they want – normal men never go there in their lives, no matter what the provocation. This leads me to a little-talked-about type of woman – the man beater.

WOMEN WHO HIT MEN

Basically the above information also applies to women who beat men – a man should get out of a physically abusive relationship IMMEDIATELY. I was violent on occasion when I was a young woman, driven insane by pain and anger. I threw a few things and delivered a few slaps, and then I grew out of it. I like to think I'm not a man beater, although my behaviour certainly makes it easier for me to understand people who do it. If you are already angry from your childhood and had a parent who belted you, you are likely to have a short fuse, in the sense that you are already over-sensitive. Women who regularly slap, punch, abuse and even kill men are not as uncommon as you might think. They have mostly been abused themselves sexually or physically or both. Controlling men is their way of regaining control over their lives. Like men who are abusive, violent women use isolation as a major part of their control system – they ensure that the man loses his friends, work colleagues, job even, and family – so he feels he has no one to turn to.

Interestingly, although men are bigger and stronger than their women partners, beaten men almost never defend themselves, restrain the woman or retaliate. The men say that to do this makes things much worse and the situation can escalate dramatically. If they hit the woman in self-defence they feel they will get the blame for the whole thing. On average, it takes thirty-five violent incidents before the man will report it to the police. Why do men stay in these relationships? The most common reasons are (a) attachment to the children; (b) love for the woman; and (c) awareness of the woman's abusive past, feeling sorry for her and hoping to save her.

Advice for the man: it is very difficult to leave an abusive relationship, but it can be done – there is a way out – you get support and tell someone. Advice for the woman: you can stop being violent by taking stock, understanding your past and learning how to manage anger so that when you get annoyed, it doesn't need to tip over into uncontrollable rage. If you can feel it boiling up in you but feel powerless to stop it, you can learn with therapy to not go there, respect boundaries and learn to communicate properly.

THE PROTOTYPE LIAR

It was while I was sewing pin tucks into an unbleached cotton skirt one day that I met the man I was to fall truly, madly, deeply in love with. The first man I set up house with, the man who would drive me to the heights of passion and the mad depths of despair. I had never loved like this before, whether because he was the first really serious relationship or because he was my true other half, I don't know. Stewart (Screw) sauntered – he did a lot of sauntering – into my sewing room wearing a leather jacket, tight jeans and a smirk. Screw by name, screw by nature. 'Oooh, this looks dangerous,' I thought. 'I think I'll try some.' There I was sitting pretty in a little tie-dyed sundress, my ears weighted down with rings, dark hair layered in big waves, smiling trustingly and radiating robust health. How could he not fall for me? There he was, leaning on the door frame, oozing cool confidence, sex appeal in boots. How could I not fall for him? What chance did I have?

Screw drove a motorbike, as did most of my male friends. We lost a lot of our friends to motorbike accidents – wild young men who, stoned and drunk, wrapped themselves around power poles on the way home from parties. Young men hooked on youth, intelligent and testosterone-poisoned; driving and laughing at eighty miles an hour head on into oblivion. Strangely, Screw was not like that. He was a safe driver, always wore a crash helmet and never took risks when a passenger was on the back of the bike. When we rode together we were always well wrapped up in his supply of protective clothing. I loved motorbikes, feeling no fear, only freedom and exhilaration. Best of all I loved the grace and beauty of bike-riding with another person, the twinned movements, the intimate embrace of balance. It was co-dependence in the nicest possible way.

Screw's first memory of me was seeing me at a party in Ponsonby. I wore a silver satin dress cut on the cross and may possibly have been wearing a slash of lipstick. Suffice to say I was wonderful and gorgeous to him. We danced, he took me home, I felt very comfortable. My women friends who were rampant feminists said, 'Screw can't relate to a woman unless he's slept with her, and he relates to a lot of women.' I tried to be careful, I confronted him about these issues, grilling him over what is now called political correctness but what was then called covering your arse. He was as smooth as water, silver tongued in his slow soft way of speaking. 'I am a feminist,' he said. 'I want you to be your own person, independent and equal politically, financially and sexually.' I was impressed with this banter, but later found out that lots of men embraced feminism because it helped them to get laid, a tactic I found quite sophisticated.

Screw had short reddish/brown hair, trimmed dark red beard, dark brown eyes, an endearing slight stutter, slim build and a shyness he covered up with dimpled coolness. Once we had moved in together, it was clear in my mind that I had made a commitment, had fallen, this was my man and I assumed he felt the very same way. My parents had rarely fought in front of us kids, there was no violence or drinking, no infidelity, no hate – just a lot of nuttiness which I thought was normal. On the other hand, his family had split asunder when he was a child, his mother running off with the night class philosophy lecturer, leaving Screw and his siblings with a morose father. Although I was now twenty-two, I was still immature emotionally and had unrealistic notions of what a live-in relationship was about. The only experience we had with relationships was within our own families. Screw was withdrawn and cautious, where I was open, naive and endlessly positive. I loved him madly and thought I could make him better with adoration, good cooking and laughter. We did laugh a lot, but his mistrust and slight depressiveness were always there. On a quotidian level, we got along very well. Screw was domesticated, organised and caring. We cooked meals together and threw huge parties using the student method of catering, which consisted of telling everyone at the university pub there was a do on and could they bring food and alcohol.

I just liked being with Screw. In our good moments we were very good. I was strong-willed and capricious and he was tolerant and calm – we had the right personality mix to make a successful match. I knew right away this was the man I would spend my life with, I submerged myself in his odour, slept wound in his body, injected his love into my veins. Having survived a convent education, betrayals – starting with Marcel when I was six years old – and two sexual assaults, it was a big thing for me to give myself entirely to a man. It required enormous amounts of trust and I trusted him with my mistakes, my faults, my past and my love. I gave them to him on a silver platter. Everything about Screw was wonderful in my eyes – his good looks, his discipline in his architecture studies, his style, his even temperament. He was an alternative middle-class person just like me. Once I had made my decision about him, I walked to his side without a wrong step or flicker of an eyelid. I entered his heart and stayed there, humming to the thump of it regulating my life.

However, when we fought it became obvious our alter egos were in the room. The four of us battled it out.

Me: 'Where have you been, Screw, until three in the fucking morning?'

My Alter Ego: 'What filth were you up to while I was alone in bed?'

Screw: 'I was out drinking with my friends.'

Screw's Alter Ego: 'I am not your baby, I am not answerable to you and there were lots of better-looking chicks than you at the party.'

Me: 'I was worried about you. I thought maybe you were wrapped around a power pole or something. I would like to go out with you too sometimes, you know.'

My Alter Ego: 'You prefer your low-life friends to me. What slut were you polluting yourself with, you lying bastard?'

Screw: 'Calm down, Peta. We're not attached at the hip, are we? I just like to go out with the boys. And it's none of your business what time I get home, anyway.'

Screw's Alter Ego: 'You're going to eat me alive. If I leave you, you might go mad or die or worse. If I stay *I* might go mad or die or worse.'

Me: 'How dare you talk to me like that? I'm supposed to be the woman you love. You sleep in my bed. What do you mean it's none of my business what time you get home?'

My Alter Ego: 'You're lucky to be alive, you snivelling, single-cell bit of ectoplasm. If it wasn't for me you wouldn't even know the meaning of the words "medium rare" let alone "alfalfa sprout".'

Screw: 'Look darlin', don't crowd me. Go to sleep and we'll talk about it in the morning.'

Screw's Alter Ego: 'Okay, okay, excuse me for breathing. At least I'm still here.'

Me: 'All right, cowboy. You bet we're going to talk about this in the morning.'

My Alter Ego: 'Don't worry about me, worry about yourself. I'll be fine. One day you'll be sorry.'

Things were great for the first year, but much as Screw wanted to love and sink into me he was profoundly mistrustful of women. He adored and respected not only me but all women, and at the same time feared intimacy, feared being swallowed up by the matriarch who would desert him anyway. Every woman was the matriarch; every woman could drag him down into a spiral of controlling asphyxia. Life was to be played with most of the cards under the table. Women were interesting and sexy, but also vicious and unpredictable. I was no exception. Most of his friends were women, but only the ones he had desexualised or who were not sexual to start with. I played with all my cards not only on the table but turned up. I never caught on to the idea of hedging my bets. If I had had half the brains God gave cement I would have learned that from Screw. But no, having lied pathologically all my life to parents, teachers and employers I was now honest. I found it humiliating when people lied to me and was embarrassed for them. But Screw found it easy to lie.

The first time I found hair clips that were not my own in our bed it took a while to figure out what it meant. People had been telling me things I didn't want to hear and others were protecting both Screw and me by covering for him. A man can be having an affair right under a woman's nose and she will never know unless she allows her heart and mind to translate the information. Everyone else knows. EVERYONE. Her friends, her family, his friends, his family, the household dog, the students reading the toilet walls. Everyone. She knows something is wrong but she does not think of the obvious because it is unthinkable. It's unthinkable that the man she has trusted and who trusts her would do the same intimate things with another woman he has done with her.

When I saw the hair clips I felt myself sinking, slipping away, imploding, fighting invading information. I had no tools for dealing with it, no idea what the proper protocol was in such a circumstance. The idea of me, Peta, sleeping with another man was something that had never entered my head, so besotted was I with my one true love, the man I gave up a peaceful night's sleep for. Screw, of course, had no idea how the hair clips got there, there was a big scene, recriminations, tears, threats to jump off the ferry halfway across the channel, threats to leave him and promises from him to be good in future. The wounds healed, I forgave him, did not go mad and the calm waters after the storm were quite enjoyable. Life went on, nothing was ever really discussed, but I assumed that Screw and I would stay together, he would graduate, get a job, we would buy a house, et cetera, et cetera.

But eventually women started calling the house again looking for him and more ribbons and foreign objects of betrayal appeared in my bed. One night he didn't come home and by the time he staggered in the next afternoon I had girded my loins. This was the first time he had ever absented himself from our bed for a whole night so he had a vague idea a line had been crossed. He slowly approached the battlefield armed with arrogance and protected by his mates. Blind with rage, grief and jealousy, I waited in our bedroom until he entered, swung my arm back and slapped him on the face so hard he fell into the hallway.

'Stand up, you bastard,' I screamed. 'Where have you been?'

'Don't do this,' he said in a very quiet voice, his brown eyes a mixture of surprise and granite.

'Where have you been?'

'I stayed the night with my friends.'

He had lied to me again and again. Again and again he undermined my trust. I shrieked like a banshee going under the bog, 'You spent the night with a woman!'

'You're mad,' he said, and started to get up off the floor as I stood over him, white and sweating cold saline.

'Stop hurting me! Stop hurting me!' I screamed. 'Get out!' I actually felt I was going mad and he was deliberately helping me.

His tough friends took one look at me in full Shakespearean flight, said, 'See you, mate', and ran. He manoeuvred me into the bedroom where we continued our war. He started by sweeping the precious contents of my dressing table onto the floor. I dragged all his clothes out of the wardrobe and all his university papers off the desk onto the floor. Into the night I vented my fury as I deconstructed the first year of our relationship. He began dismantling our bed – if he couldn't sleep in it then neither could I. To be told with unwavering eye by he in whom I had placed my trust and my horrible personal truths that black was white, betrayal was fidelity, no was yes, was more than I had the tools to deal with. I couldn't get through his wall of denial and neither could I passively accept his cruelty. So I flipped. Going mad is like dropping acid. You don't actually go anywhere; someone else moves in to the part of the brain you have vacated.

I knew that Screw would never strike me but I was unprepared for his next move. Not knowing what else to do he locked me in the bedroom and walked away. Wild-eyed, I rattled and kicked the door then picked up a chair and threw it at the window. It bounced off. I had not taken into account the strength of the old-fashioned windows, so I stood back and swung a few times to gather momentum. The third time worked sending glass everywhere and I regained my freedom. Having broken something I felt much better – it wasn't Screw's head but it would have to do. Back inside and slightly calmer, I walked down the hall wearing a nightie and one sock to call one of my friends to come and get me. By this time, Screw was looking for me, so I hid in the hedge until my friend arrived in her Mini. She turned up with two ferocious Rottweilers to protect and escort me, hair billowing out the windows, to her place, where she gave me wine and tender, loving care. I lay exhausted on her floor and dreamt I was a scampi that crawled around parched, asking everyone for water to drink and pleading with them not to step on me.

Late the next morning, I returned home to collect some belongings. I would stay at my friend's place until I found another house. Screw had also spent the night with a friend and to my astonishment I found him on our bedroom floor piecing my precious ornaments together, tears streaming down his face. I felt nothing. I couldn't afford to. His moral and emotional destruction was my passport to survival.

'Peta, I . . .' he said in a smashed-up voice.

'Don't think I've come back to see you,' I spat. 'I am here to pick up my things.'

'I'm sorry. I'm sorry. I'm sorry,' he wept.

'It is too late, Screw.'

'Peta, I love you.'

I left him there and had a long shower before returning to Armageddon to pack. Screw made me sit on the floor, put his arms around me and said, 'We have to talk. Now's the time to talk.'

I sighed. 'Why do we have to go through this before you will ever talk to me and be honest?'

We stayed that way on the floor for hours talking, weeping, talking, renegotiating. He mended my ornaments and the window and I cooked him a meal. Healing through food.

After that terrible night he was faithful to me as far as I knew. Life continued fairly tranquilly for a year, with Screw showing a new devotion, but I hadn't really recovered – there had been nerve and soul damage. Big scars grew over my heart and girlish trust flew out the window away, away, to some other mystical, innocent meadow, a meadow I would never have access to again. The cold winds of lamentation cemented the corrosion I now knew had settled in. He knew he had hurt me deeper than he ever intended and wanted to fix it, wished he could be a better mate, wished he hadn't done it, wished he wasn't so weak. I felt sorry for him, but it seemed like a matter of time before I would become like *Ishtar*, the mythical goddess of war, and woe betide anyone who got in my way. In future I would have any man I wanted and get rid of him when I wanted. I saw what my life with Screw would be – we would get married, have children, he would be an architect and run around on me, I would beat the kids and run around on him. Or I wouldn't beat the kids – I would just go mad, and he would be known as that nice man with the difficult wife.

I felt I needed to fly the coop for a while. We had Canadian friends who had stayed at our place while visiting New Zealand. I didn't know where to go so I decided to emigrate to Canada.

England didn't appeal to me and places where they spoke foreign languages were too scary. My arrangement with Screw was that either I would come home in six months or he could come and join me, whichever happened first. But I knew I wasn't returning.

At the airport the mother cried, surrounded by her other children. 'Be careful,' she said. 'When are you coming back?'

'Never,' I said, through a wall of tears.

'Don't get lost and don't talk to bodgies,' the father said, being staunch.

'I'll talk to every bodgie I see. I talk to you, don't I?'

'I'll miss you,' said Screw. 'It'll be quiet without you.'

'Something tells me you'll manage,' I smiled.

I was hardly on the plane when Screw leapt into my best friend's bed. Another nail in *his* coffin, not mine. But what did I care? I was winging my way to freedom.

Believe it or not Screw and I continued to torture each other for many years. He went to London; I visited him several times and he always had another woman when I got there. Once, he talked me into sponsoring him for immigration into Canada so we could be together. I paid all the fees, did all the interviews, arranged all the papers, went to the airport in Vancouver to pick him up, but he never got on the plane. Another time he talked me into moving to London to be with him and when I got there he had another woman in his bed. The final straw was when I was living in London and he invited me and his friends to a party. At the party he announced that it was a wedding celebration and he had just wedded a young woman. You'll be pleased to know she dumped him and took him for everything he had.

Many years later he contacted me out of the blue – he was home visiting his family. Much as I didn't want to see him, I thought it might be interesting to see how he had turned out – now he was in his mid-forties. I invited him to a party at my home and explained to my friends that the man who had ruined my life was coming. My friends stared at him open-mouthed. They had been told the story in gruesome detail.

'This is the man who ruined your life?' they asked, in shock. 'This is the sexy, good-looking devil who had women falling at his feet?' they gasped.

'Yeah,' I said.

'But this man is grey and boring and unconfident and not good-looking. We wanted George Clooney here.'

'I know. Isn't it incredible?'

'What has happened to him?'

'I don't know. Life, I suppose.'

'We cannot believe he did so much damage.'

'Neither can I, looking at him now.'

LESSONS LEARNED

- None.
- The biggest liar of all, the Fraudster, has never grown up and is still basically lying to Mummy, who he has never forgiven for withdrawing the breast. I made this up – there is no scientific proof.
- Women like to say we're over Bad Boys. No we're not, that's crap. We like edgy and slightly dangerous men. Most men are Bad Boys underneath anyway, and the nicest guys are the worst because we never see them coming.

Selected Bibliography

Amies, Hardy, *The ABC of Men's Fashion*, Harry N. Abrams, London, 2007

Biddulph, Steve, *Manhood*, Finch, Sydney, 2002

Farrell, Warren, *The Myth of Male Power*, Fourth Estate Ltd, London, 1994

Ford, Anna, *Men*, Guild Publishing London, 1985

Hamilton, Maggie, *What Men Don't Talk About*, Penguin, Melbourne, 2006

James, Oliver, *Affluenza*, Vermillion, London, 2007

Lashlie, Celia, *He'll Be OK*, HarperCollins, Auckland, 2005

McGee, Greg, *Foreskin's Lament*, Victoria University Press, Wellington, 1981

Nelson, Mariah Burton, *The Stronger Women Get the More Men Love Football*, The Women's Press, London, 1994

Pease, Allan and Barbara, *Why Men Don't Listen and Women Can't Read Maps*, Orion, London, 2001

Pert, Candace B, *Molecules of Emotion*, Scribner, New York, 2003

Ratcliffe, Gail and Keith, Hamish, *Being Single and Happy*, Simon & Schuster, Sydney, 1992

Salt, Bernard, *Man Drought*, Hardie Grant Books, Melbourne, 2008

Sheehy, Gail, *New Passages*, HarperCollins, London, 1997

Street-Porter, Janet, *Life's Too F****ing Short*, Quadrille, London, 2008